Critical Essays on Ambrose Bierce

Critical Essays on Ambrose Bierce

Cathy N. Davidson

G. K. Hall & Co. • Boston, Massachusetts

Library of Congress Cataloging in Publication Data

Davidson, Cathy N., 1949–
  Critical essays on Ambrose Bierce.

  (Critical essays, on American literature)
  Bibliography
  Includes index.
  1. Bierce, Ambrose, 1842–1914?—Criticism and interpretation—
Addresses, essays, lectures.   I. Title.
II. Series.
PS1097.Z5D3   813'.4   81–7218
ISBN 0–8161–8393–7   AACR2

This publication is printed on permanent/durable acid-free paper
MANUFACTURED IN THE UNITED STATES OF AMERICA

CRITICAL ESSAYS ON AMERICAN LITERATURE

This series seeks to collect the most important previously published criticism on writers and topics in American literature along with, in various volumes, original essays, interviews, bibliographies, letters, manuscript sections, and other materials brought to public attention for the first time. Cathy N. Davidson's volume on Ambrose Bierce is the most comprehensive collection of scholarship ever assembled on this intriguing and controversial writer. It contains thirty essays and reviews by such distinguished scholars as Daniel Aaron, H. L. Mencken, Van Wyck Brooks, Wilson Follett, Jay Martin, and Eric Solomon. In addition, there are original essays by David D. Anderson and Lawrence I. Berkove along with Professor Davidson's own primary and secondary bibliography. We are confident that this collection will make a permanent and significant contribution to American literary study.

JAMES NAGEL, GENERAL EDITOR

Northeastern University

CONTENTS

INTRODUCTION

> How many times, and covering a period of how many years, must one's unexplainable obscurity be pointed out to constitute fame? Not knowing, I am almost disposed to consider myself the most famous of authors. I have pretty nearly ceased to be "discovered," but my notoriety as an obscurian may be said to be worldwide and apparently everlasting.
>
> —Bierce in a letter to George Sterling[1]

Ambrose Bierce is certainly the most *rediscovered* writer in American literary history. As his letter to George Sterling attests, Bierce himself was well aware of his "notorious obscurity." As the letter, however, does not make clear, Bierce at least partly insured that his reputation would be, in the term of a 1909 reviewer, "underground." For example, Bierce refused to publish his short stories in national magazines that customarily edited contributions to conform to the popular stylistic and sentimental standards of the time, standards that Bierce rightly despised. When an editor of *Metropolitan Magazine* approached him on the matter, the inimitable Ambrose replied: "I know how to write a story . . . for magazine readers for whom literature is too good, but I will not do so so long as stealing is more honorable and interesting."[2] Instead of seeking a national audience Bierce preferred to publish his stories in brief collections of limited editions that were often produced by small California presses run mostly by friends who did not insist upon the extensive editing required by many major Eastern-based publishing companies. Furthermore, those stories that were printed by the big houses (Putnam, for example, published *In the Midst of Life—Tales of Soldiers and Civilians* in 1898) were not widely reviewed partly because the work had already appeared earlier elsewhere and partly because Bierce himself was a caustic reviewer who had offended many of the other established reviewers of his day. Neither would Bierce take the standard route to literary prominence and produce novels: "I'll die first!" he insisted.[3] And he did.

Bierce's attitude toward his obscurity was characteristically defiant: "My independence is my wealth; it is my literature."[4] Yet it would be grossly inaccurate to maintain that Bierce really was, in Wilson Follett's phrase, "America's neglected satirist."[5] On the contrary, this "neglected satirist" was one of America's best known—and, by his targets, most hated—newspaper columnists during the 1890s. His vituperative attacks on fellow journalists, on novelists (most notably "Miss Nancy" Howells and "Miss Nancy" James), and on self-serving businessmen and politicians enlivened such newspapers as the San Francisco *Examiner* and the New

York *Journal*. His columns were widely read and highly praised by those who did not elicit his eagle-eyed—and eagle-clawed—attention.

Today, of course, Bierce is best known as a short story writer, and Bierce himself seems to have taken somewhat less pride in his journalism than in his other literary endeavors. The twelve volume *Collected Works*, published between 1909 and 1912 and supervised by the author himself, includes relatively little of his estimated four million words of journalistic writing.[6] Disorganized, inaccurate, incomplete, the *Collected Works* is a collection of undated selections, a scholar's nightmare that has not at all served to preserve Bierce's reputation as a journalist. So it is not surprising that most commentary on Bierce written in the decades since his peculiar "passing" should focus on his fiction. His journalism simply is not accessible to a large audience, although collections such as *The Ambrose Bierce Satanic Reader*, edited by E. J. Hopkins, and Lawrence I. Berkove's recent *Skepticism and Dissent* do give the general reader a sampling of Bierce at his journalistic best.[7]

But if the focus of Bierce criticism is on the fiction, it must be emphasized that such attention has taken an unusual form. We see various literary critics who, at odd intervals and in different generations, "rediscover" the same "lost" writer. As early as 1928 Wilson Follett could note that "nearly all" of the criticism of Bierce begins with the "conviction that in the general purport of Bierce there is something far greater than has yet got itself recognized in American literary history of the official sort."[8] In his fine introduction to a 1957 edition of *The Devil's Dictionary*, Carey McWilliams sounds much the same note when he comments on Bierce's current "rediscovery after long intervals of neglect," a neglect "that continues to the present time."[9] Still more recently, Jeffrey F. Thomas observes that "writers of dissertations on Ambrose Bierce and his works often proclaim their desire to call critical attention to an unjustly neglected artist."[10] Even a cursory survey of the essays in the present collection can affirm one's sense that Bierce criticism does not so much "evolve" as play at "lost and found." Something is clearly wrong here if for nearly seventy-five years the standard essay on Bierce must begin by attempting to reclaim him—again—from critical obscurity.

One can hypothesize that Bierce has enjoyed or endured such a checkered history precisely because his own writing is a mixed bag. Bierce himself delighted in opposing the reigning assumptions of his day. He regularly played the devil's advocate and violated many of the accepted rules of life and art in late nineteenth-century America, the Gilded Age in which he incongruously flourished. And since he broke the rules of his time, he often does not fit our contemporary retrospective categories. The historical critic, for example, might have a difficult time placing Bierce amongst his fellow realists. Bierce, it will be remembered, defined "realism" as "the art of depicting nature as it is seen by toads."[11] Only an *expanded* definition of realism accommodates Bierce's idiosyncratic writing. Thus Howard Bahr, in his fine essay, "Ambrose Bierce and Literary Realism," carefully redefines realism to include the subconscious and inexplicable realms that more traditional realists ignored. As Bahr notes, Bierce himself redefined the reigning literary mode and thought of himself as a *true* realist, a realist who knew that the full measure of reality could not be taken by inchworms.

Neither can Bierce be called a naturalist—at least not without qualification. As such stories as "The Coup de Grâce" and "Chickamauga" amply attest, Bierce's sense of human suffering is certainly as keen as Theodore Dreiser's or Jack London's. Yet Bierce would never fully absolve humans of the responsibility for their own misfortunes by the naturalist's ploy of blaming the environment or "crass Casualty." Nor does Bierce take human mortality with the naturalist's deadly seriousness. As M. E. Grenander shows in "Bierce's Turn of the Screw: Tales of Ironical Terror," Bierce's perspective is generally cosmic, and from that perspective human failings—war, superstition, religion, science—seem paltry, comical. Naturalists are rarely as funny—or as wise—as Bierce.

Nor is Bierce's humor always in good taste (a term he would despise). In some senses he was a black humorist before his time. For example, the story "An Imperfect Conflagration" begins with the memorable line: "Early one June morning in 1872 I murdered my father—an act which made a deep impression on me at the time."[12] The unnamed narrator of the same tale later experiences a certain regret:

> That afternoon I went to the chief of police, told him what I had done and asked his advice. It would be very painful to me if the facts became publicly known. My conduct would be generally condemned; the newspapers would bring it up against me if ever I should run for office. The chief saw the force of these considerations; he was himself an assassin of wide experience.[13]

A reflective patricide operates in a world as absurd as he himself is. Such tales do not represent the forms of humor we commonly associate with the late nineteenth-century and the tall tale tellers or local colorists, writers such as Joel Chandler Harris or Bret Harte.[14]

Bierce can seem to be an historical misfit. He can also offend more formalistically-oriented critics such as the neo-Aristotelians or the New Critics. Intentionally, and blithely, violating the concept of "unity of action" or effect; preferring, it seems, the inappropriate to the fitting; disrupting linear plot lines to give a disjointed rendering of a tale, Bierce does not fit the categories of those who prefer that art be orderly. If, for example, Cleanth Brooks and Robert Penn Warren represent New Criticism at its finest, or at least its most consistent, we can easily see how Bierce's fiction eludes these critics' categories. Brooks and Warren, in their discussion of "An Occurrence at Owl Creek Bridge," discover, despite ample evidence to the contrary, only an action tale with a trick ending. So they dismiss the whole story as if Bierce were some inept O. Henry.[15] As F. J. Logan points out in his essay on this same story, these critics did not read the story with the attention to detail that the New Critic is supposed to prize. They should have discovered that, as Logan puts it, "the ending is in the beginning and throughout." The story is all of a piece but the piece is more complicated than their terms will admit.

Bierce has eluded standard critical categories, but he certainly has not eluded a popular audience. Presently his fiction is available in several editions and virtually every anthology of short fiction intended for classroom use includes a Bierce story or two. But despite the many attempts that have been made to elevate him into the "canon" of major American writers, he still is not generally accorded that status. As already suggested, one reason for the exclusion is the fact that Bierce's fiction does not fit readily into standard critical categories. Another might be that his corpus, as a fiction writer, amounts to less than one hundred stories, not a substantial hook upon which to hang the designation of "major" writer. Bierce is, and may well remain, a "major minor" or "minor major" writer—which means that he will undoubtedly continue to enjoy a wide popular appeal and will also be the subject of many more essays which attempt at the outset to oust him from his half-respectable niche into the full light of acceptability—an elevation which the man himself would have abhorred. The reader versed in Bierce will recall that that master of aphorisms defined "famous" as "conspicuously miserable."[16]

Unfortunately, however, Bierce's "obscurity" as a man of letters did not render him conspicuously happy. As a number of essays in the present collection indicate, Bierce was rarely pleased with either his life or the life of the times in which he lived. He earned such contemporary appellations as "Bitter Bierce" or the "Wickedest Man in San Francisco" and seemed to work as hard at cultivating the fiction of the man as he did at creating fictions of a more literary order. There are numerous (and possibly apocryphal) representative stories. He supposedly kept a skull (of a friend?) on his desk. His ash tray, according to other reports, was a cigar box filled with ashes (of another friend?) to which Bierce added the ashes of his own cigars. His marriage, we know, disintegrated. His sons met tragic deaths. His bitterest enemies tended, more often than not, to be former friends. Yet he showed a singular tendency to help upstart writers—especially if they fawned. He also despised writers who advocated reform in their fiction but nonetheless championed important social causes in his journalism. One social objective Bierce often (and happily) accomplished was the debunking of other dubious social causes. He could, in his public writings, seem misogynistic, anti-Semitic, racist, elitist. Yet as Lawrence I. Berkove demonstrates in an original essay published in this volume, Bierce could also stand up for the rights of women, Blacks, Jews, immigrants, and often did so on occasions that brought him neither credit nor profit.

Obviously Bierce was an impressive man, a man of striking contradictions. So perhaps it is fitting that his reputation as a character has,
until recently, out-stripped his reputation as an author. His bizarre and
unpredictable life—culminating in his even more puzzling disappearance
and, presumably, death—has provided material for numerous biographies, not all of which are exercises in careful scholarship and critical
restraint. Indeed, in 1929 four myth-making studies appeared, each por-
traying a different Bierce and, in the case of three of them, a Bierce
markedly different from any possible original.[17] Only Carey McWilliams'
Ambrose Bierce: A Biography can be seen as having any lasting value. But
McWilliams more than makes up for the obvious failings of the other
three. His biography, still in print, remains one of the more reliable and
well written studies of Bierce's life even though it does not adequately
concern itself with Bierce's accomplishments as an author. The substance
and merit of this full length study are intimated by the essay by
McWilliams included in the present volume.

Between the 1929 biographical treatments of Bierce, the character,
and the more contemporary criticism of Bierce, the author, fall the important, although somewhat inaccurate works of Franklin Walker and
the more impressive biographical efforts of Paul Fatout. Walker's *San
Francisco's Literary Frontier* (1939) profitably places Bierce within a context and a literary milieu. But Walker's subsequent volume, *Ambrose
Bierce: The Wickedest Man in San Francisco* (1941), is a reversion to the
earlier school of pseudo-biographical pseudo-criticism, for this second
study perpetuates numerous exaggerations and falsehoods found in the
early biographies.[18] In contrast, works such as Fatout's *Ambrose Bierce:
The Devil's Lexicographer* (1951) and his subsequent *Ambrose Bierce and
the Black Hills* (1956) show how dubious many of these myths are.[19]
Fatout uses primary sources to formulate an accurate view of Bierce's life
that serves as a useful counterbalance to Walker and to his predecessor's in
Bierceology, Walter Neale, "Adolphe de Castro," and C. Hartley
Grattan.

More recent biographies, such as Richard O'Connor's *Ambrose
Bierce: A Biography* (1967), are mostly a reworking of earlier material.[20]
O'Connor especially relies on Fatout's books and essays. The resulting
volume, neither original nor thoroughly accurate, is nevertheless lively
and appeals to a broad, popular audience. Which is precisely the author's
intention. It is unfortunate, however, that O'Connor could not achieve
that end without dwelling on the more lurid "suppositions" that have ac-
crued around Bierce's life story.

Moreover, as the opening biographical chapters of M. E.
Grenander's Twayne study, *Ambrose Bierce* (1971), amply demonstrate,
one can write an entertaining account of Bierce's life without compromis-
ing the factual or sensationalizing the supposed.[21] Of course, Grenander
has distinguished herself for over two decades now as a diligent scholar of
all things Biercean. As the concluding bibliography to this volume attests,

she has discovered and published significant Bierce letters, she has done important bibliographical work, and she has written careful discussions of Bierce's journalism and his fiction. She also approaches Bierce with a sense of humor, a requisite interpretive tool that many critics of Bierce decline to employ—frequently with unhappy results.

M. E. Grenander's book on Bierce also indicates the way in which Bierce criticism of the seventies has tended to use the facts of Bierce's biography to support interpretations of his writing, rather than to extrapolate from those facts to present still more strange tales *about* the writer. David D. Anderson, in an essay written for the present collection, also effectively employs this same methodology and in "The Old Northwest, the Midwest, and the Making of Three American Iconoclasts" uses what we know of Bierce's biography to fit him within a particular pattern of American demography in the middle and latter portions of the last century. As Anderson demonstrates, a number of the more cynical critics of the Gilded Age were born to parents who believed the myths of westward expansionism and Manifest Destiny, but who found no pots of gold at the end of the wagon train's westward trek. The sons of these pioneers grew up in poverty. They experienced firsthand the shabbiness of an earlier version of the American dream and therefore tended to criticize in their writings later manifestations of that same dream. Professor Anderson's essay also assesses a work rarely analyzed by Bierce scholars, *The Monk and the Hangman's Daughter*. Admittedly the novella—co-published by Bierce and de Castro, and Bierce's longest work—was "adopted" (some would say plagiarized) from a German tale. But what Anderson finds significant is not what was borrowed but what was changed. Even in an ostensibly medieval German tale we find reflections of Bierce's mid-American views. He dresses nineteenth-century Protestant Revivalism in Catholic robes, and thus opposes the standard religion of his time and place.

Grenander and Anderson demonstrate a fact of Bierce criticism that other prospective Bierceophiles would do well to note. It is possible to write on Bierce, to write on Bierce's life even, without being caught in the fruitless, mythologizing tangle in which the earlier biographers labored. Yet, ironically, there are still crucial biographical questions that have yet to be answered. For example, although there are myriad conjectures (some of them quite plausible), we still do not know *exactly* what happened to Bierce when, in 1914, as a seventy-one-year-old war correspondent, he disappeared in Mexico. Similarly, although much has been made of the fact that Bierce is the only important American author who both served in and wrote about the Civil War, there are still questions about his military service. In fact, only in the past few years have critics even begun to examine carefully Bierce's military record to determine precisely what he did or did not do while serving. Only after this task has been completed can we sort out Bierce's war stories, his journalistic accounts, and his many personal yarns (often factually fictionalized) of the injustices done him by military bureaucracy and trace the genesis of each.[22] The point is that despite the proliferation of often fanciful biographies, the hard work of establishing the relevant facts is as yet incomplete. The Bierce correspondence, for example, could provide many important facts about his life as well as significant comments on his own aesthetic theories. But as M. E. Grenander has often remarked, we do not have an edition of Bierce's complete letters for the simple reason that few publishers are willing to go to the expense of printing the letters of a "minor major" writer. So the diligent Bierce scholar must track down letters which are scattered about the country—from Yale University Library to the Huntington—or which remain, uncatalogued, in private collections.[23]

An MLA-sponsored textual project could resolve most of these difficulties. But such a solution is most unlikely. Definitive editing takes a long time and money is short. The best one can hope is that a new generation of Bierce scholars and doctoral students might piece by piece do the more important tasks. Particularly welcome would be a definitive and well-annotated edition of the stories, complete with variorum texts. The complete letters (or even the relatively complete letters) should at last be collected between two covers. More of the journalistic writings, especially from the first decade of this century, could be made available to a larger audience. Perhaps benevolent, philanthropic private publishers would even underwrite the expense of publishing these volumes.

The textual problems facing the Bierce scholar are indeed imposing. Yet I do not mean to suggest that we should abandon interpretive studies and give ourselves over totally to textual scholarship. There are significant omissions in the literary criticism of Bierce, too. For example, there is only one book-length treatment of the fiction, Stuart C. Woodruff's *The Short Stories of Ambrose Bierce: A Study in Polarity*.[24] Unfortunately, Woodruff begins with the assumption that Bierce is successful in only a "handful" of the war tales and ends with the assumption that, of this handful, only "An Occurrence at Owl Creek Bridge" has any lasting worth—and even that classic has serious flaws. Woodruff assesses in depth only five or six stories; he briefly discusses barely a dozen more. His study can in no way be considered a comprehensive treatment of the fiction.

In contrast, Grenander's *Ambrose Bierce* touches on dozens of the stories and many of the fables, aphorisms, and journalistic writings as well. As implied before, her book is one of the single most important contributions to Bierce studies. Yet, the very inclusiveness demanded by the introductory nature of her study means that she cannot devote lengthy discussions to individual major stories and neither can she fully assess Bierce's complexity as a narrative strategist. Still, few critics have read with more insight or wit than Grenander and hers is a good starting place for any serious (or amateur) student of Bierce.

I would suggest, however, that we still need several kinds of books and articles on Bierce, and that the essays that follow mark several starts in promising directions. First, as already noted, we need thoroughly edited texts and texts of works other than the stories and *The Devil's Dictionary*.[25] Other work, particularly the journalism, should also be fit into a larger social context. Here, it should be noted, Lawrence I. Berkove, in the extensive introduction to the recently published *Skepticism and Dissent*, has performed much of that important task, a task that will certainly be carried further with his soon to be published *A Braver Man Than Anybody Knew*.[26] We also need more discussions of Bierce's fiction that move beyond the standard thematic categories. Most criticism, however good, still focuses on the comic *or* the grotesque elements in Bierce's writings; on the war tales *or* the ghost stories. Even the present table of contents shows how pervasive the established categories have become and the bibliography attests even more to that same fact. Yet as I have earlier suggested, Bierce can be comic in his most grotesque tales; his most comic works can also verge on the macabre. Thus one of the grisliest scenes in "Chickamauga" occurs when the small child tries to mount the back of one of the hideously wounded men who can barely crawl upon the ground. The boy, playing horsey, laughs happily. He has played the game before with his father's slave and knows that it is fun. The parable is obvious and made more obvious by the merging of the comedy of small errors and the tragedy of huge ones—both of which are equally human, equally mundane.

Similarly, one cannot conclusively divide the ghost from the war stories. Into which category does one fit Bierce's most famous tale, "An Occurrence at Owl Creek Bridge"? Does Peyton Farquhar's perseverance in the face of hanging illustrate the nature of men at war or the preternatural powers of the expiring (and expired?) consciousness? Obviously the answer to that question is both, and this story is frequently discussed in essays that focus on Bierce's portrayal of war and in essays that focus on his portrayal of the supernatural. Consider also "A Tough Tussle" and "One of the Missing." In both stories we have characters who die in battle but who also die as victims of their own imagined fears and not from bullets fired by any external enemy. In tales of soldiers *and* civilians, characters often war with themselves, often succumb to horrors of their own making. In nearly every Bierce story the action turns on a perceiver who must determine a response to reality but who often does not know what is real, what imagined, and what an inextricable intermingling of both.[27] Or a comic intermingling. The same author who penned the appalling scenes in "The Coup de Grâce" could also write the hilarious "Jupiter Doke, Brigadier-General"—an 1890s predecessor of *Catch-22* and an early portrayal of war as a colossal breakdown in communication.

But whether writing of war or of ghosts, in a comic vein or in a tragic, Bierce always focuses on the question of how one knows what one thinks one knows and how one reacts to what is finally unknowable. To do so, to convey the impressionistic quality of reality, Bierce deploys a range of fictional strategies that make him one of the major technicians of his time. Perhaps the major critical task yet to be accomplished is the careful study of those techniques and the demonstration of how Bierce's fiction explores the formalistic possibilities of the short story as a genre.

So there are yet several different objectives that Bierce scholarship can profitably pursue. Textual critics are invited to sort out the letters and papers. Literary historians might better place Bierce within the context of his time and show how other important writers of the 1890s and after—Crane and Chopin, certainly—borrowed Bierce's flowing narrative techniques and were influenced by his intricate experiments with subjective languages and diverse rhetorical stances. Literary critics might well be encouraged to study Bierce's narrative methods—his manipulation of subjective and objective time, his concern with perception, his ploy of testing perceptions by subjecting his protagonists to seeming life and death crises that are, often, crises only because they seem so. The postmodernist critic might also consider some of Bierce's more unusual narrative excursions in stories like "The Moonlit Road" or "The Death of Halpin Frayser." As William Bysshe Stein implies in his discussion of "The Death of Halpin Frayser," in Bierce's most complex works statement and counterstatement so turn on one another that the reader must admit the subjectivity of any provisional reading. Like more contemporary authors—Jorge Luis Borges or Julio Cortazar, for example—Bierce delights in strewing red herrings in the path of the careless and the careful reader.[28] But the alternative to an obvious misreading is not necessarily some straight and narrow path to the heart of the tale. Bierce's best stories—whether war tales, ghost stories, or the so-called "tall tales"—cannot be so simply pinned down or summed up. In the realm between the conscious and the subconscious, the world of darkness and dreams as well as the world of common daytime experience are all subsumed into the waking nightmare. The only reality is the reality of the "haunted mind."

The following essays are offered to the reader as an attempt to move once again beyond previously established preconceptions about Bierce as man and as writer. The earliest reviews included here indicate that Bierce was early on recognized as a great *and* flawed writer.[29] But after his strange disappearance in 1914, one notices that reviewers become more ready to resolve the contradictory estimation that had characterized the living man. We begin to encounter the "great and neglected" writer or the "mean and overestimated" man. The contemporary criticism included in the present volume attempts a more even-handed appraisal of Bierce's contributions in his day and in ours. Taken together, the selections present an overview of the contemporaneous and the current assessments of Bierce as well as a representative sampling of the best Bierce criticism to date. They also discuss all of the major phases of Bierce's life and letters. But of course one volume cannot contain all the selections that I wished.

The bibliography will direct the interested reader to other studies, many of them excellent, of Bierce the man and the literary figure.

The timing of this volume is fortunate. Judging from the number of editions of Bierce's work currently in print, the amount of criticism that is now being published on his work, and the frequency with which dissertations on Bierce are appearing, one could even surmise that he is enjoying a kind of "renaissance"—yet another period of rediscovery. That rediscovery is not surprising. Considering the current popular interest in fantasy and the occult, the present academic concern with formalistic ingenuity and structuralist mappings of the "real" and "unreal," Bierce's fiction does sound a number of contemporary notes. Like such writers as John Barth, Donald Barthelme, and Joseph Heller, Bierce exhibits a taste for the comically grotesque and a disdain for standard convention. As previously observed, his narrative techniques can well be compared to those used by Borges and a number of the other contemporary South American and Latin American fantasists. So maybe *that* is what Bierce has been doing all of these years south of the border: influencing writers there after having given up at home. But more seriously, although Bierce is much read these days, I hesitate to suggest that we claim him as a writer for our time. He has achieved that dubious distinction too often in the past hundred years. Suffice it to say that he is an *enduring* writer who has endured the exaggerated vicissitudes of his literary reputation for quite long enough.

I wish to thank the Michigan State University Humanities Research Institute for a grant which allowed me to accomplish some of the editing on the present collection. I also want to thank Professor James Nagel for putting up with the inconvenience of overseeing a book edited partly from the midwest—the *Japanese* midwest. Special thanks to Mrs. Betty Uphaus, a superb typist. And, finally, I am grateful to my friends and colleagues at Michigan State University, particularly Professors Linda W. Wagner and Nancy Ainsworth and my doctoral student, Ms. Judy Funston. They have attended to last minute details and unexpected editorial problems, details and problems that would have been most difficult for me to resolve while a Visiting Professor of American Literature at Kobe College. Their assistance in these matters (and others) is most appreciated.

Cathy N. Davidson

Notes

1. Bertha Clark Pope, ed., *The Letters of Ambrose Bierce* (San Francisco: Book Club of California, 1922), p. 148; with a memoir by George Sterling.

2. Pope, p. 102.

3. Pope, p. 74.

4. Quoted by Walter Neale in *Life of Ambrose Bierce* (New York: Walter Neale, 1929), p. 97.

5. Wilson Follett, "America's Neglected Satirist," *The Dial*, 65 (July 1918), 49–52.

6. See the "Introduction" to Ernest Jerome Hopkins, ed. *The Complete Short Stories of Ambrose Bierce* (Garden City, N.Y.: Doubleday, 1970).

7. Ernest Jerome Hopkins, ed., *The Ambrose Bierce Satanic Reader: Selections from the Invective Journalism of the Great Satirist* (Garden City, N.Y.: Doubleday, 1968); and Lawrence I. Berkove, ed., *Skepticism and Dissent. Selected Journalism from 1898–1901* (Ann Arbor: Delmas, 1980).

8. Wilson Follett, "Ambrose Bierce: An Analysis of the Perverse Wit that Shaped His Work," *Bookman*, 68 (1928–29), 284–89.

9. "Introduction," *The Devil's Dictionary* (New York: Sagamore Press, 1957), p. v.

10. Jeffrey F. Thomas, "Ambrose Bierce," *ALR*, 8 (Summer 1975), 198.

11. *The Devil's Dictionary* (1911; rpt. New York: Dover, 1958).

12. *The Complete Short Stories of Ambrose Bierce*, p. 405.

13. *The Complete Short Stories*, p. 406.

14. However, E. J. Hopkins does use the term "tall tale" to designate Bierce's more macabre stories and notes that "to a Westerner no explanation should be needed for the fact that Ambrose Bierce wrote twenty-three 'tall tales,' since this was one form of literature that the pioneers had brought across the plains. . . . The essence of the 'tall tale' was high exaggeration presented in a deadpan manner as truthful fact; it was a hoax aimed at the listener who might be sucker enough to take the wild tale seriously" (p. 403). It should be emphasized, however, that Bierce's tales of gruesome patricides, matricides, infanticides, and various other "-cides" are rather different than those tall tales of Paul Bunyan and his famous ox, Babe.

15. See *Understanding Fiction*, 2nd ed. (New York: Appleton, 1959), p. 52.

16. This definition is from *The Devil's Dictionary*.

17. The four biographies are: Adolphe de Castro [Gustav Adolph Danziger], *Portrait of Ambrose Bierce* (New York: Century, 1929); C. Hartley Grattan, *Bitter Bierce: A Mystery of American Letters* (Garden City: Doubleday, 1929); Carey McWilliams, *Ambrose Bierce: A Biography* (New York: A. and C. Boni, 1929); and Walter Neale, *Life of Ambrose Bierce*.

18. *San Francisco's Literary Frontier* (New York: Alfred A. Knopf, 1939) and *Ambrose Bierce: The Wickedest Man in San Francisco* (San Francisco: Colt Press, 1941).

19. *Ambrose Bierce: The Devil's Lexicographer* (Norman: Univ. of Oklahoma Press, 1951) and *Ambrose Bierce and the Black Hills* (Norman: Univ. of Oklahoma Press, 1956). See also the Fatout entries in the "Articles" section of the bibliography in this volume.

20. Richard O'Connor, *Ambrose Bierce: A Biography* (Boston: Little, Brown, 1967).

21. M. E. Grenander, *Ambrose Bierce* (New York: Twayne, 1971).

22. One of the most thorough examinations of Bierce's actual war records is Matthew C. O'Brien's "Ambrose Bierce and the Civil War: 1865," *AL*, 48 (1976), 377–81.

23. This is not to imply that no work has been done with Bierce's letters. On the contrary, even a cursory survey of the "Published Letters" section of the bibliography in this volume indicates the quantity of scholarship already accomplished. The quality is equally impressive. Yet there is much still to be done.

24. *The Short Stories of Ambrose Bierce: A Study in Polarity* (Pittsburgh: Univ. of Pittsburgh Press, 1964).

25. Again the problem is finding a publisher. At least three notable Bierce scholars of my acquaintance have tried to publish excellent collections using an appealing "best of Bierce" format, but to no avail. Such lack of interest by publishers does not bode well for future *scholarly* editions of Bierce's work.

26. Lawrence I. Berkove, *Ambrose Bierce: A Braver Man Than Anybody Knew* (Ann Arbor: Ardis, forthcoming 1980 or 1981).

27. For a further discussion of Bierce's experiments with perceptual awareness as well as an exploration of his fictional techniques, see my essay "Literary Semantics and the Fiction of

Ambrose Bierce," *ETC., A Review of General Semantics*, 31 (Sept. 1974), 263–71.

28. For a fuller discussion of the similarities between Bierce and Borges, see Howard M. Fraser's "Points South: Ambrose Bierce, Jorge Luis Borges, and the Fantastic," *STCL*, 1 (1977), 173–81.

29. Early reviews tended to discuss both the man and his work. Sometimes, indeed, the emphasis was on the former. A number of these commentaries might now be called "review essays" rather than, strictly speaking, "reviews." But as I have already emphasized, one cannot be too categorical in discussing Bierce—and certainly his early critics, friends and foes alike, dealt with him fast and loose.

REVIEWS AND
REVIEW ESSAYS

[Review of *In the Midst of Life*]

Anonymous*

Mr. Bierce's collection of American tales of horror is occasionally marred by extravagance of style, and some of the more terrible descriptions of solitary suffering are too long drawn out. His themes are chosen for the most part from the Civil War, and it is characteristic of the nature of that struggle that the pride of soldiership nowhere appears in these descriptions. We read of nothing but the minutest details of bodily and mental pain: of tragedies like 'A Horseman in the Sky,' where a skirmisher shoots his father (of the opposite faction), who has bound him to "do his duty" in the war; like 'Coulter's Notch,' where an artillerist plays upon his own house, held by the enemy, and slaughters unwittingly his wife and child; like the frightful story of panic, 'A Tough Tussle,' when a man in an agonizing state of nervous tension takes the corpse of an enemy for an assailant, and is slain himself while engaged in his ghastly onslaught. The hapless man was on outlying picket in a forest, alone, while his lunacy grew on him.

> He to whom the portentous conspiracy of night and solitude and silence in the heart of a great forest is not an unknown experience needs not to be told what another world it all is—how even the most commonplace and familiar objects take on another character. The trees group themselves differently; they draw close together, as if in fear. The very silence has another quality than the silence of the day. And it is full of half-heard whispers, whispers that startle—ghosts of sounds, too, such as are never heard under other conditions: notes of strange night-birds, the cries of small animals in sudden encounters with stealthy foes, or in their dreams, a rustling in the dead leaves—it may be the leap of a wood-rat, it may be the footstep of a panther. What caused the breaking of that twig? what the low, alarmed twittering in that bushful of birds? There are sounds without a name, forms without substance, translations in space of objects which have not been seen to move, movements wherein nothing is observed to change its place. Ah, children of the sunlight and the gaslight, how little you know of the world in which you live!

*This item is reprinted by permission of *The Huntington Library, San Marino, California*, from *The Atheneum*, 20 February 1892, p. 241.

It will be seen the writer can give a vivid description. Perhaps the most gruesome of all the military stories is that of the lost child at Chickamauga, who slept through the battle, and, guided by the wounded crawling to the river, found its home burnt, its mother slain, and was struck deaf and dumb with the shock. In this the details are given with the sort of power one sees in a Russian battle-piece, and will repel more readers than they attract. Incidentally one can realize something of the visible experiences of that most strange, Titanic, and unorthodox of wars, with its ambitious strategy and confused manœuvring, and its incessant embarrassment owing to the vastness and complexity of natural obstacles. We should consider this part of the book extremely unsuitable for young readers, to whom it is surely more wholesome to present the nobler side of war. Of the civilian stories, 'A Holy Terror' and 'The Middle Toe of the Right Foot' quite correspond to the promise of their titles, and are calculated to be read with most result after a heavy supper, though 'A Watcher by the Dead' and 'The Man and the Snake' may also affect the nerves. In 'Haita the Shepherd' and 'An Heiress from Redhorse' the author endeavours, most inadequately, to reassure his readers. Is "Sepoy," by the way, established American for British India?

[Review of *In the Midst of Life*]

Anonymous*

No one who ever read Ambrose Bierce's 'Tales of Soldiers and Civilians,' published originally under this title in San Francisco in 1891, and now reissued, with a few additions, by G. P. Putnam's Sons (as it has meanwhile been in London and Leipzig), under the major title of 'In the Midst of Life'—no one, we say, could forget the impression of these grimly powerful vignettes chiefly of our civil war. Tolstoi himself might praise the psychology of dying in "One of the Missing" or in "The Occurrence at Owl Creek Bridge"; and what an allegory is "Chickamauga," with the strayed child, wooden sword in hand, leading the crawling troop of hideously wounded men to the blazing ruins of his own home and the mangled body of his own mother! This little volume could not have been revived at a more opportune moment, and deserves the widest circulation as a peace tract of the first order, in the present craze for bloodshed. Mr. Bierce's imagination, his poetic feeling, his humor (which can be sardonic on occasion) have long been known to be above the ordinary. They are here fitly and truthfully applied in the depiction of organized human slaughter.

*Reprinted by permission of *The Nation*, 333 Sixth Avenue, New York, New York. Copyright, 1898, The Nation Associates. From *The Nation*, 66 (March 1898), 225.

[Review of *In the Midst of Life*]

Anonymous*

Ambrose Bierce was a writer of high ambitions and uncommon powers, who never quite reached his mark and is already half-forgotten. At his best, he comes nearer than any other to the company of Hawthorne and Poe. This collection of tales was first printed in 1891, with the following preface by the author: "Denied existence by the chief publishing houses of the country, this book owes itself to Mr. E. L. G. Steele, merchant, of this city [San Francisco]. In attesting Mr. Steele's faith in his judgment and his friend, it will serve its author's main and best ambition." More than half these stories come straight from Bierce's experience as an officer in the Civil War. Like the others, they deal pretty monotonously with blood and terror and death. No doubt the chief publishing houses of the early nineties dismissed the book as "morbid." Taken as a whole, it is morbid, and rather tiresome as well—a supper of horrors too long drawn out. Even the four or five among these tales which are touched with tragic pity and terror are compromised by their enforced fellowship with stories which are mere grewsome inventions. No modern realism has rendered more ruthlessly the bloody items of war: "The greater part of the forehead was torn away, and from the jagged hole the brain protruded, overflowing the temple, a frothy mass of gray, crowned with clusters of crimson bubbles—the mark of a shell." The grisly, the ironic, the macabre, are more frequently achieved than the tragic. Now and then, however, as in "Chickamauga," the story of the deaf and dumb child playing among the horrors of war till dreadfully awakened to their reality, a deep and haunting note is struck. On the whole, the tales rest their effect too much on the surprise ending which Bierce, before "O. Henry," somewhat overemployed. Yet he does not eschew the simpler kind of narrative condemned by current magazine editors as the "sketch."

*Reprinted by permission of *The Nation*, 333 Sixth Avenue, New York, New York. Copyright, 1918, The Nation Associates. From *The Nation*, 107 (August 1918), 232.

[Review of *The Collected Works*, Vol. I]

Anonymous*

This volume, which is published in sumptuous style, consists, in almost equal parts, of political satire and personal reminiscence, the former occupying the place of prominence. Satire of one kind and another is so redoubtable a faculty of our author that many good people identify him with it alone. This opinion is due, no doubt, to their want of acquaintance with the full range of his work, and more obviously to his having made a memorable appearance in journalism as a flagellator of corruption. The satire which gives its title to the present volume—'Ashes of the Beacon'—is a notable and well-wrought production of its kind. Cast in the form of a succinct philosophical monograph, in which one of the scholars of an exceedingly far future reviews the causes of the 'Decline and Fall of the Connected States of America,' it is a forcible indictment of some of the notions and practices which are the conspicuous and less admirable attributes of a generally astonishing people. The most sacred things are submitted to contemptuous touch by a critic whose attitude towards "the ancient Americans"—gone several millenniums into the dim disastrous past—is very much what ours might be towards *Pithecanthropus erectus*, had that worthy left a sufficiency of documents for a study of his polity and social life. None of their follies, we learn, was quite so curious as their general fatuity, especially in regard to the excellence and originality of their form of government. "Republican government was thought by them to have been established"—for the first time on earth, of course—

> by the god Washington, whose worship, along with that of such *dii minores* as Gufferson, Jaxon and Lincon (identical probably with the Hebru Abrem), runs like a shining thread through all the warp and woof of the stuff which garmented their moral nakedness.

With another worship of theirs, which he somewhat illiterately calls gyneolatry, the historian holds less civil terms. That woman was regarded as a deity is shown by the fact that the American woman had permission to kill a man whenever she felt disposed. Some vestiges of an extinct custom might cause her, even so late as the twentieth century, to be put on trial for murder; but no American jury would think of convicting. Presumably their wives would not let them. Woman is, indeed, by her incursion into the world of work and wages, the remoter cause of the terrific downfall in which American civilization perishes. But before it comes to that, many other factors of weakness and corruption are submitted to a

*This item is reprinted by permission of *The Huntington Library*, San Marino, California. From *The Atheneum*, 3 July 1909, p. 8.

criticism which is rarely rendered innocuous by any excessive touch of wildness or even of humour. Not that humour is entirely lacking. Witness the account of an anarchist insurrection, with its accompaniments of vast slaughter, ending thus:—

> Of all the principal cities, only Chicago and San Francisco escaped. The people of the former were all anarchists, and the latter was valorously and successfully defended by the Chinese.

The form in which this satire is cast has a chastening effect on the writer's style, saving him from some besetting faults. As the survey is made in a large historic manner, so the writing touches at times a gravity and finish which recall Gibbon. Let one example (slightly condensed in transcription) show Mr. Bierce at his best:—

> Nor must we forget that ages before the inception of the American republics this form of government had been discredited by emphatic failures among the most enlightened and powerful nations of antiquity. . . . To the lesson of these failures the founders of the eighteenth and nineteenth century republics were blind and deaf. Have we, then, reason to believe that our posterity will be wiser because instructed by a greater number of examples? Or is the number of examples which they will have in memory really greater? Already the instances of Egypt, China, Greece and Rome are almost lost in the mists of antiquity: they are known, except by infrequent report, to the archæologist only, and but dimly and uncertainly to him. The brief and imperfect record of yesterdays which we call History is like the travelling vine of India, which, taking new root as it advances, decays at one end while it grows at the other, and so is constantly perishing and finally lost in all the spaces which it has over-passed.

'The Land beyond the Blow' introduces us to a manner which is, we fear, more characteristic. The narrator, turning with disgust from a brutal street scene, is followed by a bully, who wantonly strikes him senseless. The incident is etched unforgettably in a few lines; but we feel that the greatest writers of earlier literatures would have devised a less repulsive way of launching a man upon his dream-travel into strange lands. The lands are more strange than wonderful. No great powers of mind are needed in order to imagine countries where the grass is sky-blue, and the trees have long tresses reaching to the ground instead of leaves, or where the jutting rocks are of bronze veined with brass. The proofs of power would be in giving to such aberrations symbolic value and affinity with the psychology of the scene: which the author seldom achieves. But they are fantastic lands, inhabited by fantastic beings, who are pleased to give practical effect to certain moral truisms (as, that wealth is a disadvantage, that labour is a blessing, or that persecution invigorates a good cause) which among us are kept in due subordination to the requirements of sense and comfort. The 'Land beyond the Blow' is a land without an atmosphere, and therefore comparisons with Lucian and with Swift can only be made to the damage of the modern. On the other hand, the story forcibly recalls Mr. Chesterton, except that it is by a writer in whom the gifts of grace—as fancy and fun—are less, and the mental specific gravity greater.

The 'Bits of Autobiography' deal, in vividly written, but disconnected sections, with Mr. Bierce's experiences as a soldier in the Civil War, as a Treasury official doing risky work in the South later, as an engineer explorer crossing the plains, and as a journalist in London in the early seventies. Mr. Bierce seems to have taken very seriously the somewhat raffish celebrities of Fleet Street to the honour of whose acquaintance and orgies he was admitted; and would have us think that not Jamshyd himself gloried and drank deep as he and they. As a fact, we do not believe that they did his morals any material harm, but we suspect that they influenced his literary standards for life, and that, conscious of it or no, his aim ever since has been to write what any one of these judges would have declared to be "damned good stuff." The commodity which can be justly so described contains many elements admired in literature; but it is doubtful whether it ever ceases to be journalism.

[Review of *The Collected Works*, Vol. II]

Anonymous*

The second volume of the *Collected Works of Ambrose Bierce* (New York, Neale Publishing Company) confirms our opinion of that author's native power without quite cancelling our first impression of ability warped by a wrong choice of admirations. Entitled 'In the Midst of Life,' this collection of short stories might fitly have borne the name of one of them, 'A Holy Terror.' From the dedication we learn that some twenty years ago the book "was denied existence by the chief publishing houses of the country," and first reached the light in 1891 through the maieutic offices of a San Francisco merchant. We admire the merchant ("Mr. E. L. G. Steele of this city") without wondering greatly at the rejecting publishers. Twenty years ago such abstention from morality as Mr. Bierce affects was not well understood; nor was such crashing thoroughness of presentment as his (not to call it brutality) accounted a legitimate resource of literature in English. Twenty years earlier still, for that mat-

*This item is reprinted by permission of *The Huntington Library*, San Marino, California. From *The Atheneum*, 26 March 1910, p. 367.

ter, the idyllized realism of Bret Harte was endured rather than welcomed by many as a rough, uncivil inroad upon the clean carpet of polite letters—justified to the sensibilities usually by an ending in tears. There are no tears in Mr. Bierce, or they are as severely restrained as if there were no pity; but there is an abundance of terror. Nearly every story in the second part, indeed, is a study of the workings of fear. In 'A Watcher of the Dead' the illusion—the sense of being in the room with a corpse—even survives the explanation of the scene and the ensuing tragedy, leaving the reader with an uncomfortable feeling that Dr. Mancher is somebody else or a dead man at large. 'The Man and the Snake' is surely one of the most awful things in literature. What would in other hands have been an anticlimax—the revelation that the snake which killed the man by fright was a stuffed snake, its unearthly eyes mere shoe-buttons—actually enhances the awe of the story. Perhaps 'The Boarded Window' reaches the outer limit of the terrible.

The power of the treatment is not to be denied, but the style is imperilled by Mr. Bierce's journalistic experience, his sense of an audience: and his pose of contempt. Yet it is only fair to say that the better influence triumphs, and that in nearly every case the artistic aim controls the character of the writing and keeps it dignified. This is especially true of the war stories in the first part.

[Review of *The Collected Works*, Vol. III]

Anonymous*

The third volume of the *Collected Works of Ambrose Bierce* (New York, Neale Publishing Company) contains some two score short stories under the general title 'Can Such Things Be?' Most readers will fervently hope that they cannot be, and may find comfort in applying to the whole forty-odd the euphemistic sub-title of one of them—'A Story which is Untrue.' They are not so much ghost stories as stories of the unearthly and diabolic. Here corpses, already highly mature for burial, struggle with, stab, or strangle living men. A hound, not of heaven, but certainly not of earth, "materializes" in a closed room to tear with his fangs the jugular vein of his master's murderer, after the long torture of a nightly obsession. An unholy piece of mechanism, losing a game of chess to its creator, loses therewith its self-control, and, amid an appalling crescendo of whirring wheels, murders and mangles him with the fiendish brutality of an Edward Hyde. These are almost pleasant opponents compared with an in-

*This item is reprinted by permission of *The Huntington Library*, San Marino, California. From *The Atheneum*, 11 July 1910, p. 702.

discriminate beast called the Damned Thing, which belongs to the actinic region of the spectrum, and so has the advantage in a tussle of being viewless.

A good deal of this sounds fairly cheap, but what makes the difference here is the fact that Mr. Bierce's powers are better than the use he puts them to, and invest the use with something of their own value. We could ask for a happier choice of theme, but hardly for a more impeccable execution. To the author's hardness is here added more than a flavour of the unhallowed, and once at least an odour of the disgusting. The story of the cat in the coffin, "found among the papers of the late Leigh Bierce," should certainly have been buried with that gentleman. But even the wildest themes have underlying them some sort of metaphysical notion or conjecture.

[Review of *The Collected Works*, Vol. VII–X]

Anonymous*

The sumptuous edition of "The Collected Works of Ambrose Bierce" (New York, Neale Publishing Company), which was begun over two years ago, is now completed.

Vol. VII, *The Devil's Dictionary*, appears for the first time under its own desperate and predestined title. It seems that an earlier publisher liked well the matter of the book, but lacked the courage for the name, so it appeared as 'The Cynic's Word-Book,' "a name," says Mr. Bierce sententiously, "which the author had not the power to reject nor the happiness to approve." The book called forth a swarm of unworthy (and occasionally dishonest) imitations—"The Cynic's This, The Cynic's That, and The Cynic's t'Other," say the present publishers, taking up the tale of wrongs—"and among them they brought the word 'cynic' into disfavour so deep that any book bearing it was damned in advance of publication." What would have occurred had the run been started on the word "Devil," we shudder to guess.

The book is an alphabetical list of remarks on things in general—most of them cynical, and devoutly intended, we can believe, to be diabolic. Dealing with a wide range of topics as well as a great number of words, it presents a sort of summary index of the author's characteristic views as well as his literary aptitudes and poses. A sameness in the intention tends to tire, especially when it is ill-intention; and many things are not bewilderingly new. "BRUTE, *n*. See HUSBAND" owes its merit to its position, as it follows the article Bride. Collocation has its uses in other

*This item is reprinted by permission of *The Huntington Library*, San Marino, California. From *The Atheneum*, 16 September 1911, pp. 322–23

cases also: "ACADEME, *n.* An ancient school where morality and philosophy were taught. ACADEMY, *n.* (from Academe). A modern school where football is taught." The second of these words has in America a definite meaning, like Public School among us, which gives force to the sarcasm. Sometimes irony sophisticated and ponderous is conjoined with fun of a more simple sort, as in "HONORABLE, *adj.* Afflicted with an impediment in one's reach. In legislative bodies it is customary to mention all members as honorable; as 'the honorable member is a scurvy cur.' " We discover frankness and the humility of true learning in other notices. For instance, "HASH, *n.* There is no definition for this word—nobody knows what hash is." Affiliation with certain older English writers is suggested by "HEARSE, *n.* Death's baby carriage," and "PATIENCE, *n.* A minor form of despair, disguised as a virtue." Those to whom the term applies may find either consolation or rebuke in "JEALOUS, *adj.* Unduly concerned about the preservation of that which can be lost only if not worth keeping." We are left to guess whether the reference intended by "ONCE, *adv.* Enough" is marriage or electrocution; but the author sees in the adoption of the latter form of capital punishment by New Jersey "the first instance known to this lexicographer of anybody questioning the expediency of hanging Jerseymen."

Substantial intellectual value belongs to a great many entries that deal with a few large groups of subjects (politics, philosophy, &c) but are individually too long for quotation.

Regarding the *Negligible Tales* of Vol. VIII, we need only say that they are fitly named, and might well have been overlooked by the author in making this collection. Murder as a Good Joke is a theme that soon tires, and poor tales of the sea make dry reading ashore or anywhere else. A perplexed speculation as to the precise nature of the mental difference (national and personal) which makes this sort of boyish humour seem worth while to a mature American is the only drop of interest we have been able to extract from the bulk of these tales. We except a few which reflect exuberantly on the Fourth Estate as it exists in America and 'The Major's Tale,' a first-rate example of the raconteur's art in matter and manner.

More interesting are 'On with the Dance,' and the 'Epigrams' which complete the volume. The former, a long philosophical and historical vindication of the dance against the foolish charge of being per se of immoral tendency, is a notable piece of writing and reasoning, and pleasantly redolent of cited literature, old and new.

Vols. IX and X are entitled *Tangential Essays* and *The Opinionator* respectively. Both titles seem to indicate a disposition on the author's part to hedge, or at least to deprecate a too rigid construction of his text from page to page. That is natural enough; for in making a selection from the miscellaneous output of forty years of journalism a writer may reasonably have an eye to other things than the presentation of his full and final opinion on the subjects of discourse.

We should like to think that perversity alone was Mr. Bierce's aim in some instances in which he seems to us to have written rather rudely and noisily. His animadversions on the novel, for example, we should like to be able to explain as having been written with the tongue in the cheek and the eye exclusively fixed on Mr. Howells. Not because we ourselves bear an ill will towards Mr. Howells and his stories (very much the reverse), but because Mr. Bierce's onslaught on the novel might be held justified, or at least excused, if read as belonging to the warfare waged against 'The Lady of the Aroostook' and her sister novelettes what time (in the late eighties) these seemed to many the end, if not the apex, of prose fiction.

Unfortunately, that historical explanation is not available. For though Mr. Bierce's hostile intention towards Mr. Howells specially is manifest and avowed, he broadens the scope of his disrespect, and writes of the novel generally in a way which really puts him out of court. It might be interesting to consider what are the prepossessions, the constituents of the berating view of life, which make such a solecism possible in an intelligence so acute. Lacking space for that excuses, let us say that, though our author's other critical pronouncements (most of which are placed in 'The Opinionator') are tangential enough, none is so flagrantly wide of the mark, and many must have been a distinct mental acquisition to the public which Mr. Bierce instructs. It is paradoxical, but pleasing, to find a writer so ruthless, and with such an aptitude for contempt, defending the gentle poetry of Mr. Austin against the disparagements which sometime rioted among the superior persons of the Middle (and Farther) West. After some excellent quotations and as excellent comments thereon, he transcribes the beautiful sonnet, 'Love's Wisdom,' and asks, with characteristic determination to insult the unworthy:—

> Will the merry Pikes of the Lower Mississippi littoral and the gambolling whalebackers of the Duluth hinterland be pleased to say what is laughable in all this?

They probably said something else first; but the reference reminds us that Mr. Bierce is entitled to the liberties which he claims for others—of being judged, namely, by the best, and not the worst, that they have done. The best that he has done is not in these two volumes, but in those (Vols. II and III of this collection) containing his greater short stories. Nevertheless the last two volumes, dealing with a great variety of themes and occasions in many mental keys—satirical and serious, controversial and playful—offer too full a sampling of their author's quality not to contain much that can be admired and enjoyed. The great fault or misfortune of Mr. Bierce is that, when he is not kept right by the pressure of an artistic purpose serious enough to exhibit the characteristic sallies of his intelligence, his writing is apt to be punctuated with lapses and excesses, tags of humour or extravagances of verbiage, which bring it into line, for the moment at least, with very common matter. He has more wits, and even (though this may seem a contradiction in terms) more power and character, than he has known how to manage to his own best credit in literature.

The Underground Reputation
Of Ambrose Bierce

Anonymous*

Ambrose Bierce, whose collected works have recently been issued in a luxurious edition (*The Collected Works of Ambrose Bierce*, New York: The Neale Publishing Company), occupies a unique position in the literature of the world, being apparently both a cult and an author. California, mother of many eminent authors, regards him as one who enjoys "the full wide world's testimony of his worth." His fellow writers nurtured in the same soil speak of him in terms of hyperbolic laudation. Says Edwin Markham: "Bierce is our literary Atlas. His is a composite mind—a blending of Hafiz, the Persian; Swift, Poe, Thoreau, with sometimes a gleam of the Galilean." Gertrude Atherton affirms that Bierce has "the best brutal imagination of any man in the English-speaking race." J. O'Hara Cosgrove, formerly editor of *The Wave*, now editor of *Everybody's*, speaks in awestruck tones of Mr. Bierce's stylistic attainments. "Here," he says, "is a literary quality that is a consecration. A perfect arrangement of words expressing an idea, an attitude, a form as imperishable as stone." The Hearst papers idolize Bierce, he is the oracle of Hearst's monthly, *The Cosmopolitan*. Promising young Californians like George Sterling dedicate their books to him as one lays precious offerings at the feet of some idol. His publisher's literary notes are apotheoses; they are honestly convinced that in the history of American literature no more important announcement has been made than that the collected works of Ambrose Bierce, edited and arranged by himself, and representing the best of his life's work, have been published by them in ten gorgeous volumes.

Yet, in spite of all these distinguished spokesmen, the literary reputation of Ambrose Bierce is confined to a narrow circle. America, as well as England, has turned a deaf ear to his verbal cascades. The complete edition of Mr. Bierce's works, significantly enough, is limited to 250 expensive sets.

Mr. Bierce has been writing for a good many years: he is no longer a young man; he has addressed through his journalism a vast number of people. And yet, Jacob Tonson remarks in *The New Age* (London), the question that starts to the lips of ninety-nine readers out of a hundred,

*From *Current Literature*, 47 (September 1909), 279–81.

even the best informed, will assuredly be: Who is Ambrose Bierce? "I scarcely know," Mr. Tonson admits, "but I will say that among what I may term 'underground reputations' that of Ambrose Bierce is perhaps the most striking modern example. You may wander for years through literary circles and never meet anybody who has ever heard of Ambrose Bierce, and then you may hear some erudite student whisper in awed voice: 'Ambrose Bierce is the greatest living imaginative prose writer.' I have heard such an opinion expressed. I think I am in a position to deny it. Altho I have read little of Ambrose Bierce, I have read what is probably his best work, to wit, his short stories. After I had read the first I was almost ready to arise and cry with that erudite student: 'This is terrific.' But after I had read a dozen I had grown calmer. For they were all composed according to the same recipe, and they all went off at the end like the report of the same pistol. "Nevertheless," Mr. Tonson goes on to say, "he is a remarkable writer. His aim, in his short stories, is to fell you with a single blow. And one may admit that he succeeds. In the line of the startling—half Poe, half Merimée—he cannot have many superiors." To quote further:

> A story like "An Occurrence at Owl Creek Bridge"—Well, Edgar Allan Poe might have deigned to sign it! And that is something. If Mr. Bierce had had the wit to write only that tale and 'A Horseman in the Sky,' he might have secured for himself the sort of everlasting reputation that, say, Blanco White enjoys. But, unfortunately, he has gone and imitated himself, and, vulgarly, given the show away. He possesses a remarkable style—what Kipling's would have been had Kipling been born with any understanding of the significance of the word "art"—and a quite strangely remarkable perception of beauty. There is a feeling for landscape in 'A Horseman in the Sky' which recalls the exquisite opening of that indifferent novel "Les Frères Zemganno" of Edmond de Goncourt, and which no English novelist except Thomas Hardy, and possibly Charles Marriott, could match. It is worthy of W. H. Hudson (whose new book of English travel I urge upon you). Were Ambrose Bierce temperamentally less violent—less journalistic—and had he acquired the wisdom of a wider culture, he might have become the great creative artist that a handful of admirers believe him to be. As it is, he is simply astonishing. It occurs to me that Stephen Crane must have read him. If you demand why Ambrose Bierce is practically unknown in England, and why an expensive edition of him should suddenly appear as a bolt from the blue of the United States, I can offer no reply. I do not even know if he is living or dead, or where he was born, or if any of his books are published in England.

This article called forth a letter from Mr. William Purvis, from which it appears that Bierce never attained the distinction of book publication in England, altho Robert Barr and James Payne have praised him. In vain, Mrs. Atherton, years ago, tried to work up a London interest in Bierce. Mr. Cowley Brown coupled Bierce with Bret Harte, Joaquin Miller and Mark Twain as the pride of the Golden Gate, and, to the best of his power, blew the Bierce trumpet across the sea. Nevertheless, Bierce failed not only of recognition but even of a livelihood in London, where some of his earlier stories were written.

The comparative obscurity of the Californian seems all the more surprising if we consider the range of his work. He is a poet and an essayist, a short-story writer, a critic, a political writer, and, above all, a powerful satirist. Like Poe, he has dwelt with the occult and the terrible; like Poe also, he has been fascinated by science, and, again like Poe, he has depicted in a grotesque satirical tale the downfall of the American republic. He has tried his hand at everything that Poe has tried, but, unlike Poe, he always seems to fall short of finality. As some English critic has pointed out, there is a journalistic streak even in his most ambitious productions. In "Bits of Autobiography" he tells of his experiences as a soldier in the Civil War, as a treasury official in the South, and as a journalist in London in the early seventies. "Mr. Bierce," remarks the London *Atheneum*, in connection with his residence in London,

> seems to have taken very seriously the somewhat raffish celebrities of Fleet Street to the honor of whose acquaintance and orgies he was admitted; and would have us think that not Jamshyd himself gloried and drank deep as he and they. As a fact, we do not believe that they did his morals any material harm, but we suspect that they influenced his literary standards for life, and that, conscious of it or no, his aim ever since has been to write what any one of these judges would have declared to be "damned good stuff." The commodity which can be justly so described contains many elements admired in literature; but it is doubtful whether it ever ceases to be journalism.

The admirers of Mr. Bierce are no doubt prepared to crucify the reviewer of the English periodical; they seem to clothe the figure of their idol with glory even when it is hardly deserved. Thus Mr. S. O. Howes, in his introduction to Bierce's essays (*The Shadow of the Dial.* By Ambrose Bierce. A. M. Robertson, San Francisco), recently published, hails Mr. Bierce as a prophet. "The note of prophecy," he boldly exclaims, "sounds sharp and clear in many a vibrant line, in many a sonorous sentence of the essays herein collected for the first time." President Hadley, we are told, attracted wide-spread attention to himself by his recommendation of social ostracism for malefactors of great wealth; Edwin Markham made a stir by advancing the application of the Golden Rule to temporal affairs as a cure for evils arising from industrial discontent; and Mr. Sheldon, it will be remembered, created a nine days' wonder by undertaking to conduct for a week a newspaper as Christ would have conducted it;—but all these things, it seems, have been foreshadowed by Mr. Bierce. "I am sure," concludes Mr. S. O. Howes, "that Mr. Bierce does not begrudge any of these gentlemen the acclaim they have received by enunciating his ideas, and I mention this instance here merely to forestall the folly of any other claim to priority." The introducer's attitude and his hero worship strike one as distinctly provincial.

Mr. Bierce is undoubtedly to be regarded as one of the vital personalities in the world of American letters; he seems to have been critic and inspirer of many Californian writers of wider popularity than he has ever attained. His personal fascination has evidently hypnotized those who have been in immediate contact with him. He seems to be the living center of the Bohemian Club in San Francisco. His works, however, while striking, are not extraordinary; and his genius has been warped by provincial adulation. If he were as great as his admirers maintain, it is almost unthinkable that his fame and fortune should never have penetrated beyond the esoteric coterie of those who have made him a cult.

Ambrose Bierce: An Appraisal

Frederic Taber Cooper*

In the preface to the fourth volume of his collected works, the volume containing under the title of *Shapes of Clay* the major portion of purely personal satiric verse, Mr. Ambrose Bierce emphatically expresses his belief in the right of any author "to have his fugitive work in newspapers and periodicals put into a more permanent form during his lifetime if he can." No one is likely to dispute Mr. Bierce's contention; but it is often a grave question as to what extent it is wise for the individual to exercise his inalienable rights. And in the case of authors the question comes down to this: How far is it to their own best interests to dilute their finer and more enduring work with that which is mediocre and ephemeral? For it is unfortunately true that no author is measured by his high lights alone, but by the resultant impression of blended light and shade; and there is many a writer among the recognized classics who today would take a higher rank had a kindly and discriminating fate assigned three-quarters of his life work to a merciful oblivion.

To the student of American letters, however, the comprehensive edition of Ambrose Bierce's writings now being issued in ten portly and well-made volumes cannot fail to be welcome. It places at once within

*Reprinted from *Bookman*, 33 (July 1911), 471–80.

convenient reach a great mass of material which, good, bad or indifferent, as the case may be, all helps to throw suggestive side lights upon
the author, his methods, and his outlook upon life. It forces the reader
who perchance has hitherto known Mr. Bierce solely as a master of the
short story, to realise that this part of his work has been, throughout a
long and busy life, a sort of side issue and that the great measure of his
activities has been expended upon social and political satire. And similarly, those who have known him best as the fluent producer of stinging
satiric verse suddenly recognize how versatile and many sided are his
literary gifts. The ten volumes are divided as follows: three volumes of
prose fiction; two volumes of satiric verse; two volumes of literary and
miscellaneous essays; and three volumes consisting mainly of satiric prose,
including a greatly amplified edition of that curiously caustic piece of
irony, *The Cynic's Word Book*, now for the first time published under the
title of Mr. Bierce's own choosing, *The Devil's Dictionary*. It seems,
therefore, most convenient to consider Mr. Bierce, the Man of Letters,
under three separate aspects: the Critic, the Satirist and the Master of the
Short Story.

I   The Critic

Regarding literary criticism, Mr. Bierce says quite frankly "the sad-
dest thing about the trade of writing is that the writer can never know,
nor hope to know, if he is a good workman. In literary criticism, there are
no criteria, no accepted standards of excellence by which to test the
work." Now there is just enough truth in this attitude of mind to make it a
rather dangerous one. If there were literally no accepted standards in any
of the arts, no principles to which a certain influential majority of critical
minds had given their adhesion, then literature and all the arts would be
in a state of perennial anarchy. But of course any writer who believes in
his heart that there are no criteria will necessarily remain in lifelong ignorance regarding his own worth; for it is only through learning how to
criticise others sanely and justly that one acquires even the rudiments of
self-criticism. And incidently, it may be observed that no better proof of
Mr. Bierce's fundamental lack of this valuable asset could be asked than
the retention in these ten volumes of a considerable amount of journalistic
rubbish side by side with flashes of undoubted genius. Mr. Bierce's entire
essay on the subject of criticism is a sort of literary agnosticism, a gloomy
denial of faith. He has no confidence in the judgment of the general
public nor in that of the professional critic. He admits that "in a few centuries, more or less, there may arrive a critic that we call 'Posterity;' " but
Posterity, he complains, is a trifle slow. Accordingly, since the worth of
any contemporary writer is reduced to mere guess work, he, Ambrose
Bierce, has scant use for his contemporaries. He has very definite ideas
regarding the training of young writers and tells us at some length the

course through which he would like to put an imaginary pupil, but he adds:

> If I caught him reading a newly published book, save by way of penance, it would go hard with him. Of our modern education he should have enough to read the ancients: Plato, Aristotle, Marcus Aurelius, Seneca and that lot—custodians of most of what is worth knowing.

In spite of the pains to which Mr. Bierce goes to deny that he is a *laudator temporis acti*, the term fits him admirably—and nowhere is this attitude of mind more conspicuous than in his treatment of the modern novel. It is important, however, to get clearly in mind the arbitrary sense in which he uses the word novel as distinguished from what he chooses to call romance. His occasional half definitions are somewhat confusing; but apparently by the novel he means realistic fiction as distinguished from romantic fiction—a distinction complicated by the further idiosyncrasy that by realism he understands almost exclusively the commonplaces of actuality and by romanticism any happening which is out of the ordinary. The novel, then, in his sense of the word is "a snow plant; it has no root in the permanent soil of literature, and does not long hold its place; it is of the lowest form of imagination." And again: "The novel bears the same relation to literature that the panorama bears to painting; with whatever skill and feeling the panorama is painted, it must lack that basic quality in all art, unity, totality of effect." He seems utterly unaware that the great gain in modern fiction, the one indisputable factor that separates it from the fiction of half a century ago, is precisely the basic quality of unity. The modern novel whose technique most nearly approaches perfection is the one which when read rapidly with "a virgin attention at a single sitting"—to borrow Mr. Bierce's own phrase—gives an impression of as single-hearted a purpose as one finds in the most faultless of Maupassant's three-thousand-word masterpieces. It is quite possible for any well-trained reader to go through even the longest of novels at a single sitting. The present writer would feel himself grievously at fault if he interrupted his first reading of any novel that had been given him for the purpose of review; and he well remembers that in only two recent cases did he become conscious of the prolonged strain: namely, Mr. Kipling's *Kim*, which required an uninterrupted attention of eight and one-half hours, and *The Golden Bowl*, of Mr. James, which required somewhat more than eleven. Mr. Bierce's attitude, however, is partly explained by his *obiter dictum* that "no man who has anything else to do can critically read more than two or three books in a month"—and of course, if you make your way through books at the snail's pace of one in ten days, the most perfect unity of purpose is inevitably going to drop out of sight.

All of this helps us to understand how it happens that Mr. Bierce, otherwise a man of intelligence, can say in all seriousness that "in

England and America the art of novel writing is as dead as Queen Anne."
Listen also to the following literary blasphemy:

> So far as I am able to judge, no good novels are now
> "made in Germany," nor in France, nor in any European
> country except Russia. The Russians are writing novels which
> so far as one may venture to judge . . . are in their way ad-
> mirable; full of fire and light, like an opal . . . ; in their hands
> the novel grew great—as it did in those of Richardson and
> Fielding, and as it would have done in those of Thackeray and
> Pater if greatness in that form of fiction had been longer pos-
> sible in England.

Or again:

> Not only is the novel . . . a faulty form of art, but because
> of its faultiness it has no permanent place in literature. In
> England it flourished less than a century and a half, beginning
> with Richardson and ending with Thackeray, since whose
> death no novels, probably, have been written that are worth
> attention.

Think for a moment what this means. Here is a man who has ven-
tured to speak seriously about the modern novel, and who confessedly is
unaware of the importance of Trollope and Meredith and Hardy, of
Henry James and Rudyard Kipling and Maurice Hewlett—and who
deliberately ignores the existence of Flaubert and Maupassant and Zola,
Galdos and Valdès, Verga and d'Annunzio! It is not astonishing after that
to find Mr. Bierce seriously questioning the value of epic poetry: "What
more than they gave," he asks, "might we not have had from Virgil (*sic*),
Dante, Tasso, Camoens and Milton if they had not found the epic poem
ready to their misguided hands?"

The fact is that Mr. Bierce as a critic is of the iconoclastic variety. He
breaks down but does not build up. He has no patience with the historical
form of criticism that traces the intellectual genealogy of authorship
showing, for instance, Maupassant's debt to Poe or Bourget's debt to Stendhal. He is equally intolerant of that analytical method—the fairest of
them all—that judges every written work by its author's purpose as nearly
as this may be read between the lines. Nothing is more certain, he says,
than if a writer of genius should bring to his task the purposes which the
critics trace in the completed work "the book would remain forever unwritten, to the unspeakable advantage of letters and morals." Yes, he
tears down the recognised methods of criticism but suggests nothing better
in their place. And when he himself undertakes to criticise, it is hardly
ever for the purpose of paying tribute to excellence—with the noteworthy
exception, *mirabile dictu,* of his extraordinary praise of George Sterling's
poetic orgy of words, "The Wine of Wizardry." Tolstoy, for instance, he
defines as a literary giant: "He has a giant's strength and has unfortun-

ately learned to use it like a giant—which means not necessarily with conscious cruelty, but with stupidity." The journal of Marie Bashkirtseff—the last book on earth that one would expect Mr. Bierce to discuss—he sums up as "morbid, hysterical and unpleasant beyond anything of its kind in literature." Among modern critics he pronounces Mr. Howells "the most mischievous, because the ablest, of all this sycophantic crew."

The truth is that the value of Mr. Bierce as a critic lies solely in his fearlessness and downright sincerity, his unswerving conviction that he is right. He has to a rather greater extent than many a better critic the quality of consistency; and no matter how widely we are forced to disagree with his conclusions there is not one of them that does not throw an interesting side light upon Mr. Bierce, the man.

II   The Satirist

The short stories and the serious critical papers of Mr. Bierce have appeared in a spasmodic and desultory way, but from first to last he has been at heart a satirist of the school of Lucilius and Juvenal, eager to scourge the follies and the foibles of mankind at large. The fact that Mr. Bierce is absolutely in earnest, that he is destitute of fear and confessedly incorruptible accounts for the oft repeated statement that he was for years the best loved and the most hated man on the Pacific Coast. Now the ability to use a stinging lash of words is all very well in itself; it is a gift that is none too common. But to be effective it must not be used too freely. The two ample volumes of Mr. Bierce's poetical invectives form a striking object lesson of the wisdom in Hamlet's contention that unless you treat men better than they deserve none will escape a whipping. And when fresh from a perusal of the contents of *Shapes of Clay* and *Black Beetles in Amber*, one has become so accustomed to seeing men flayed alive that a whole skin possesses something of a novelty. Now there is no question that there is a good deal wrong with the world, just as there always has been, if one takes the trouble to look for it. But when any one man takes upon himself the task of reprimanding the universe it is not unreasonable that we should ask ourselves in the first instance: What manner of man is this? What are his standards and beliefs? And if he had his way what new lamps would he give us in place of the old? In the case of Mr. Bierce it is a little difficult to make answer with full assurance. Somewhere in his preface he has said that he has not attempted to classify his writings under the separate heads of serious, ironical, humorous and the like, assuming that his readers have sufficient intelligence to recognise the difference for themselves. But this is not always easy to do, because in satire these different qualities and moods overlap each other so that there is always the danger of taking too literally what is really an ironical exaggeration. Here, however, is a rather significant passage taken from a serious essay entitled "To Train a Writer;" it sets forth the convictions and the general attitude toward life which Mr. Bierce believes are essential to any young author before he can hope for success—and it is only fair to infer that they represent his own personal views:

> He should, for example, forget that he is an American and remember that he is a Man. He should be neither Christian nor Jew, nor Buddhist, nor Mahometan, nor Snake Worshipper. To local standards of right and wrong he should be civilly indifferent. In the virtues, so called, he should discern only the rough notes of a general expediency; in fixed moral principles only time-saving predecisions of cases not yet before the court of conscience. Happiness should disclose itself to his enlarging intelligence as the end and purpose of life; art and love as the only means to happiness. He should free himself of all doctrines, theories, etiquettes, politics, simplifying his life and mind, attaining clarity with breadth and unity with height. To him a continent should not seem wide, nor a century long. And it would be needful that he know and have an ever-present consciousness that this is a world of fools and rogues, blind with superstition, tormented with envy, consumed with vanity, selfish, false, cruel, cursed with illusions—frothing mad!

Now this strikes the average fairminded person as a rather wholesale indictment of what on the whole has proved to be a pretty good world to live in. In fact, it is difficult to conceive of any one honestly and literally holding such an extreme view and yet of his own volition remaining in such an unpleasant place any longer than the time required to obtain the amount of gunpowder or strychnine needed to make an effective exit. But of course Mr. Bierce does not find life half so unpleasant as he makes out: in fact, he gives the impression of hugely enjoying himself by voluntarily looking out upon a world grotesquely distorted by the lenses of his imagination. He has of course a perfect right to have as much or as little faith as he chooses in any human religion or philosophy, moral doctrine or political code—only it is well when studying Mr. Bierce as a satirist and reformer to understand clearly his limitations in this respect and to discount his views accordingly. It is well, for instance, to keep in mind, when reading some of his scathing lines directed at small offenders who at most have left the world not much worse off for having lived in it, that Mr. Bierce has put himself on record as proclaiming Robert Ingersoll "a man who taught all the virtues as a duty and a delight—who stood, as no other man among his countrymen has stood, for liberty, for honour, for good will toward men, for truth as it was given him to see it."

To the present writer there is much that is keenly irritating in Mr. Bierce's satiric verse for the reasons above implied. It is, of course, highly uncritical to find fault with a writer for no better reason than because you find yourself out of harmony with his religious and moral faith, or his lack of it—for an author's personal beliefs should have no bearing upon the artistic value of what he produces. But putting aside personal prejudice, it may be said in all fairness that Mr. Bierce made a mistake in giving a permanent form to so large a body of his fugitive verses. It is not quite true that satiric poetry is read with the same interest after the people at whom it was directed are forgotten. Aristophanes and Horace and Juvenal cannot be greatly enjoyed to-day without a good deal of patient delving for the explanation of local and temporal allusions; and in modern times Pope's *Dunciad*, for instance, is probably to-day the least important and the least read of all his writings. It is impossible to take much interest in vitriolic attacks made twenty years ago upon various obscure Californians whose names mean nothing at all to the world at large. But on the other hand, any one can understand and enjoy the sweeping irony as well as the sheer verbal cleverness of a parody like the following:

A Rational Anthem
My country, 'tis of thee,
Sweet land of felony,
    Of thee I sing—
Land where my fathers fried
Young witches and applied
Whips to the Quaker's hide
    And made him spring.

My knavish country, thee,
Land where the thief is free,
    Thy laws I love;
I love thy thieving bills
That tap the people's tills;
I love thy mob whose will's
    All laws above.

Let Federal employees
And rings rob all they please,
    The whole year long.
Let office-holders make
Their piles and judges rake
Our coin. For Jesus' sake,
    Let's *all* go wrong!

One is tempted to devote considerably more space than is warranted to that extremely clever collection of satiric definitions, *The Devil's Dictionary*. It represents a deliberate pose consistently maintained, it is pervaded with a spirit of what a large proportion of readers in a Christian country would pronounce irreverent, it tells us nothing new and can hardly be conceived of as an inspiration for higher or nobler living. But it is undeniably entertaining reading. Almost any one must smile over such specimens as the following, taken almost at random:

Monday, *n*. In Christian countries, the day after the base-ball
   game.
Bacchus, *n*. A convenient deity invented by the ancients as an
   excuse for getting drunk.
Positive, *adj*. Mistaken at the top of one's voice.

III   The Story Teller

But it is as a writer of short stories that Mr. Bierce's future fame rests
upon a firm foundation. It is not too much to say that within his own
chosen field—the grim, uncompromising horror story, whether actual or
supernatural—he stands among American writers second only to Edgar
Allan Poe. And this is all the more remarkable when we consider his expressed scorn of new books and modern methods and his implied indifference to the development of modern technique. He does understand and
consciously seeks for that unity of effect which is the foundation stone of
every good short story; yet in sheer technical skill there is scarcely one
among the recognised masters of the short story to-day, Mr. Kipling, for
instance, and the late O. Henry, Jack London and a score of his contemporaries, from whom he might not learn something to his profit. What
Mr. Bierce's habits of workmanship may be the writer does not happen to
know; it is possible that he has always striven as hard to build an underlying structure, a preliminary scaffolding, for each story as ever Edgar
Allan Poe did. But if so he has been singularly successful in practising the
art which so artfully all things conceals. He gives the impression of one
telling a story with a certain easy spontaneity and attaining his results
through sheer instinct. He seldom attempts anything like a unity of time
and place; and many of his short tales have the same fault which he
criticises in the modern novel, namely, that of having a panoramic quality, of being shown to us in a succession of more or less widely separated
scenes and incidents.

   Nevertheless, in most cases his stories are their own best justification.
We may not agree with the method that he has chosen to use, but we cannot escape from the strange, haunting power of them, the grim, boding
sense of their having happened—even the most weird, most supernatural,
most grotesquely impossible of them—in precisely the way that he has
told them.

   The stories, such of them at least as really count and represent Mr.
Bierce at his best, divide themselves into two groups: first, the Civil War
stories, based upon his own four years' experience as a soldier during the
rebellion, and unsurpassed in American fiction for the unsparing
clearness of their visualisation of war. And secondly, the frankly supernatural stories contained in the volume entitled *Can Such Things
Be?*—stories in which the setting is immaterial because if such things
could be they would be independent of time and space. The war stories

range through the entire gamut of heroism, suffering and carnage. They are stamped in all their physical details with a pitiless realism unequalled by Stendhal in the famous Waterloo episode in the *Chartreuse de Parme* and at least unsurpassed by Tolstoy or by Zola. Indeed, there is nothing fulsome or extravagant in the statement that has more than once been made that Mr. Bierce is a sort of American Maupassant. And what is most remarkable about these stories is that they never fail of a certain crescendo effect. Keyed as they are to a high pitch of human tragedy, there is always one last turn of the screw, one crowning horror held in reserve until the crucial moment. Take, for example, "A Horseman in the Sky." A sentinel whose duty it is to watch from a point of vantage overlooking a deep gorge and a vast plain beyond, to see that no scout of the Southern army shall discover a trail down the precipitous sides of the opposite slope, suddenly perceives a solitary horseman making his way along the verge of the precipice within easy range of fire. The sentinel watches and hesitates; takes aim and delays his fire. The scene shifts with the disconcerting suddenness of a modern moving picture and we see the sentinel back in his Southern home at the outbreak of the war; and we overhear the controlled bitternesss of his parting with his Southern father after declaring his intention to fight for the Union. A modern story teller would consider this shifting of scene bad art; nevertheless, Mr. Bierce, in theatrical parlance, "gets it over." Back again he shifts us with a rush to the lonely horseman, shows him for a moment motionless upon the brink and the next instant launched into space, a wonderful, miraculous, awe-inspring figure, proudly erect upon a stricken and dying horse, whose legs spasmodically continue their mad gallop throughout the downward flight to the inevitable annihilation below. This in itself, told with Ambrose Bierce's compelling art, is sufficiently harrowing, but he has something more in reserve. Listen to this:

> "Did you fire?" the sergeant whispered.
> "Yes."
> "At what?"
> "A horse. It was standing on yonder rock—pretty far out. You see it is no longer there. It went over the cliff."
> The man's face was white, but he showed no other signs of emotion. Having answered, he turned away his eyes and said no more. The sergeant did not understand.
> "See here, Druce," he said, after a moment's silence, "it's no use making a mystery. I order you to report. Was there anybody on the horse?"
> "Yes."
> "Well?"
> "My father."

And again, there is that extraordinary *tour de force* entitled "An Occurrence at Owl Creek Bridge." It is the story of a spy caught and about to be hanged by the simple expedient of allowing the board on which he stands to tilt up and drop him between the cross beams of the bridge. The story is of considerable length. It details with singular and compelling vividness what follows from the instant that the spy feels himself dropped, feels the rope tighten around his neck and its fibres strain and snap under his weight. His plunge into the stream below, his dash for life under cover of the water, his flight, torn and bleeding through thorns and brambles, his miraculous dodging of outposts and his passing unscathed through volleys of rapid fire, all read like a hideous nightmare—and so in fact they are, because the entire story of his rush for safety lasting long hours and days in reality is accomplished in a mere fraction of time, the instant of final dissolution—because, as it happened, the rope did not break and at the moment that he thought he had attained safety his body ceased to struggle and dangled limply beneath the Owl Creek Bridge. Variations upon this theme of the rapidity of human thought in the moment of death are numerous. There is, for instance, a memorable story by Morgan Robertson called, if memory is not at fault, "From the Main Top," in which a lifetime is crowded into the fraction of time required for the action of gravity. But no one has ever used it more effectually than Mr. Bierce.

But it is in his supernatural stories that Mr. Bierce shows even more forcefully his wizardry of word and phrase, his almost magnetic power to make the absurd, the grotesque, the impossible, carry an overwhelming conviction. He will tell you, for instance, a story of a man watching at night alone by the dead body of an old woman; a cat makes its way into the room and springs upon the corpse; and to the man's overwrought imagination it seems as though that dead woman seized the cat by the neck and flung it violently from her. "Of course you imagined it," says the friend to whom he afterward tells the tale. "I thought so, too," rejoins the man, "but the next morning her stiffened fingers still held a handful of black fur."

For sheer mad humour there is nothing more original than the tale called "A Jug of Syrup." A certain old and respected village grocer who through a lengthy life has never missed a day at his desk dies and his shop is closed. One night the village banker and leading citizen on his way home drops in from force of habit at the grocery, finding the door wide open and buys a jug of syrup, absent-mindedly forgetting that the grocer who served him has been dead three weeks. The jug is a heavy weight to carry; yet when he reaches home he has nothing in his hand. The tale spreads like wildfire through the village and the next night a vast throng is assembled in front of the brightly lit up grocery, breathlessly watching the shadowy form of the deceased methodically casting up accounts. One by one, they pluck up courage and make their way into the grocery—all but the banker. Riveted to the spot by the grotesque horror of the sight he stands and watches, while pandemonium breaks loose. To him in the road the shop is still brilliantly lighted but to those who have gone within it presents the darkness of eternal night and in their unreasoning fear they kick and scratch and bite and trample upon one another with the primordial savageness of the mob. And all the while the shadowy figure of the dead grocer continues undisturbed to balance his accounts.

It is a temptation to linger beyond all reason over one after another of these extraordinary and haunting imaginings, such for instance, as "Moxon's Master," in which an inventor having made a mechanical chess-player makes the mistake of beating it at the game and is promptly strangled to death by the revengeful being of his own creation. But it is impossible to do justice to all these stories separately and it remains only to single out one typical example in which perhaps he reached the very pinnacle of his strange, fantastic genius, "The Death of Halpin Frayser." The theme of this story is this: it is sufficiently horrible to be confronted with a disembodied spirit, but there is one degree of horror beyond this, namely, to have to face the reanimated body of some one long dead from whom the soul has departed—because, so Mr. Bierce tell us, with the departure of the soul all natural affection, all kindliness has departed also, leaving only the base instincts of brutality and revenge. Now in the case of Halpin Frayser, it happens that the body which he is fated to encounter under these hideously unnatural conditions is that of his own mother; and in a setting as curiously and poetically unreal as any part of "Kubla Kahn" he is forced to realise that this mother whom he had in life worshipped as she worshipped him is now, in spite of her undiminished beauty, a foul and bestial thing intent only upon taking his life. In all imaginative literature it would be difficult to find a parallel for this story in sheer, unadulterated hideousness.

Mr. Ambrose Bierce as a story teller can never achieve a wide popularity, at least among the Anglo-Saxon race. His writings have too much the flavour of the hospital and the morgue. There is a stale odour of mouldy cerements about them. But to the connoisseur of what is rare, unique and very perfect in any branch of fiction he must appeal strongly as one entitled to hearty recognition as an enduring figure in American letters. No matter how strongly he may offend individual convictions and prejudices with the flippant irreverence of his satiric writings it is easy to forgive him all this and much more besides for the sake of any single one of a score or more of his best stories.

Personal Memories of Ambrose Bierce

Bailey Millard*

> Great poets fire the world with faggots big
>   That make a crackling racket,
> But I'm content with but a whispering twig
>   To warm some single jacket.

Thus sang Ambrose Bierce in his old San Francisco days when, as the licensed lampooner of everybody that happened to displease him, he made his *Examiner* "Prattle" the most wickedly clever, the most audaciously personal and the most eagerly devoured column of causerie that probably ever was printed in this country. "Prattle," the sub-title of which was "A Transient Record of Individual Opinion," bristled with cynical sallies against the great and the small in public and private life, ridiculed nearly every pretension to morality, particularly of a churchly sort, and made ducks and drakes of all the popular idols. And this railing against people who upheld the established order of things he continued in one paper or another during the rest of his career on earth.

It seems strange to one who knew Bierce so well during his restless, red-corpuscled life to be writing of him in the past tense, and yet any other is hardly admissible, for after nine months of anxious waiting for any sort of word from him his friends and relations have given him up as lost. He was serving upon the staff of General Villa in the Mexican insurrection and has been missing since the terrible battle of Torreon, so the daily journals have recorded. He was ever a fighter—in the Civil War, where he was brevetted major for gallantry in action as in civic life—so this "one fight more" was naturally sought by him, and he went into it with all the fierce joy of the old soldier who loves war for war's sake.

Cavalierly handsome of face, Bierce's singularly expressive, keen, grey eyes, his visage so full of vigour, freshness and refined power, his strong, erect, military figure, which revealed no sign of decrepitude, even at seventy-two—the age of his passing—marked him for a man of power—a power amply exhibited in his writings, especially in his critical essays and stories.

It was Bierce the satirist that we Californians first knew, not Bierce the poet or Bierce the story-teller, as he is more generally recognised, wherever he *is* recognised, though the limits to the recognition of him, once merely parochial, are widening with the years. He came to us from London, where he had gone from his Ohio home after the war. In his anecdotage, as he used to term his later period of table-talk, he used to tell of his adventures among the London literati, by whom, because of his caustic satires, he was known as "Bitter Bierce." He frequented a certain

*Reprinted from *Bookman*, 40 (February 1915), 653–58.

tap-room in Ludgate Station, where regularly gathered such rare spirits as George Augustus Sala, young Tom Hood and Captain Mayne Reid. When Joaquin Miller went to England in the early 'seventies he joined this convivial set, which was greatly addicted, as Bierce expressed it, "to shedding the blood of the grape." "We worked too hard," he confessed, "dined too well, frequented too many clubs and went to bed too late in the forenoon. In short, we diligently, conscientiously and with a perverse satisfaction burned the candle of life at both ends and in the middle." As the fact that he afterward enjoyed robust health would seem to indicate, this life did Bierce no permanent injury, but once it resulted in his financial downfall. There was a certain London publisher named John Camden Hotten, who for a long time had owed Bierce a considerable sum, and, being without tangible assets, the young satirist hounded Hotten day and night for his due. Finally the implacable creditor got the publisher at a disadvantage and Bierce was sent to negotiate with Hotten's manager, Mr. Chatto, who afterward, as a member of the publishing firm of Chatto and Windus, succeeded to his business. After two mortal hours of "Bitter Bierce" in his most acidulated mood, Chatto pulled out a cheque for the full amount, ready signed by Hotten in anticipation of defeat. The cheque bore date of the following Saturday.

"Before Saturday came," said Bierce in telling the story, "Hotten proceeded to die of a pork pie in order to beat me out of my money. Knowing nothing of this, I strolled out to his house in Highgate, hoping to get an advance, as I was in great need of cash. On being told of his demise I was inexpressibly shocked, for my cheque was worthless. There was a hope, however, that the bank had not heard. So I called a cab and drove furiously bank-ward. Unfortunately my gondolier steered me past Ludgate Station, in the bar whereof our Fleet Street gang of writers had a private table. I disembarked for a mug of bitter. Unfortunately too, Sala, Hood and others of the gang were in their accustomed places. I sat at board and related the sad event. The deceased had not in life enjoyed our savour, and I blush to say we all fell to making questionable epitaphs to him. I recall one by Sala which ran thus:

> Hotten,
> Rotten,
> Forgotten.

At the close of the rites, several hours later, I resumed my movements against the bank. Too late—the old story of the hare and the tortoise was told again! The heavy news had overtaken and passed me as I loitered by the wayside.

"I attended the funeral, at which I felt more than I cared to express."

In London Bierce wrote over the signature of "Dod Grile," and that name appeared on the cover of two books of his published in the 'seventies. One of these books was called *Cobwebs from an Empty Skull*. Years later Gladstone fished up one of the "Dod Grile" books from the table of a second-hand dealer, read it through, was delighted with it and helped to revive in England the identity of Ambrose Bierce. Gladstone, the maker of literary reputations, also assisted the author not a little by sounding the praises of his stories of the occult—tales that were, however, a trifle too strong for the tea-drinking bourgeoisie of modern Britain.

While Bierce was in London the Empress Eugenie, then in exile in England, employed him to write for her several numbers of the *Lantern*, a journal she began to publish there to forestall her bitter enemy, Henri de Rochefort, who, like herself, had been banished from France after the Prussian conquest of 1870. Rochefort, who had persistently attacked the Emperor and Empress in *La Lanterne*, of Paris, going to the length of denying the legitimacy of the Prince Imperial, was outwitted by Eugenie when he announced his intention of reviving his paper in London. Before he could do so she had copyrighted the title, the *Lantern*, and herself proceeded to publish a paper bearing that name, though at the time she was not known to be connected with it in any way. Not only did she thus win a great triumph over her enemy, but she employed Bierce to flagellate him. This he did in number after number. And as he afterward said, he never was employed in so pleasant and congenial a pursuit. But the *Lantern* did not last long and there were times when Bierce, for lack of employment, was destitute of funds. His "Little Johnny" essays on zoology which a London journal "featured" as rare bits of humour, were the means by which he refilled his purse. These essays contained amazing descriptions of actual as well as inconceivable animals and afforded an attractive vehicle for his satire.

He went from London to San Francisco for no particular reason save that he thought he would like the Far West. And he did like it—like it so well that he lived there twenty-five years, save for a brief period during which he was mining near Deadwood, South Dakota, where he had some hair-raising adventures with road-agents and other bad men. One night in 1880 he was driving in a light wagon through the wildest part of the Black Hills. In the wagon was thirty thousand dollars in gold belonging to the mining company of which he was manager. Beside him on the wagon seat was Boone May, a famous gunman of those days, who was under indictment for murder, but had been paroled from jail on Bierce's promise that he would see him into custody again. May sat doubled up in rubber poncho, his rifle between his knees. Bierce thought him a trifle off guard, but said nothing. Suddenly they heard a shout, "Throw up your hands!" Bierce reached for his revolver but it was quite needless. Quick as a cat, almost before the words were out of the highwayman's mouth, May had thrown himself backward over the seat, face upward, and with the muzzle of his rifle within a yard of the robber's throat, had fired a shot that put an end to his usefulness as a highwayman.

Bierce had many adventures with bad men in the West, and his assaults in print upon citizens who were inclined to underscore their resentment by a flourish of firearms, occasionally got him into trouble, but the fact that he was famous as a dead shot generally acted as a damper upon the ambition of those who harboured the fancy of effacing him. In San Francisco he made the *News Letter* and the *Wasp* conspicuous examples of personal journalism, some of his philippics against prominent men and women being of the most biting nature. It is safe to say that his vocabulary of acrimonious invective exceeded in volume that of any other modern journalist. You stood aghast at his bold characterisations and yet, being human, you read on with a grim smile. He was particularly happy in his poetic quips, though some of these were of the most contumelous nature. His idea of attack was to fell you at a single blow. One must apologise for quoting some of them, as in the case of the following quatrain aimed at a gentle popular poet of national reputation whom it pleased Bierce to hold in contempt:

> His poems—says that he indites
>   Upon an empty stomach. Heavenly
>   Powers,
> Feed him throat-full, for what he writes
>   Upon his empty stomach empties ours!

And mind you, the name was not a blank in the original stanza.

Once when a great English novelist visited San Francisco and ran afoul of Bierce who proceeded to show in "Prattle" that the man's reputation was based upon utterly false claims, the surprised and indignant Briton, heedless of the advice of his friends, replied in print. The delighted Bierce, affecting to disdain the retort, slapped the great man in the face with this:

> Dispute with such a thing as you,
>   Twin show to the two-headed calf?
>   Why, sir, if I repress my laugh,
>   'Tis more than half the world can do.

In his serious essays Bierce always took the most unconventional and often the most cynical views of life. He revered nobody's opinion but his own, and in this idea of his greatness he was upheld by a flattering literary coterie who acknowledged him as master. These constituted an esoteric cult whose adulation Bierce accepted as a matter of course. They laid their literary work before him, rejoiced in his praise, however stinted, and received his harshest criticism without murmur. He dominated many young literary lives, but if by his criticism he smothered whatever tenderness they sought to convey in their writings and thereby restricted and hardened them, he also helped them to clarity of expression and to more nearly perfect diction. For technically his pencraft was of the purest, as is shown on nearly every page. He prided himself upon being ruled wholly by intellect, never by emotion. But being, after all, human, he could not successfully live up to his vaunt, and occasionally we see him lapsing into tender passages in spite of himself. On the whole, however, his philosophy worked itself out according to his own hard rule. Of civilisation, for example, he was the sternest critic. He declared that it made the race no better and that the cant of it was boresome.

"We have," he said, "hardly the rudiments of a true civilisation. Compared with the splendours of which we catch dim glimpses in the fading past, ours are as an illumination tallow candles. We know no more than the ancients; we only know other things, but nothing in which is an assurance of perpetuity and little that is truly wisdom."

When a disciple of Bierce broke his leading-strings and dared to declare his independence the wrath of the master was terrible to see and the loyal ones would echo it and help to put down the apostate. And yet as the years passed nearly all of the cult deserted him or were deserted by him. The reason for this is plain. No dominant factor in literature ever gave himself such liberty of expression as Bierce. This expression extended even to the personal conduct of the members of his flock, and in some cases concerned itself with their most sacred family affairs. In time this came to rankle. Here and there an insurgent spirit manifested itself and there was a cleavage of the cult. But while his primacy lasted—and it lasted a long time—his ego made itself felt not only in the inner circle, but throughout a nebular outer ring which included many who were not under his personal influence. Whatever of import came up for discussion the question invariably would be asked, "What does Bierce think of it?"

When literary California rang with the bugle note of "The Man with the Hoe," the literati turned to Bierce as to one who should say whether the poem should be permitted to live or die. Probably for no other reason in the world than that the Markhamic strain was tremendously popular Bierce turned down his thumbs. He admitted that Markham previously had written good poetry, but now he had become an anarchist and no true work might be expected of him. He hammered hard and long with his journalistic gavel to drown the chorus of approval of "The Man with the Hoe," and his thunder strokes of condemnation convinced his disciples; but the poem went abroad into a field where his words could not follow. Once Markham was told to his face by this modern Dr. Johnson that his famous poem was merely a cheap bid for popularity and that as a poet he had killed himself by publishing it.

"The mistake you make is a common one," observed Bierce. "You let your heart get into your head. No great artist ever did that."

"Well," said the urbane Markham, "I do not profess to be a great artist; but to me it seems that the heart always should rule rather than the intellect, and what confirms me in the belief are the finer passages of Keats, Shelley, Tennyson and other true poets."

But Bierce would not be convinced, and ever after in print made sport of "The Man with the Hoe."

Intense and inexorable were his literary prejudices, extending even to the most venerated of authors. Once when the present writer mentioned to him the fact that French scholars considered Poe and Whitman our greatest voices, he said: "Poe, yes; but Whitman never. There isn't a line of poetry in *The Leaves of Grass*."

"Not in 'Out of the Cradle Endlessly Rocking?' " he was asked.

"Sentimental twaddle of the worst order," he replied with Johnsonian curtness.

One thing that tended to embitter Bierce was his neglect at the hands of the publishers. Beginning in the early 'eighties he wrote story after story, but nearly all were considered by magazine editors to be impossible for their pages; and when he sent a lot of manuscript tales to book publishers they would have none of them. These men admitted the purity of his diction and the magic of his haunting power, but the stories were regarded as "revolting." Bierce revelled in the horrible. His tales of war make the reader see red for weeks. His stories of the occult freeze the spinal marrow and set the flesh a-shiver. With his fetching method of realism went a crystal-pure style in which words were chosen as a jeweller chooses diamonds for the necklace of an empress. His imagination was of the most riotous, nay, of the most brutal order. His psychological effects did not fall short of Maupassant's. His surprise of climax always was complete.

Bierce, as has been said, loved war, and often dilated upon "the horrors of peace," which, he held, were more terrible than the carnage of battle. Such army tales as "Chickamauga," "A Son of the Gods," "A Horseman in the Sky" and "An Affair of Outposts" afford a feast in which one may sup full of horrors. But let us not look altogether upon the gory and grisly side of his fiction. His tales of war celebrated such heroism as thrills the pulses and makes the reader forget that he is a mere reader; he feels himself an onlooker, if not a participant. Death, death, death! is the note sung over and over in a deep, compelling, almost pitiless cadence. Knowing war so well and the art of depicting it even better Bierce could give the colour and tone of it with the terrible effect of a Vereshchagin. And yet, in spite of that cold aloofness which he contended to be the true attitude of the artist, occasionally he would give a glimpse of the compassion he really felt for war's victims. Take this finale of that amazing exploit described in "A Son of the Gods," where a single officer charges a whole battalion of the enemy:

> The skirmishers return, gathering up their dead.
> Ah, those many needless dead! That great soul whose body is lying over yonder, so conspicuous against the sere hillside—could it not have been spared the bitter consciousness of a vain devotion? Would one exception have marred too much the pitiless perfection of the divine, eternal plan?

Such tales as this, from *In the Midst of Life* and those stories of the occult in *Can Such Things Be?* were enough to establish any author's reputation, and it seems strange that Bierce, as a writer of fiction, did not sooner find his public. A San Francisco merchant, E. L. G. Steele, who was a great admirer of his work, finally defrayed the expenses of the publication of *Tales of Soldiers and Civilians*, afterward republished in England and America as *In the Midst of Life*. The book, though it awed and compelled the Biercean cult, enjoyed nothing that might be termed vogue. Reviewers shook their heads over such stories as "The Affair at Coulter's Notch," in which an officer of artillery feels it his duty to train his guns upon a house that shelters his own wife and children, and the *débâcle* of "Chickamauga" challenged resentment for its bloody detail. Even when *Can Such Things Be?* and *The Monk and the Hangman's Daughter* made their appearance in book form the critics were slow to give their approval. But where a reviewer dared to let himself become a champion he generally was a fierce one. Never was an author more discussed in a private way than Bierce, and yet it is hardly fair to say, as has been averred, that his was simply an "underground" reputation. As the years went by the *cognoscenti* came to know him very well and to say good words of him. This counted by way of publicity, but he never had a popular audience. That he was "unknown" even up to his death, as many writers will tell you, is a statement not to be seriously accepted. In his latter years he took exception to this curious manner of reference to him, and wound up a breezy journalistic jingle about himself with the satirical line:

Five thousand critics crying "He's unknown!"

To him his trunkful of clippings established the fact that he was not only not unknown, but very well known and recognised. In truth it was easy for him to assume the character of a celebrated literary personage. Once he accepted an invitation from a wealthy New Yorker, who received him very hospitably in his Fifth Avenue home. After dinner, when Bierce was told that he was expected to go with his host and a number of others to the theatre where a box had been engaged for them, he declared hotly:

"Do you think I'll let you show me about like a monkey in a cage? No, sir! I'm going home."

And home he went in high dudgeon, leaving his friend the most amazed man in New York that night.

Perhaps he enjoyed making a scene, as this story tends to show: At a large gathering in a Washington drawingroom the host presented Bierce to a street railway magnate, who extended his hand cordially.

"No!" thundered Johnson the Second, drawing back in magnificent rage. "I wouldn't take your black hand for all the money you could steal in the next ten years! I ride in one of your cars every night and always am compelled to stand—there's never a seat for me."

The black hand was speedily withdrawn.

For over thirty years Bierce enjoyed an income of five thousand dollars a year, besides which he received a pension of thirty dollars a month from the Government—"cigar money" as he termed it. He was a good liver. About twenty years ago he told the writer that in his old age he wanted to look like "one of those red-faced, full-blooded English squires." In this he had his wish. He was liberal with those who made demands upon him for charity. Several outworn hack writers in Washington where he lived during the fifteen years preceding his fateful campaign in Mexico, knew where to go to "borrow" five dollars or so when their pockets were empty. They knew, too, that Bierce would promptly forget the indebtedness, Although he was rather inclined to prodigality, Bierce was possessed of a goodly estate. Before going to Mexico he made his will and left nearly all of his property, which consisted of stocks, money and real estate, in the hands of a trustee. It is said that the bulk of his estate will go to his daughter, who lives in Ohio.

There are those who believe that General Villa and the Constitutionalists owe much of their military success to Bierce, who was well skilled in the art of war. He was much stirred by the cause of the Constitutionalists, and on leaving Washington for Mexico to join them in the fray, he said he could not understand why thousands of liberty-loving Americans did not take up arms against the tyrannical Huerta.

Yes, this strange and seemingly hard and cold philosopher loved liberty, and his greatest poem, "An Invocation," from which Kipling is said to have received inspiration for his "Recessional," was addressed to that benign goddess. But he fulminated against the American idea of freedom, which he called "blind idolatry." The most illustrative though by no means the best stanza of his "Invocation" is this:

> Let man salute the rising day
> Of Liberty, but not adore.
> 'Tis Opportunity—no more—
> A useful, not a sacred ray.

That despite all his scoffings at churchly folk and despite all that they regarded as his heterodoxy, he should still have made profession of a profound Christian faith seems paradoxical, and yet he made such profession. And this paper can have no fitter or more significant finale than the following exalted tribute to Jesus of Nazareth from his pen:

> This is my ultimate and determinate sense of right—
> "What under the circumstances would Christ have
> done?"—the Christ of the New Testament, not the Christ of
> the commentators, theologians, priests and parsons.

The orthodox will frown at this, but in any scale of logic it seems clear that no man holding such a view of Christ could have been the hopelessly agnostic and altogether Mephistophelean being which some of the critics of Ambrose Bierce have pictured him.

An English Tribute to the
Genius of Ambrose Bierce

Anonymous*

The mystery of the present whereabouts of Ambrose Bierce does not seem to have been cleared up. The statement was made and denied that the American author had been discovered drilling recruits in England. It has remained for a British periodical—the London *Spectator*—to point out that Bierce was a pioneer in presenting the realities of war. "He did not fail to render justice to its heroic side, but he stripped it of its pageantry." So the English paper notes in a review of Bierce's book, "In the Midst of Life," a cheap edition of which was recently published in England. "He made no attempt to deal with it as a vast panorama in the manner of Tolstoy, or with the cumulative and circumstantial detail to be found in Zola's 'Débâcle' or the 'Désastre' of the brothers Margueritte. He confined himself to episodes—none of these stories run to more than twenty pages—and their essential interest is psychological. In this regard he naturally suggests comparison with another and later American writer of war stories, Stephen Crane, but his style was simpler and less spasmodic, and while Crane wrote his best stories before he had seen any fighting, Bierce had himself served in the fighting line throughout the campaign of 1861–1865. Stephen Crane's 'Red Badge of Courage' was a triumph of reconstructive imagination; but Bierce brought to bear on his first-hand knowledge an imagination even more horrifying than that of the younger writer." Altho, as the reviewer points out, there is only one of Bierce's books in the catalog of the London Library, the American is one of the greatest masters in depicting the horrors of war. He is the veritable Goya of literature:

> No one has ever reproduced the grotesque horrors of war more vividly than Ambrose Bierce. In this vein he reaches a climax in the story of the deaf-mute child who wandered away from his home and, coming across a number of wounded soldiers crawling painfully from the battlefield of Chickamauga, thought they were playing a game, in which he tried to take part, finally returning to his home to find it burned down and his mother lying dead and shattered by a shell. But the kind of narrative peculiar to Bierce is the analysis of a man's thoughts during the brief moments in which he is being sent from life to eternity. Thus, in the description of the death

*Reprinted from *Opinion*, 58 (June 1915), 427.

of the Southern spy, we escape with him by the breaking of the rope, drop into the stream, reach the river bank, and are on the point of reaching home, when the narrative breaks off, and we realize that all these incidents have taken place in the doomed man's imagination, and his death follows instantly. Perhaps the best comment on Ambrose Bierce's somber genius and the best explanation of his limited appeal is to be found in the remark made to the present writer by a friend. On being asked whether he had ever read Bierce's war stories, he answered: "O yes. I read them years ago, and shall never forget them. But I could never read them again. They are too terrible." It may, however, be fairly urged that, while there is nothing in them to blunt the resolution of those who are fighting for a righteous cause, they form the most powerful indictment conceivable of war for war's sake. Sherman's often-quoted saying, "War is hell!" never found more convincing literary illustration than in the stories of Ambrose Bierce.

Another Attempt to Boost Bierce Into Immortality

Anonymous*

For the third time in three decades, an American publisher has rediscovered the genius of Ambrose Bierce, and a new effort is being made, with the new edition of "In the Midst of Life" (Boni & Liveright), to establish the great San Francisco satirist as one of the supreme storytellers of America. In 1890 Bierce's volume of tales of soldiers and civilians was refused by every publishing house to which it was offered. It was finally brought out in 1892 by an obscure printer, under the patronage of E. L. G. Steele, a merchant. In 1898 it was issued again, under the imprint of a prominent New York publishing house. In 1909, Bierce's complete works were published by the Neale Company in a limited and expensive edition. And now, practically ten years later, the new house of Boni & Liveright is making a valiant attempt to secure for Bierce his own particular niche among the immortals of American literature.

The persistent obscurity of Ambrose Bierce's genius is the more puzzling because of the praise that has been lavished upon his work by the most discriminating critics of England and America. His works have been translated into every European language, including Russian and Norwegian. Henry Irving, Austin Dobson, Clement Scott, Arthur Machen and Arnold Bennett all eulogized his genius. Joel Chandler Harris, Gertrude Atherton, Edwin Markham, the late Percival Pollard, Owen

*Reprinted from *Current Opinion*, 65 (September 1918), 184–85.

Wister and a score of other critics and writers swore to his supremacy in the field of satire and the short story. But for years his work was out of print in this country or unavailable at popular prices. This anomaly is to be corrected at last by Messrs. Boni & Liveright.

When, in 1909, a limited edition of 250 copies of the complete works of Bierce was published, Arnold Bennett, writing as "Jacob Tonson" in the London *New Age*, declared that Bierce's was the most striking example of the "underground reputation" that he knew of. Admitting the superb power of Bierce's imagination, Bennett nevertheless declared that all of these stories were composed according to the same recipe. "His aim, in his short stories, is to fell you with a single blow. And one may admit that he succeeds. In the line of the startling—half Poe, half Mérimée—he cannot have many superiors." Bennett continues:

> A story like "An Occurrence at Owl Creek Bridge"—well, Edgar Allan Poe might have deigned to sign it. And that is something. If Mr. Bierce had had the wit to write only that tale and "A Horseman in the Sky" he might have secured for himself the sort of everlasting reputation, that, say, Blanco White enjoys. But, unfortunately, he has gone and imitated himself, and, vulgarly, given the show away. He possesses a remarkable style—what Kipling's would have been had Kipling been born with any understanding of the significance of the word "art"—and a quite strangely remarkable perception of beauty. There is a feeling for landscape in "A Horseman in the Sky" which recalls the exquisite opening of that indifferent novel, "*Les Frères Zemganno*," by Edmond de Goncourt, and which no English novelist except Thomas Hardy, and possibly Charles Marriott, could match. It is worthy of W. H. Hudson (another recipient of belated appreciation). Were Ambrose Bierce temperamentally less violent—less journalistic—and had he acquired the wisdom of a wider culture, he might have become the great creative artist that a handful of admirers believe him to be. As it is, he is simply astonishing. It occurs to me that Stephen Crane must have read him.

The imagination that goes into Bierce's most successful tales, asserts a critic in the New York *Evening Post*, is the imagination of genius, no less. Had this genius been adequately recognized during the period of its virility, this critic discerningly notes, Bierce could have avoided journalistic paths, and gained a much larger place in the history of American literature.

> The story of the soldier who, about to fire his cocked rifle at the retreating Confederates from an abandoned house, is caught in its ruins as it is demolished by a shell; who returns to consciousness to find the apparently loaded rifle pointing straight at his forehead, and so fixed in the débris that his slightest movement will fire it; and who dies of fright as he

finally makes a convulsive effort to escape, the rifle, which had been previously discharged, falling harmlessly by his side—this is admirably effective. Pierre Mille has done it the honor of appropriating its plot for one of his French volumes. A finer fancy goes into the "Occurrence at Owl Creek Bridge," where a Confederate spy, executed by having a fastened rope tied about his neck and being pushed from a bridge, has a vision of an escape and a return home that seem to last for days, in the instant before his neck is broken.

In the tales of the supernatural the narrowness of range, which annoys us slightly if we read a dozen of the war stories, is even more evident. The same motives, or more correctly, similar motives, recur in one tale after another; there are too many abandoned houses and too many sheeted corpses. But some striking effects are nevertheless achieved. The story which bears some such title as 'The Middle Toe of the Right Foot'—unfortunately not included here—shows remarkable ingenuity in compounding all the elements of horror possible in Southwestern lawlessness and a ghostly setting. The story of the weary pioneer who sat at night in his solitary cabin with his dead wife, and, worn by days of nursing, fell asleep till he was awakened by a panther which had entered to carry the body off, might have been written by Poe. But the breadth of Poe's imagination, and its finer delicacy, is in general wanting.

In his war stories, writes "A. Non" (Cowley Brown) in the Chicago *Musical Leader*, Bierce blazed a path where few may follow. "The fact that Stephen Crane, attempting that path, reached a sort of passing notoriety, has bearing only on the history of our amateurish, ludicrous crowd of American criticasters, not of literature." Bierce's fame, this critic writes, will rest Gibraltar-like upon the nineteen stories included in "In the Midst of Life." He explains why:

The grimmest of subjects combined with psychologic analysis of the clearest, the method of realism, a style crystal-clear, went with imaginative vision of the most searching and the most radiant. Death, in warfare and in the horrid guise of the supernatural, was painted over and over. Man's terror in the face of each death gave the artist the cue for his wonderful physical and psychologic microscopics. You could not pin this work down as realism, or as romance; it was the greatest human drama—the conflict between life and death—fused through genius. Not Zola in the endless pages of his "Débâcle," not the great Tolstoi in his great "War and Peace," had ever painted war, horrid war, more faithfully than any of the war stories in this book; not Maupassant had invented out of war's terrible truths more dramatically imagined plots. The very color and note of war itself are in those pages. There painted an artist who had seen the thing itself, and, being a genius, had made of it art still greater.

Death of the young, the beautiful, the brave, was the closing note of every one of the ten stories of war in this book. The
brilliant, spectacular death that came to such senseless bravery
as Tennyson hymned for the music-hall intelligence in his
"Charge of the Light Brigade"; the vision-starting, slow, soul-
drugging death by hanging; the multiplied, comprehensible
death that makes rivers near battle-fields run red; the death
that comes from sheer terror—death actual and imagined—every sort of death was in these pages, so painted as to
make Pierre Loti's 'Book of Pity and of Death' seem but feeble
fumbling.

In the field of satire, Bierce can be compared only with the most dar-
ing of the ages. Edwin Markham once described him as "a blending of
Hafiz the Persian, Swift, Poe, Thoreau, with sometimes a gleam of the
Galilean." His literary career in London, where, under the pseudonym of
"Dod Grile," his astonishing power of invective was revealed, stirred
London as no writer had done since Swift. But this satire was too savage,
too relentless, for the politer tastes. It would be impossible to-day for
anyone to express the misanthropic thought Bierce gave vent to in his "col-
umn" in the San Francisco *Examiner*. As the *Evening Post* reviewer notes:

Bierce's satirical work will not catch the taste of the moment as his Civil War tales may; he was too fierce a hater of
our democratic society, and declared too insistently that
republican government does not govern. A characteristic contribution to thought on international questions is his cynical
comment that "International arbitration may be defined as the
substitution of many burning questions for a smouldering
one." He remarked even before the first Balkan war that "All
languages are spoken in hell, but chiefly those of Southeastern
Europe." The volume entitled "The Shadow on the Dial"—the
well-phrased title is typical—was a labored but not very
coherent or thoughtful contention that the shadow on the dial
of civilization is receding. "The men and women of principle,
he declared, "are a pretty dangerous class, generally speaking—and they are generally speaking."

It was Ambrose Bierce's misfortune, Wilson Follett writes in the
Dial, to be a satirist alone. His wit was perhaps the most brilliant of its
kind since Voltaire, but it coruscates *in vacuo*. Unlike the first Samuel
Butler, he found no sharp social contrast to draw; all he could see in
America was a perfect homogeneity of smugness, and, like the second
Samuel Butler, he was forced to create fictitious worlds to be the media of
his criticism of the real one. "If in one sense he is unmodern, it is because,
with Lucian and Juvenal, Dryden and Pope, Swift and Voltaire, he chose
to explore the possibilities of hate as a form of creative energy."

His savagery, as exemplified in such overwhelming satire as "My
Favorite Murder," is every bit as devastating as that of the Frenchman

Octave Mirbeau. And Bierce had the same power as Leon Bloy to kill a reputation or to destroy a "masterpiece" in a few vitriolic words. This type of literary power is never conducive to popularity. And yet Bierce was not only one of the best-known littérateurs of California in his own time but the object almost of what one critic rather unjustly terms "provincial adulation." It cannot be said of Bierce that he was without honor in his own country. At a certain period California children were almost "brought up" on Bierce and Biercisms. He was the critic and dynamic inspiration of scores of California writers, many of a wider popularity than he ever himself attained. He was the literary "pope" for a period out there; his faults may have been pontifical. As a journalist he was too soon forgotten; but with the new wave of permanent recognition now coming to him and the example France is giving us in the naming of streets, there may yet be an Ambrose Bierce Avenue in San Francisco!

The mystery of Ambrose Bierce's final disappearance in 1912–13, at the age of 70, has never been adequately cleared up. He was reported in Texas, on his way to Mexico. It is believed that, despite a severe illness, he did go into Mexico, where he may have been killed in the revolutionary fighting of the Villistas. He never returned.

The Art of Ambrose Bierce

William M. Clemens*

Ambrose Bierce is a literary artist, one of the most delicate and finest that English literature has known. He has the savageness of Swift with the polish of Pope, and in intellect and literary feeling is the equal of both. His tales are forbidding, in the sense that they are not pleasant, and the running judgement is that he cannot be read because he is not agreeable. For example, here is a letter that I have received from a lady who thinks she is without prejudice, and who has a mind:

> What an anatomist of the unnatural! What a sense for the hidden and mysterious eccentricities and tricks of man's brain this Bierce has! I have always suspected he was the devil; now I know it. Bierce is but a non-de-plume, and "Ambrose" a dash of cynicism. I read and read until my head beat, and the beat became intolerable. Poe never was so horrible—for Poe sounds like a delirious fancy. These tales have a dreadful air of truth. What a fiendish, what a fine touch is there in that moon-lit picture of the soldier—a modern gentleman without superstition—watching a corpse and becoming a slave to his action-compelling imagination. The doctor, turning to the other and indicating the unbleeding wounds of the dead foe, was a

*Reprinted from *The Biblio*, 4 (July 1924), 676–77.

finishing horror. And the "Horseman in the Sky"—what a piece of sculpture that is! The thing could be done in bronze. Yet it is all morbid. I simply shudder. That is Bierce's effect.

That's the devil of it. Bierce is always forbidding. His stories make the flesh creep, and you turn to your wife and children and the lamp to reassure yourself. But what of it? I say it is an indictment of the intelligence and taste of the present generation that this man of genius was not recognized and rewarded. His was one of the brains that comes not twice in a century. He fooled his powers away on the newspapers of San Francisco. Cities are ordinarily more conscious of their sewers than of their children of light. It is my judgment—and I give it only for what an individual judgment is—that in the next century San Francisco will base her claim to distinction on the circumstance that Ambrose Bierce made it his dwelling place. He was a great man. He did not know it, which is a minor proof of the fact. With his wit, his scorn—which he can express—for twenty years he ameliorated the ferocity of the manners of the new rich and made dishonesty and pretense feel not only ashamed but conscious that there was a man in their habitat. Bierce could not be bought; he could not be silenced. Cork him one way and he would break out in another. Bierce was to be neither collared nor silenced. He was the only one of his kind. He was a voice crying in the wilderness. He had no fads, no theories. He was simply a natural man. Consequently everybody, including my lady friend, was more or less afraid of him. I said to him once, "You go into a rose garden and you see nothing but the manure about the roots of the bushes. It is there undoubtedly, but there are other things to be looked at—roses for instance."

"Yes, yes, undoubtedly.

But everybody else sees the roses."

Every one has his function, and Bierce's was to get at the root of things. That he is not appreciated is a phenomena to which twenty years of literary life have accustomed him.

"How do you think my book will go?" he asked me before he placed his dish of tales on the table d'hote.

My answer: "I won't be surprised if it makes a world hit or falls as dead as a landed salmon. You haven't in all you write, a trace of what we call sympathy. The pretty girl never appears."

"Darn the pretty girl," said Bierce.

"That's the matter with you," I said.

And that is the secret of Ambrose Bierce's lack of popularity.

But he is a man of genius, and this generation should take shame to itself that it does not see the realness of his incidents, and the incomparable literary art with which he relates them. One always has the impulse, if he writes at all, to take off his hat to Ambrose Bierce.

Bierce's Devil Dictionary

H. Greenbough Smith*

Ambrose Bierce, man of letters, writer of fiction, essays, fables, satires, epigrams, and verse, is known in England, if he is known at all, by a single volume of supremely fine short stories entitled In the Midst of Life. Even in America, where the main part of his work was written, he has by no means come into his kingdom. Something has to be done, however. Since he went to Mexico in 1914, and vanished forever from the eyes of men, his complete works have been collected from a host of periodicals and issued in a limited edition of twelve volumes. It is to one of these that I purpose to draw attention—surely one of the oddest volumes ever given to the world.

Dr. Johnson, as we are aware, took a sly delight at times in "gingering" his dictionary with an epigram, in the mere flash and outbreak of his petulant wit. Thus, Exise he defined as a hateful tax, adjudged by wretches; Oats, as the food of horses in England and of men in Scotland; a Lexicographer as a harmless drudge. Now, all the Doctor's sallies of this kind would find a fit and proper home in Bierce's pages. Indeed, it would almost seem as though he had turned them over in his mind and resolved to make a volume of such coruscations, all satire, sting, and sparkle, and of nothing else. The result was The Devil's Dictionary, or, as it was first entitled, The Cynic's Word Book.

Let us turn the pages and select, almost at random, a few examples that will serve to show its scope and quality.

Bierce was a soldier—which is perhaps the reason why he seems to have thought little of the rulers of the Navy. Here is his definition of an Admiral: "That part of a warship which does the talking while the figurehead does the thinking." There is a touch of Johnson about this, and yet the peculiar tang of it is Bierce's own.

As a short-story writer pure and simple, he has a jape at writers of long works of fiction—at least those of his own time. "Novel—A short story padded. The art of writing novels is long dead. Peace to its ashes, some of which have a large sale."

The Law has been the butt of satirists since laws have had existence. Bierce has a dart or two to throw. Here is his definition of a Litigant: "A person about to give up his skin in the hope of retaining his bones." Then we have the following on the word Appeal: "To put the dice into the box for another throw." And, if brevity is the soul of wit, how shall we better this: "Court Fool: The Plaintiff"?

His views of women vary strangely. Sometimes he is wormwood, as in "Belladonna: In Italian, a beautiful lady; in English, a deadly poison. A striking example of the essential identity of the two languages." And yet Bierce was no woman-hater. What can be more of a subtle sweetness than

*Reprinted from The Biblio, 4 (July 1924), 678–80.

his remark on Wine: "Wine, madam, is God's next best gift to man"? And what truer compliment, however whimsical, was ever paid to her all-conquering charm than this, under the word Garter: "An elastic band, intended to keep a woman from flying out of her stockings and devasting the country."?

I have called this whimsical, though it is more than that. But some of his definitions are pure whimsies—just freaks of fun and fancy, quaintly put. Such, for example, is the definition of an Auctioneer: "A man who proclaims with a hammer that he has picked a pocket with his tongue." Or this one, of a Jews-harp: "An unmusical instrument, played by holding it fast with the teeth and trying to brush it away with the finger." Or the definition of the word Positive: "Mistaken at the top of one's voice." There is, alas, no whimsy in his definition of the word Peace: "A period of cheating between two periods of fighting."

Sometimes he is not satisfied to give a single definition, but provides the reader with a rich selection. Such an example is the word Platitude: "A thought that snores in words that smoke. The wisdom of a million fools in the diction of a dullard. All that is mortal of a departed truth. A jelly-fish withering on the shore of the sea of thought. The cackle surviving the egg."

But the book is not all jibe and jeer—it is very far from that. "Brain: The apparatus with which we think we think." This is a sneer at human folly, or a truth, "deep as the centre," as we may choose to take it. Such a truth also "Accident: An inevitable occurrence, due to the action of immutable laws."

But the best example of this kind is that given under the word Magnitude:—

> Size: Magnitude being purely relative, nothing is large and nothing is small. If everything in the universe were increased in bulk one thousand diameters, nothing would be any larger that it was before, but if one thing remained unchanged, all the others would be larger than they had been. To an understanding familiar with the relativity of magnitude and distance, the spaces and masses of the astronomer would be no more impressive than those of the microscopist. For anything we know to the contrary, the visible universe may be a small part of an atom, with its component ions, floating in the lifefluid (luminiferous ether) of some animal. Possibly the wee creatures peopling the corpuscles of our own blood are overcome with the proper emotion when contemplating the unthinkable distance from one of these to another.

Rather striking, is it not, to find the theory of relativity expressed some twenty years before Professor Einstein had been heard of?

A Tribute to Ambrose Bierce

Walter Blackburn Harte*

Only fools are entirely lacking in egoism! A man without individuality is a mere shadow of a man. This world is filled with shadows, who pride themselves, poor imbeciles! on their complete vacuity. They are like a photographer's plates. They may possibly receive impressions, if they do not get fogged; but they can produce none.

Ambrose Bierce possessed an irrefragable individuality. He is at once wit, philosopher and genius. His style is peculiar to himself; it is like that of no other writer. His stories are unique in contemporary literature. If they suggest any influence at all, it is that of Edgar Allan Poe. Bierce is a past-master of the realistically horrible and the unexpected. Like Poe, he has weighed every word; not one could be replaced by a synonym without losing the delicate shades of meaning of the sentence. He has, too, like Poe, solved the difficulty of creating an atmosphere of horror. There are but few ghost stories in literature which are not really transparently commonplace. Ambrose Bierce's "The Middle Toe of the Right Foot," is a master-piece of mystery. The admixture of realism and romance is perfect. It is the wildest improbability told with pitiless realism. Of course, the very orthodox realists could not say anything good of such work; but who among them has written anything as powerful as "The House of Usher," "The Pit and the Pendulum," "The Descent into the Maelstrom," or "The Cask of Amontillado"? I do not say that Ambrose Bierce is following in exactly the same lines as Poe, but he has more nearly approached his intensely logical illogicalness than any other writer in English.

"Chickamauga," with its marvellous portrayal of a child's impressions of a battlefield, and the child's terrible awakening to its horrors upon finding his mother's dead body, is a masterpiece of descriptive writing. The making the child a deaf mute was the final touch of artistic perfection, which nine out of ten of the "reportorial" realists would have omitted. Every word in Ambrose Bierce's work shows that he is a consummate artist. "The Boarded Window" holds one in a thrill of expectation; but the climax, told so tersely, comes with the shock of a sudden horror. "The Affair at Coulter's Notch" and "One of the Missing" reveal the tragedy of war as I have never seen it revealed before, in English literature. Certainly, no living American could equal these two stories. These alone prove that Ambrose Bierce is possessed of more than ordinary abilities. "Parker Adderson, Philosopher," is a magnificent study of resignation and sudden terror. It is a pitiless piece of mental surgery, absolutely true in every detail. Bret Harte's Mr. Oakhurst is not more real than Parker Adderson. It is a story worthy of Dickens, as he is at his very best, in The Tale of Two Cities.

*Reprinted from *The Biblio*, 4 (July 1924), 680–81.

Ambrose Bierce is not only a philosopher and a student of character, but he has a strong poetic sense and a splendid talent for painting natural scenery in a few words.

ESSAYS

Ambrose Bierce

H. L. Mencken*

The reputation of Ambrose Bierce, like that of Edgar Saltus, has always had an occult, artificial drug-store flavor. He has been hymned in a passionate, voluptuous, inordinate way by a small band of disciples, and he has been passed over altogether by the great majority of American critics, and no less by the great majority of American readers. Certainly it would be absurd to say that he is generally read, even by the *intelligentsia*. Most of his books, in fact, are out of print and almost unobtainable, and there is little evidence that his massive Collected Works, printed in twelve volumes between 1909 and 1912, have gone into anything even remotely approaching a wide circulation. I have a suspicion, indeed, that Bierce did a serious disservice to himself when he put those twelve volumes together. Already an old man at the time, he permitted his nostalgia for his lost youth to get the better of his critical faculty, never very powerful at best, and the result was a depressing assemblage of worn-out and fly-blown stuff, much of it quite unreadable. If he had boiled the collection down to four volumes, or even to six, it might have got him somewhere, but as it is, his good work is lost in a morass of bad and indifferent work. I doubt that any one save the Bierce fanatics aforesaid has ever plowed through the whole twelve volumes. They are filled with epigrams against frauds long dead and forgotten, and echoes of old and puerile newspaper controversies, and experiments in fiction that belong to a dark and expired age. But in the midst of all this blather there are some pearls—more accurately, there are two of them. One consists of the series of epigrams called "The Devil's Dictionary"; the other consists of the war stories, commonly called "Tales of Soldiers and Civilians." Among the latter are some of the best war stories ever written—things fully worthy to be ranged beside Zola's "L'Attaque du Moulin," Kipling's "The Taking of Lungtungpen," or Ludwig Thoma's "Ein Bayrischer Soldat." And among the former are some of the most gorgeous witticisms in the English language.

Bierce, I believe, was the first writer of fiction ever to treat war realistically. He antedated even Zola. It is common to say that he came out of the Civil War with a deep and abiding loathing of slaughter—that he wrote his war stories in disillusion, and as a sort of pacifist. But this is

61

certainly not believed by any one who knew him, as I did in his last years. What he got out of his services in the field was not a sentimental horror of it, but a cynical delight in it. It appeared to him as a sort of magnificent *reductio ad absurdum* of all romance. The world viewed war as something heroic, glorious, idealistic. Very well, he would show how sordid and filthy it was—how stupid, savage and degrading. But to say this is not to say that he disapproved it. On the contrary, he vastly enjoyed the chance its discussion gave him to set forth dramatically what he was always talking about and gloating over: the infinite imbecility of man. There was nothing of the milk of human kindness in old Ambrose; he did not get the nickname of Bitter Bierce for nothing. What delighted him most in this life was the spectacle of human cowardice and folly. He put man, intellectually, somewhere between the sheep and the horned cattle, and as a hero somewhere below the rats. His war stories, even when they deal with the heroic, do not depict soldiers as heroes; they depict them as bewildered fools, doing things without sense, submitting to torture and outrage without resistance, dying at last like hogs in Chicago, the former literary capital of the United States. So far in this life, indeed, I have encountered no more thorough-going cynic than Bierce was. His disbelief in man went even further than Mark Twain's; he was quite unable to imagine the heroic, in any ordinary sense. Nor, for that matter, the wise. Man to him, was the most stupid and ignoble of animals. But at the same time the most amusing. Out of the spectacle of life about him he got an unflagging and Gargantuan joy. The obscene farce of politics delighted him. He was an almost amorous connoisseur of theology and theologians. He howled with mirth whenever he thought of a professor, a doctor or a husband. His favorites among his contemporaries were such zanies as Bryan, Roosevelt and Hearst.

Another character that marked him, perhaps flowing out of this same cynicism, was his curious taste for the macabre. All of his stories show it. He delighted in hangings, autopsies, dissecting-rooms. Death to him was not something repulsive, but a sort of low comedy—the last act of a squalid and ribrocking buffoonery. When, grown old and weary, he departed for Mexico, and there—if legend is to be believed—marched into the revolution then going on, and had himself shot, there was certainly nothing in the transaction to surprise his acquaintances. The whole thing was typically Biercian. He died happy, one may be sure, if his executioners made a botch of dispatching him—if there was a flash of the grotesque at the end. Once I enjoyed the curious experience of going to a funeral with him. His conversation to and from the crematory was superb—a long series of gruesome but highly amusing witticisms. He had tales to tell of crematories that had caught fire and singed the mourners, of dead bibuli whose mortal remains had exploded, of widows guarding the fires all night to make sure that their dead husbands did not escape. The gentleman whose carcass we were burning had been a literary critic.

Bierce suggested that his ashes be molded into bullets and shot at publishers, that they be presented to the library of the New York Lodge of Elks, that they be mailed anonymously to Ella Wheeler Wilcox. Later on, when he heard that they had been buried in Iowa, he exploded in colossal mirth. The last time I saw him he predicted that the Christians out there would dig them up and throw them over the State line. On his own writing desk, he once told me, he kept the ashes of his son. I suggested idly that the ceremental urn must be a formidable ornament. "Urn hell!" he answered. "I keep them in a cigar-box!"

There is no adequate life of Bierce, and I doubt if any will ever be written. His daughter, with some asperity, has forbidden the publication of his letters, and shows little hospitality to volunteer biographers. One of his disciples, the late George Sterling, wrote about him with great insight and affection, and another, Herman George Scheffauer, has greatly extended his fame abroad, especially in Germany. But Sterling is dead and Scheffauer seems indisposed to do him in the grand manner, and I know of no one else competent to do so. He liked mystification, and there are whole stretches of his long life that are unaccounted for. His end had mystery in it too. It is assumed that he was killed in Mexico, but no eyewitness has ever come forward, and so the fact, if it is a fact, remains hanging in the air.

Bierce followed Poe in most of his short stories, but it is only a platitude to say that he wrote much better than Poe. His English was less tight and artificial; he had a far firmer grasp upon character; he was less literary and more observant. Unluckily, his stories seem destined to go the way of Poe's. Their influence upon the modern American short story, at least upon its higher levels, is almost nil. When they are imitated at all, it is by the lowly hacks who manufacture thrillers for the cheap magazines. Even his chief disciples, Sterling and Scheffauer, did not follow him. Sterling became a poet whose glowing romanticism was at the opposite pole to Bierce's cold realism, and Scheffauer, interested passionately in experiment, and strongly influenced by German example, has departed completely from the classicism of the master. Meanwhile, it remains astonishing that his wit is so little remembered. In "The Devil's Dictionary" are some of the most devastating epigrams ever written. "Ah, that we could fall into women's arms without falling into their hands"; it is hard to find a match for that in Oscar himself. I recall another: "Opportunity: a favorable occasion for grasping a disappointment." Another: "Once: enough." A third: "Husband: one who, having dined, is charged with the care of the plate." A fourth: "Our vocabulary is defective: we give the same name to woman's lack of temptation and man's lack of opportunity." A fifth: "Slang is the speech of him who robs the literary garbage cans on their way to the dump."

But I leave the rest to your exploration—if you can find a copy of "The Devil's Dictionary." It was never printed in full, save in the ghastly

Collected Works that I have mentioned. A part of it, under the title of "The Cynic's Word-Book," was first published as a separate volume, but it is long out of print. The other first editions of Bierce are scarce, and begin to command high premiums. Three-fourths of his books were published by obscure publishers, some of them not too reputable. He spent his last quarter of a century in voluntary immolation on a sort of burning ghat, worshipped by his small band of zealots, but almost unnoticed by the rest of the human race. His life was long sequence of bitter ironies. I believe that he enjoyed it.

The Letters of
Ambrose Bierce

Van Wyck Brooks*

The Book Club of California has done a service to all lovers of good writing and fine printing in issuing a collection of the letters of Ambrose Bierce, and I wish it were possible for more readers to possess themselves of the book. Few better craftsmen in words than Bierce have lived in this country, and his letters might well have introduced him to the larger public that, even now, scarcely knows his name. A public of four hundred, however, if it happens to be a picked public, is a possession not to be despised, for the cause of an author's reputation is safer in the hands of a few Greeks than in those of a multitude of Persians. "It is not the least pleasing of my reflections," Bierce himself remarks, "that my friends have always liked my work—or me—well enough to want to publish my books at their own expense." His wonderful volume of tales, "In the Midst of Life," was rejected by virtually every publisher in the country: the list of the sponsors of his other books is a catalogue of unknown names, and the collected edition of his writings might almost have been regarded as a secret among friends. "Among what I may term 'underground reputations'," Mr. Arnold Bennett once observed, "that of Ambrose Bierce is perhaps the most striking example." The taste, the skill and the devotion with which his letters have been edited indicate, however, that, limited as this reputation is, it is destined for a long and healthy life.

It must be said at once that all the letters in the volume were written after the author's fiftieth year. They thus throw no light upon his early career, upon his development, or even upon the most active period of his creative life, for in 1893 he had already ceased to write stories. Moreover, virtually all these letters are addressed to his pupils, as he called them, young men and women who were interested in writing, and to whom he liked nothing better than to give advice. We never see him among his equals, his intimates or his contemporaries; he appears as the benevolent uncle of the gifted beginner, and we receive a perhaps quite erroneous impression that this, in his later life, was Bierce's habitual rôle. Had he no companions of his own age, no ties, no society? A lonelier man, if we are

*From *Emerson and Others*. Copyright, 1927, by E. P. Dutton & Co. Renewal copyright, 1955, by Van Wyck Brooks. Reprinted by permission of the publisher, E. P. Dutton.

to accept the testimony of this book, never existed. He speaks of having met Mark Twain, and he refers to two or three Californian writers of the older generation; he lived for many years in Washington, chiefly, as one gathers, in the company of other old army men, few of whom had ever heard that he had written a line; he mentions Percival Pollard. Otherwise he appears to have had no friends in the East, while with the West, with San Francisco at least, he seems to have been on the worst conceivable terms. San Francisco, his home for a quarter of a century, he describes as "the paradise of ignorance, anarchy and general yellowness. . . . It needs," he remarks elsewhere, "another quake, another whiff of fire, and—more than all else—a steady trade-wind of grapeshot." It was this latter—grapeshot is just the word—that Bierce himself poured into that "moral penal colony," the worst, as he avers, "of all the Sodoms and Gomorrahs in our modern world"; and his collection of satirical epigrams shows us how much he detested it. To him San Francisco was all that London was to Pope, the Pope of "The Dunciad"; but it was a London without any delectable Twickenham villas or learned Dr. Arbuthnots or gay visiting Voltaires.

To the barrenness of his environment is to be attributed, no doubt, the trivial and ephemeral character of so much of his work; for while his interests were parochial, his outlook, as these letters reveal it, was broadly human. With his air of a somewhat dandified Strindberg he combined what might be described as a temperament of the eighteenth century. It was natural to him to write in the manner of Pope: lucidity, precision, "correctness" were the qualities he adored. He was full of the pride of individuality; and the same man who spent so much of his energy "exploring the ways of hate" was, in his personal life, the serenest of stoics. The son of an Ohio farmer, he had had no formal education. How did he acquire such firmness and clarity of mind? He was a natural aristocrat, and he developed a rudimentary philosophy of aristocracy which, under happier circumstances, might have made him a great figure in the world of American thought. But the America of his day was too chaotic. It has remained for Mr. Mencken to develop and popularize, with more learning but with less refinement, the views that Bierce expressed in "The Shadow of the Dial."

Some of these views appear in his letters, enough to show us how complete was his antipathy to the dominant spirit of the age. He disliked humanitarianism as much as he liked humanism, or would have liked it if he had had the opportunity. He invented the word peasant in Mr. Mencken's sense, as applied, that is, to such worthies as James Whitcomb Riley. "The world does not wish to be helped," he says. "The poor wish only to be rich, which is impossible, not to be better. They would like to be rich in order to be worse, generally speaking." His contempt for socialism was unbounded. Of literary men holding Tolstoy's views he remarks that they are not artists at all: "They are 'missionaries' who, in their zeal to lay about them, do not scruple to seize any weapon that they can lay their hands on; they would grab a crucifix to beat a dog. The dog is well beaten, no doubt (which makes him a worse dog than he was before), but note the condition of the crucifix!" All this is in defence of literature and what he regards as its proper function. Of Shaw and, curiously, Ibsen, he observes that they are "very small men, pets of the drawing-room and gods of the hour"; he abhors Whitman, on the score equally of sentiment and form; and of Mr. Upton Sinclair's early hero he writes as follows:

> I suppose there are Arthur Sterlings among the little fellows, but if genius is not serenity, fortitude and reasonableness I don't know what it is. One cannot even imagine Shakespeare or Goethe bleeding over his work and howling when "in the fell clutch of circumstance." The great ones are figured in my mind as ever smiling—a little sadly at times, perhaps, but always with conscious inaccessibility to the pin-pricking little Titans that would storm their Olympus armed with ineffectual disasters and popgun misfortunes. Fancy a fellow wanting, like Arthur Sterling, to be supported by his fellows in order that he may write what they don't want to read!

Bierce was consistent: his comments on his own failure to achieve recognition are all in the spirit of this last contemptuous remark. "I have pretty nearly ceased to be 'discovered'," he writes to one of his friends, "but my notoriety as an obscurian may be said to be worldwide and apparently everlasting." Elsewhere, however, he says: "It has never seemed to me that the 'unappreciated genius' had a good case to go into court with, and I think he should be promptly non-suited. . . . Nobody compels us to make things that the world does not want. We merely choose to because the pay, *plus* the satisfaction, exceeds the pay alone that we get from work that the world does want. Then where is our grievance? We get what we prefer when we do good work; for the lesser wage we do easier work." Sombre and at times both angry and cynical as Bierce's writing may seem, no man was ever freer from personal bitterness. If he was out of sympathy with the life of his time and with most of its literature, he adored literature itself, according to his lights. It is this dry and at the same time whole-souled enthusiasm that makes his letters so charming. Fortunate was the circle of young writers that possessed so genial and so severe a master.

One forms the most engaging picture of the old man "wearing out the paper and the patience" of his friends, reading to them Mr. Ezra Pound's "Ballade of the Goodly Fere." Where poetry is in question, no detail is too small to escape his attention, no day long enough for the counsel and the appreciation he has to give. "I don't worry about what my contemporaries think of me," he writes to his favorite pupil. "I made 'em think of *you*—that's glory enough for one." Every page of his book bears witness to the sincerity of this remark. Whether he is advising his "little group of gifted obscurians" to read Landor, Pope, Lucian, or Burke, or elucidating some point of style, or lecturing them on the rudiments of grammar, or warning them against the misuse of literature as an instrument of reform, or conjuring them not to "edit" their thought for somebody whom it may pain, he exemplifies his own dicta, that, on the one hand, "literature and art are about all that the world really cares for in the end," and on the other that, in considering the work of his friends, a critic should "keep his heart out of his head." Let me quote two or three other observations:

> One cannot be trusted to feel until one has learned to think.

> Must one be judged by his average, or may he be judged, on occasion, by his highest? He is strongest who can lift the greatest weight, not he who habitually lifts lesser ones.

> A writer should, for example, forget that he is an American and remember that he is a man. He should be neither Christian, nor Jew, nor Buddhist, nor Mohammedan, nor Snake Worshipper. To local standards of right and wrong he should be civilly indifferent. In the virtues, so-called, he should discern only the rough notes of a general expediency; in fixed moral principles only time-saving predecisions of cases not yet before the court of conscience. Happiness should disclose itself to his enlarging intelligence as the end and purpose of life; art and love as the only means to happiness. He should free himself of all doctrines, theories, etiquettes, politics, simplifying his life and mind, attaining clarity with breadth and unity with height.

This is evidently a "set piece"; but behind its rhetoric one discerns the feeling of a genuine humanist.

In certain ways, to be sure, this is a sad book. At seventy-one Bierce set out for Mexico "with a pretty definite purpose," as he wrote, "which, however, is not at present disclosable." From this journey he never returned, nor since 1913, has any word ever been received from him. What was that definite purpose? What prompted him to undertake so mysterious an expedition? Was it the hope of exchanging death by "old age, disease, or falling down the cellar stairs" for the "euthanasia" of death in action? He had come to loathe the civilization in which he lived, and his career had been a long tale of defeat. Of journalism he said that it is "a thing so low that it cannot be mentioned in the same breath with literature"; nevertheless, to journalism he had given nine-tenths of his energy. It is impossible to read his letters without feeling that he was a starved man; but certainly it can be said that, if his generation gave him very little, he succeeded in retaining in his own life the poise of an Olympian.

Ambrose Bierce

Bierce has been spoken of as a "notorious obscurian," but there was really nothing obscure about the man. This reputation, however, coupled with an amazing amount of esoteric writing about him, has resulted in a myth. It is impossible to deal with this myth other than by a resort to the convenient makeshift of paradox. Thus it can be said, and truly, that Bierce was a very famous man in his lifetime and yet was but little known. Little has been written about him; much has been written about him. Can fact ever be disentangled from fancy? Can the sources of myths ever be traced and analyzed? It is to be doubted. Perhaps further discussion of the man will but result in further confusion, but this is a peril to which all criticism is subject.

Bierce has been written about by the following, the mere juxtaposition of whose names will perhaps explain the growth of the myth: Haldane MacFall, Arthur Machen, A. Conan Doyle, Elbert Hubbard, Arnold Bennett, Arthur Brisbane, William E. Gladstone, Joel Chandler Harris, Eugene Field, Paul Jordan-Smith, William Marion Reedy, John Stapleton Cowley-Brown, Percival Pollard, Walter Harte, Edwin Markham, Gertrude Atherton, W. C. Morrow, Walter Jerrold, R. F. Dibble, Edward J. O'Brien, Walter A. Mursell, C. Hartley Grattan, Allen Nevins, Jay House, Ruth Guthrie-Harding, Franklin K. Lane, Michael Williams, Charles Warren Stoddard, Mark Twain, Edward H. Smith, G. R. Sims, Van Wyck Brooks, Samuel Loveman, Ella Sterling Cummins, Vincent Starrett, Benjamin De Casseres, Dana Sleath, H. G. Scheffauer, Victor Llona, Charles Willis Thompson, Mary Austin, Thomas Beer, Oscar Lewis, David Starr Jordan, Eric Partridge, George Sterling, Lewis Mumford, Wilson Follett, Harold Williams, Alfred C. Ward and Silas Bent. To the list should be added the name of Rabbi Danziger, sometimes known as Adolphe De Castro—dentist, lawyer, author, diplomat and theologian. Rabbi Danziger has written much about Bierce, and has talked to newspaper reporters with a glittering profusion of anecdote, but he has omitted to mention the most important of all his memories of Bierce: the time his friend broke a cane over his head.

*Reprinted by permission of the author and of *The American Mercury*, P.O. Box 1306, Torrance, California 90505. From *The American Mercury*, 16 (February 1929), 215–22.

Bierce has been discussed as if he were wholly a writer of short stories by such critics as Fred Lewis Pattee, Alfred C. Ward and Harold Williams. His stories, in fact, are of trivial importance when compared with the amazing bulk of his satirical writing; if he was a great short-story writer, then it was by a miracle of indirection. Others have been impressed with his talents as a political philosopher, as witness Silas Bent's article in the *Double Dealer* for January, 1921, in which grave comment is made upon the pontifical utterances of the Master. The fact is that much of Bierce's political writing is unutterably trite, Silas Orin Howes' introduction to "The Shadow on the Dial" to the contrary notwithstanding. Again an editorial writer for the *Nation* makes the common mistake of assuming that Bierce was a propagandist against war. Nothing could be further from the truth. These and many similar misapprehensions have arisen largely because Bierce's Collected Works have been accepted as the final repository of his writings. But this huge collection actually omits the most important portion of his work: his long-continued and highly characteristic "Prattle" in the *Argonaut*, the *Wasp* and the San Francisco *Examiner*. There has been too much comment about him and too little fact.

Bierce was born in Meigs county, Ohio, June 24, 1842, the son of Marcus Aurelius and Laura Sherwood Bierce. His family originally emigrated from England and settled in Lyme, Conn. They were related to Sir Charles Bell, the English anatomist. Connecticut, as is well known, made ambitious claims to the territory westward of its present boundaries, and streams of emigrants from the mother-State settled in the province known as the Western Reserve.

These settlers were very religious and the Bierce family was nothing if not orthodox. Most of the pioneers located in Ashtabula county, and, if we may accept the authority of "Ohio and the Western Reserve," by Alfred Mathews (1902), the Bierce family was among them. Later the Bierces moved to Meigs county, where Ambrose was born, and finally they settled in Indiana near Elkhart.

The history of the family in this vicinity has been laboriously exhumed by Maurice Frink, city editor of the Elkhart *Truth*. The meager but extremely interesting facts were first published in that paper in 1922, and a note containing additional material was written by Mr. Frink for *Book Notes* in August, 1923. But Mr. Frink's story is misleading in at least one particular: it assumes that the Bierces were very commonplace, mid-Western trash. The fact is that their ancestry was quite distinguished, and that many members of the family served with credit in the Civil War. They were New Englanders in the strict sense of the term, and Puritans to the bone.

Even after the settlement in Ohio and Indiana, when it may be inferred that the family had fallen in state, there were several notable members. One of these was an uncle of Ambrose, Lucius Verus Bierce. He was a gentleman of sundry distinctions. He wrote a volume of essays and served at one time as the president of a small college. In the month of December, 1838, he gathered together a band of 135 men and boarded the steamboat *Champlain* to join the so-called Canadian Rebellion. The men landed above Walkerville, Ont., and marched down to Windsor, where they set fire to the military barracks and guardhouse and to the steamer *Thames*, which was at the dock. Great damage was done: soldiers were killed, the docks were fired, and many habitations destroyed. Finally the rebellion was dispersed by Col. John Prince. The whole tale may be found in "The Story of Detroit" by George B. Catlin, published by the Detroit *News* in 1923. Lucius Verus, nothing if not versatile, later became interested in sculpture and contemplated a trip to Italy for study. He was greatly admired by his nephew for his keen mind and high courage.

Of his immediate family, however, Ambrose was never very proud. He once told George Sterling that his father and mother were "unwashed savages," and to another acquaintance he remarked that all he ever inherited from his mother was a curse—asthma. The entire family, with the exception of Ambrose and his brother Albert, who also went to the Pacific Coast, was very religious, and it was for this reason that Ambrose never returned to Indiana after the Civil War, though he did make one trip home during the war, when he was wounded. Before enlisting he had written some boyish verses to one "Fatima," which he mailed to the young lady unsigned, but never doubting that she would recognize him as their author. The verses contained this line: "Fatima is divine! For I have kissed her thrice, and she is surely mine!" When the returned hero called on his love and asked her if she had received the verses she exclaimed: "Oh, was it *you!*" This was a story that Bierce never wearied of repeating in his later years.

II

Company C of the 9th Indiana Volunteers was organized at LaPorte, Ind., in 1861. Bierce enlisted at once; he was but nineteen years old. In 1862 the regiment joined the 42nd Ohio Infantry and the 6th Kentucky Volunteers at Nashville and was assigned to the command of General W. B. Hazen. A graphic and detailed account of the service that followed may be found in General Hazen's "A Narrative of Military Service," published by Ticknor Company, at Boston, in 1885.

Bierce was a member of the general's staff during the remainder of the war, and is mentioned in his commander's book as a very brave and gallant fellow. In later years Bierce and Hazen made an engineering expedition into the West and they were always fast friends. When Bierce disappeared into Mexico, his old comrade wrote a letter to his daughter which is as fine a tribute to the man's gallantry as could be imagined. Bierce was breveted for his services and several times mentioned in dispatches. He received an ugly scalp wound at Kenesaw Mountain and was loaded on an open flat car late at night and transported back to the base hospital. The dead and dying were piled knee-deep on the car, and left with only the moon to witness their agony.

But Bierce, though war was unkind to him, was not against it. On the contrary he loved it. He wrote and thought much on military matters and once lectured at the War College in Washington. For years he carried on a correspondence with Lord Kitchener, for whom he entertained a great admiration. Bierce's stories reflect his mastery of military detail, and he has been ranked by Laurence Stallings with the greatest of war authors. In "What I Saw of Shiloh," he sings the poetry and glamour of war with naive rhetoric:

> O days when all the world was beautiful and strange; when unfamiliar constellations burned in the southern midnights, and the mocking-bird poured out his heart in the moon-gilded magnolia; when there was something new under a new sun; will your fine, far memories ever cease to lay contrasting pictures athwart the harsher features of this later world, accentuating the ugliness of the longer and tamer life? Is it not strange that the phantoms of a blood-stained period have so airy a grace and look with so tender eyes?—that I recall with difficulty the danger and death and horrors of the time, and without effort all that was gracious and picturesque?

But Bierce did not forget the horrors of war. He told many dreadful stories in his column of "Prattle," particularly in the *Wasp* between 1881 and 1886, which did not find a place in his published works. He narrated such truly Biercian episodes as the story of the cavalry officer who was to be shot for desertion. The man was placed, according to Bierce, astride his own coffin, blind-folded. The firing squad was ready to fire the fatal volley, when the doomed man spoke to the officer in charge of the execution. No one heard what was said. Later Bierce questioned the officer and was informed that the unfortunate deserter had requested that a saddle be placed on the coffin!

There is also the story of the two men to be hanged at Murfreesboro, Tenn., for committing a murder outside the day's routine of war. One of them began to tell the assembled army gathered to witness the hanging that he was "going to Jesus, boys," and just then, so Bierce says, a nearby engine emitted a harsh "Hoot, Hoot!" and the men met death to a roar of laughter. Many of Bierce's more familiar war stories are based on actual happenings, as, for example, "Killed at Resaca." Bierce was the officer who carried the news of Lieut. Brayle's death to a lovely lady on Rincon Hill in San Francisco and received the response given in the story.

But while he believed in war, he was no chauvinist. He once remarked to his daughter that General Robert E. Lee was the noblest character of the Civil War and easily the finest general in either army. He was skeptical about the justness of the cause for which he fought so gallantly. Once, when the long-lost body of a Confederate soldier was found near Washington, Bierce wrote to Sterling: "They found a Confederate soldier the other day with his rifle alongside. I'm going over to beg his pardon." He disliked noisy patriotism, as witness his remarks apropos of General Salomon that "he drew his tongue and laid it on the altar of his country." He curtly refused the offer of the government to give him some $50,000 of accumulated back pay in a note in which he said: "When I hired out as an assassin for my country, that wasn't part of the contract." And he warned his daughter never to accept a cent of the money.

Bierce was against the Spanish-American War and always spoke of it as a freak. At a time when his employer, the chromatic William Randolph Hearst, was dazzling America with gaudy tales about the imprisonment of Evangelina Cisneros, Bierce was writing in the same paper on the same page: "We can conquer these people without half trying, for we belong to the race of gluttons and drunkards to whom dominion is given over the abstemious. We can thrash them consummately and every day of the week, but we cannot understand them; and is it not a great golden truth, shining like a star, that what one does not understand one knows to be bad?"

III

Bierce's residence in London was the most important episode of his life aside from the war chapter. In 1872 he was a free lance journalist in San Francisco, writing feeble copy for a column called "The Town Crier" in the *News-Letter*. He later collected this material and published it in London as "Nuggets and Dust." It represents the entire body of his writing prior to his London residence, and I stress the point because many critics have stated that he wrote for the *Argonant* before going to England. This is erroneous, and the significance of the truth may be easily seen by comparing "Nuggets and Dust" with the column of "Prattle" which Bierce started in Volume I, No. I, of the *Argonaut* on March 25, 1877. He went to England a rough, uncouth Western humorist, and came back a wit who wrote with great finish and elegance.

It was in 1872 that Bierce married Mary Eleanor Day, daughter of Captain H. H. Day, a wealthy Nevada miner, who had participated in the Virginia City discoveries. Mollie Day, as she was called, was one of the two or three most beautiful "society belles" of early San Francisco. The marriage took place in the San Leandro home of Judge Noble Hamilton. Captain Day presented the young couple with $10,000 as a wedding gift and they left for England on a honeymoon.

In England Bierce soon came into contact with a group of writers who he thought were of the utmost literary importance, but who were really only "raffish celebrities of Fleet Street." He had corresponded with Tom Hood prior to going to England and that fact was one of the reasons for the visit. Several times it has been said that he also corresponded with

Leigh Hunt, but this, of course, is incorrect, for Hunt died in 1859. The story probably got afloat because Bierce named his younger son after Leigh Hunt. In England he learned his trade as a wit from such men as Tom Hood, G. A. Sala, George R. Sims, W. S. Gilbert, Henry S. Leigh, Arthur Stretchley, Clement Scott, Godfrey Turner, T. W. Robertson, Austin Dobson and Henry Sampson. Bierce was an eager pupil. He derived much pleasure from his association with these brilliant, if not important, scribes. He was more happy with Hood than with the others, and was a frequent visitor at Hood's home in Penge, where they enjoyed many a bowl of grog, and where they made a death pact together. In 1875 Hood died. One day, several weeks later, Bierce was walking opposite Warwick Castle when he suddenly felt the presence of his friend in the street. The experience was never forgotten and he made fantastic use of it years later in "The Damned Thing," one of his most famous stories.

Bierce left some recollections of these early London days in his Collected Works. His easy circumstances enabled him to associate with as charming a society as London possessed. G. R. Sims has some words about Bierce in his autobiography, and Gilbert Dalziel, of the Brothers Dalziel, who owned *Fun* and published Tom Hood's Comic Annual, remembers Bierce's visits to the office of the publication at 80 Fleet street. The Bierce of the London days is also remembered by Hattie O'Connor, the only child of Henry Sampson, who was editor of *Fun* after Hood's death in 1875, and by Mrs. Croston, formerly Julia Sampson, who knew him in London and visited him years later in San Francisco. Mrs. Croston's interesting memoirs of him may be found in the London *Evening Standard* for September 15, 1922.

In London Bierce published three books, one of which became quite popular by reason of Gladstone's fondness for it. At this time he was a member of the famous White Friar's Club. Years later he used to tell of attending a dinner there given in honor of Mark Twain and Joaquin Miller. Miller came attired in red hip boots, and a buckskin jacket, with a huge knife stuck in the sash he wore as a belt. Mark and Bierce did not appear at all amazed by Miller's appearance, but accepted it as though such gaudiness were common in America. With elaborate nonchalance they even failed to notice it when Miller picked a fish up from the table by its tail and swallowed it whole.

Bierce lived in London for five years, from 1872 to 1877. His two sons, Day and Leigh, were born there. Later Mrs. Day, his mother-in-law, came to London on a visit and returned to America with Mrs. Bierce and the two children. It was not long after their return that Bierce received word that his wife was again *enciente*. He immediately abandoned his work in London to return and be with her. He returned early in 1877, took up a residence in San Rafael, and began to write his "Prattle" for the *Argonaut*.

The precious criticism which has referred to this "Prattle" as "unfortunate journalese" is grounded on ignorance. I cannot help thinking it is the most important work Bierce ever did. The much vaunted war stories were written as mere fillers to occupy the space of "Prattle" when its author was indolent or there was a paucity of fools to lambast. "Prattle" appeared in the *Argonaut* from 1877 to 1879. During 1880 Bierce was in the Black Hills on a mining expedition. He returned to San Francisco in 1881 and "Prattle" then ran in the *Wasp*, one of the first colored cartoon weeklies in America, until about 1886. From approximately 1886 to 1896 it appeared every week in the San Francisco *Examiner* on the editorial page, two or three columns of the wittiest, sharpest satire ever written by an American.

The yellowing columns of "Prattle" are amusing even today. I doubt if such beautiful abuse has ever been equaled in our literature. It was so violent that once the attorney for a criminal Bierce was abusing moved for a change of venue on the ground that Bierce's writing had incensed the entire community to such an extent that an impartial jury was impossible. When he read to the court some of Bierce's couplets the court considered the matter for a moment and then granted the motion. This column continued for twenty years.

IV

About the question of Bierce's appalling cynicism much theorizing has centered. "Bierce," said David Starr Jordan, "always seemed to me a fine and brave spirit whose life had been darkened by some hidden tragedy." George Sterling, also, murmured about a hidden tragedy and mystery. There were three tragedies in Bierce's life, but I do not think they had anything whatever to do with shaping his mind.

The first had to do with his wife. Bierce separated from her about 1891, when he left the family home at St. Helena and took up his residence at Auburn. The cause of their separation was simply incompatibility. Bierce's wife was a beautiful woman, but she was conventional, orthodox and perhaps burdened with social aspirations. Bierce always said that he would never divorce her, and he never did. He told one of his oldest and dearest friends that he had never cared for any other woman. Of Mrs. Bierce's devotion to her husband there can be no question. But through a misunderstanding of his wishes she applied for a divorce in Los Angeles in 1904, and then died within three weeks after it had been granted.

However tragic this affair may have been, it must be apparent that it did not change the character of Bierce's writing. He was writing the same pungent satire in 1877, when he was living at San Rafael very happily with his wife and children, that he was writing in 1891 at Auburn after the separation. It has been suggested that Mrs. Bierce was jealous of her husband, who was, of course, lionized by women wherever he went. But the truth is that she seems to have been vastly amused by the antics of admirers, who tried every ruse imaginable to catch his fancy. On the mantel of their St. Helena home was a collection of gifts that they had sent him.

The second tragedy was that of his eldest son, Day. This boy, who was very gifted and beautiful, was living, in July of 1889, at Chico, Calif. He fell in love with a young girl, Eva Adkins. They were both about eighteen. On the eve of their marriage, the girl ran away to Stockton with young Bierce's best friend. During the elopers' absence of several weeks the local newspapers made great sport of the affair and the result was that Day, a very sensitive youngster, became insane with rage. When the couple returned, the inevitable happened: young Bierce and Hubbs, the other man, began to shoot at about the same time. Both died. The two bodies were brought out from Chico on the same train. At Sacramento they parted: young Bierce's being sent to St. Helena and Hubbs' to Stockton. The Adkins girl stood on the platform, one ear clipped off by a flying bullet from the revolver of one of her lovers, and remarked to the reporters: "Now ain't that funny—one goes one way, the other goes another!"

This occurred in 1889. A terrible shock, indeed, but the great bulk of Bierce's writing had been written by that date. It was hoped that the tragedy might result in a reconciliation between the Bierces, but it was otherwise. Bierce soon returned to Auburn. In his absence, however, his former employer, and now arch enemy, Frank Pixley, had seized upon the occasion to wax moralistic at his expense in the *Argonaut*. Pixley, who had tasted Bierce's lash, wrote with cruelty and malice. Bierce wrote an answer which may be found in the *Examiner* for August 25, 1889. In it he said, addressing Pixley:

> You disclosed considerable forethought, Mr. Pixley, in improving the occasion to ask for lenity, but I can see nothing in the situation to encourage your hope. You and your kind will have to cultivate fortitude in the future as in the past; for assuredly I love you as little as ever. Perhaps it is because I am a trifle dazed that I can discern no connection between my mischance and your solemn "Why persecutest thou me?" You must permit me to think the question incompetent, irrelevant and immaterial,—the mere trick of a passing rascal swift to steal advantage from opportunity. Your *ex post facto* impersonification of the Great Light is an ineffective performance: it is only in your undisguised character of sycophant and slanderer for hire that you shine above.

The son Leigh was the center of the third tragedy. He seems to have been a very brilliant fellow, but intemperate. When he was living with his father in Oakland, a woman who had become infatuated with him at Los Gatos grew offensive in her advances and rumors of the affair reached Bierce. He called on the woman at her hotel and told her to leave Oakland at once or he would publicly denounce her in "Prattle." She left. Leigh later went to New York and became quite well known as an editor and illustrator. He even found backing for a little publication called the *Bee*. But he made a very unfortunate marriage, and it brought down the wrath of his father, who did not write or speak to him during the two years prior to his death. One day the newspaper for which Leigh was working gave a Christmas benefit. Leigh was to escort a wagonload of provisions and supplies to the East Side. He became intoxicated *en route*, and gave the Christmas treats away. Pneumonia followed and he died. Another terrible blow to his father, but that was in 1901, and Bierce was old enough at that time to be a grandfather.

Whatever may be made of these tragedies, it is apparent that they fall short of an adequate explanation of Bierce's bitterness. It is more probable that the Civil War, and more particularly the period of corruption and dishonesty that followed, made a cynic of him. In any case, his exile in barbaric San Francisco for twenty years could hardly have made him an optimist. The asthma theory has also been put forward. Bierce suffered from asthma as a boy in Indiana; he had inherited the affliction from his mother. He was not bothered with it, however, during the war. Then followed the long expedition across the plains with Hazen, and Bierce arrived in San Francisco a cured man, so far as he could then tell. He once remarked that he would never have married had he thought the cure other than absolute. But on his return to San Francisco in 1877 he was again cursed with the disease, and his agony was doubled when he learned that his younger son, Leigh, had in turn inherited it from him.

V

In 1896 Bierce went to Washington. His friends say that he was sent there by Hearst for the sole purpose of fighting Collis P. Huntington's Southern Pacific refunding bill. But A. M. Lawrence, editor of the San Francisco *Examiner* for many years, says that Bierce came to him and requested the transfer. That he did successfully fight the refunding measure is borne out by the famous Huntington-Bierce interview, which took place on the steps of the Capitol and made a great sensation in its day.

An encounter with Roosevelt deserves to be equally famous. Sam Davis, the well known Western journalist, had mentioned to Roosevelt that he knew Bierce. The President was immediately interested and expressed a desire to meet him. A formal invitation was sent at once. Bierce replied that he was exceedingly sorry to decline the invitation, but that it so happened that he had a previous engagement with an old friend from San Francisco, and that he never "neglected old friends to make new." Roosevelt was delighted and sent another note, saying, "I quite agree with you. Come tonight and let us be old friends." The loyal Sam Davis was present at the meeting, and, true to Virginia City form, introduced the President *to* Bierce. Later in the evening the three inspected the White House and Roosevelt showed them the famous painting of San Juan Hill with the Rough Rider, well in the foreground, leading the charge. He asked Bierce what he thought of the picture, and was informed that it was inaccurate since it depicted Roosevelt at San Juan when in truth he hadn't been there!

Bierce's life was full of such incidents. He and his wife received an elaborately printed invitation to attend the coronation ceremonies of the King and Queen of the Hawaiian Islands in 1881. Bierce's wife went, along with some others from San Francisco, but the major did not attend. His friends cabled him inquiring as to his absence and he responded: "Why should I bother to see a black Negro crowned Queen of the fly-speck islands?"

One time in St. Helena the local pastor came to call on Mrs. Bierce. Young Leigh ran in from the garden and remarked, aghast, "Daddy, I just heard Day say 'Damn God'." The pastor and Mrs. Bierce were properly horrified, but Bierce's only comment was: "My child, how many times have I told you not to say 'Damn God' when you mean 'God damn'!"

Bierce's wit at all times was very lively. He once remarked to a lady in Oakland that to be really happy a good woman must possess the three B's, and when asked what they were he said: "She must be Bright, Beautiful and Barren." At a party in Oakland he remarked that a widow was "God's second noblest gift to man," and when some one asked him what the first was, he replied, very softly, "A bad girl." To a very, very proper woman in Washington, he remarked: "Madame, you are so proper that I would even hesitate to call you a woman, since a woman is only a man with a womb."

His daughter wrote to him in Washington asking him to visit her at her new home in Bloomington, Ill. His answer was a wire: "Why Bloomington?" His humor often took a grim turn. In a famous portrait by J. H. E. Partington, Bierce is shown standing by his writing table with his hand on a skull. After making some remark, he would turn to it and say: "That's so, isn't it, old fellow?" I am not at liberty to say whose skull it was. Suffice it to say that it was bequeathed to Bierce by a friend. The ashes of another friend he kept in a silver cigar-box on his desk.

When he was living at Angwin, Calif., in 1892, he met a little deaf girl, Elizabeth Walsh, who was then a waitress in a country hotel. He became interested in her and saw to it that she was sent to a school for the deaf in Berkeley. She possessed poetic talent and her premature death was a severe loss to Bierce. There is a very touching reference to this child on page 168 of his "Letters": he requests his niece to take a picture of the child's grave and send it to him.

His devotion to his disciples was memorable. Of them the following were the chief: George Sterling, H. G. Scheffauer, Flora MacDonald Shearer, Emma Frances Dawson, Gertrude Atherton, Ruth Guthrie-Harding, Blanche Partington, Ina Partington, Ina Peterson, Muriel Bailey, and Ruth Robertson (now Ruth Pialkovo). Rupert Hughes wrote

Bierce letters addressed to "My Beloved Master." Of these pupils Sterling and Scheffauer were suicides; Flora MacDonald Shearer died in a sanitarium in Livermore, Calif.; Emma Frances Dawson died a recluse in Palo Alto (the newspapers said by starvation); and Mrs. Atherton and Mr. Hughes have committed intellectual hari-kari, the one by writing bland novels, the other by falling in love with the movies.

As Bierce grew older he wrote platitudes, wondered at the banality of existence, swore at life, and was obsessed with the suspicion that the entire play had been a dream. The mystery surrounding his disappearance into Mexico remains unexplained despite the recent efforts of his daughter to unearth the facts. After joining the revolutionists, Bierce wrote to his daughter that in order to convince the men he was with that he was loyal he had shot a few Mexicans; he added: "Poor devils! I wonder who they were!" Even the glamour of war had left him. Experience had embittered him, life had enraged him, and his mistress Art had forsaken him.

As he made that last sad journey southward, lingering at Shiloh, at Franklin, at Chickamauga, what memories must have flouted his soul! Men had died here, on these sun illuminated hillcrests, and he had shot some of them. Had it actually happened? Or was it only a dream of his youth? Battle cries and death yells, and murderous volleys of shot had once torn all this loveliness into a mad medley of hell and the very skies had bled with man's incurable folly. And all for what? They had not even known what they were fighting for!

Ambrose, Son of Marcus Aurelius

Wilson Follett*

An Author saw a Laborer hammering stones into the pavement of a street, and approaching him said: 'My friend, you seem weary. Ambition is a hard taskmaster.'

'I'm working for Mr. Jones, sir,' the Laborer replied.

'Well, cheer up,' the Author resumed; 'fame comes at the most unexpected times. To-day you are poor, obscure, and disheartened, but to-morrow the world may be ringing with your name.'

'What are you telling me?' the Laborer said. 'Can not an honest pavior perform his work in peace, and get his money for it, and his living by it, without others talking rot about ambition and hopes of fame?'

'Can not an honest writer?' said the Author.
—*Fantastic Fables*

I

Ambition he defined as 'an overmastering desire to be vilified by enemies while living and made ridiculous by friends when dead.' Disclaiming it as he might and did for himself, he was not to escape plucking either of the sour fruits specified in his definition. They were, in fact, but half of his harvest, for his friends did what they could to make him ridiculous while he was living, and he had been plentifully vilified by enemies since his mysterious death.

The vilification, whether contemporary or posthumous, is certainly not hard to account for. He was, from first to last, a difficult and thorny being, and his lifelong trade was the making, chiefly gratuitous, of enemies. When a woman feature writer, hounding him for an interview on the rearing of the young, asked him if any of the ancients had bequeathed us profitable counsel on the subject, he replied: 'Study Herod, madam—study Herod.' Publicly placed 'among our three greatest writers' by that kindliest of mortals, William Dean Howells, he commented only: 'I am sure Mr. Howells is the other two.' The pieces of a cane which he

*Copyright © 1937 ® 1965, by The Atlantic Monthly Company, Boston, Mass. Reprinted with permission. From *Atlantic Monthly*, 160 (July 1937), 32–42.

81

had broken over the head of a former associate he saved to remind himself, as he said, of the nature of friendship. He recorded in cold print his sorrow because cremation had robbed him of the pleasure of spitting on a dead enemy's grave. When Theodore Roosevelt, always eclectic in his hospitality, invited him to the White House he replied that he had a previous engagement with an old friend who was visiting Washington, and that he never neglected old friends to make new. Roosevelt neatly parried with a second note ending 'Come to-night, and let us be old friends.' When, toward the close of the evening, the President showed the spirited painting of the Rough Riders at San Juan Hill, with himself leading the charge, his implacable guest stated that the picture was historically false, inasmuch as Roosevelt had not been among those present.

An imp of the perverse drove this strange man all his days, and the more inexorably as his days became many. His stories, of which by his own account he had never shown a line to any publisher east of the Rockies, he issued in San Francisco with a prefatory statement that they had been 'denied existence by the chief publishing houses of the country.' He quarreled violently with all that he hated, and twice as violently with much that he loved. From the mother of his children, the one woman whom, by his own solemn avowal late in life, he had ever loved, he parted for a no-reason which was reason enough to him, and for her remaining years he communicated with her only through an intermediary. Through an intermediary went likewise the sums he sent at intervals to the widow of his son; for he had declined to see her as either bride or widow. On the threshold of old age he could still refer to his parents, estimable Mid-West farming folk, as 'unwashed savages.' As surely as he was Ambrose Gwinett, youngest son and ninth child of Marcus Aurelius Bierce, as surely as he was born on June 24, 1842, in the hamlet of Meigs County, Ohio, then known as Horse Cave, just so surely he was writing about himself and still loathing his origins when he set down the words:—

> Ah, woe is his, with length of living cursed.
> Who nearing second childhood, had no first.
> Behind, no glimmer, and before no ray—
> A night at either end of his dark day.

II

Ambrose Bierce the man, while he was alive, both gained and lost by his brilliant perversity, the glamour of his personal legend; but Ambrose Bierce the writer has only lost by it. It is, to this day, chief among the factors which keep his genius from being seen in rational perspective.

For the forty years past, and especially during the twenty-odd since his romantic, much-publicized disappearance, he has been treated as an irresistibly fascinating character who happened to do a good deal of miscellaneous writing in his day. Insatiate curiosity about the man prompts students of the bizarre to look up the writings and glance through them; and what they see is, naturally, whatever happens to reënforce the legend of the man. This approach happens to be the one utterly futile method of prospecting for what is of ultimate importance in Bierce. Obsession with such a personality is like fixing one's eyes on a glare—it being the property of a glare to blind one to all but itself. Bierce's epigram on the sea gull which dashes itself to destruction against the lighthouse is a perfect statement of what has happened to virtually all contemplation of himself.

The ministry of light is guide, not goal.

To survey the works in the light of the man's vagaries is to be dazzled by irrelevancies and incidentals, and so to miss the steady luminosity which the works have always had in themselves and perhaps always will have.

The tide of interest in Bierce and of print about him rose steadily after his disappearance in 1914. It reached full flood in the year 1929, which brought forth no fewer than five books about Bierce. With the exception of one, Mr. Vincent Starrett's bibliography, they were preoccupied with a commanding personality to the neglect of a commanding pen. The general impression which one gets from them is that Bierce was a rocket and that his work is the charred stick which came down to prove the fact and the line of his flight.

Even the quasi-official life by Mr. Carey McWilliams, the one rich, authoritative, permanently valuable source of information about Bierce in spite of some faults of presentation, ends on this discouraging surmise: 'Perhaps the ultimate judgment will be that he was more interesting as a man than important as a writer.' Mr. McWilliams, quite properly for his purpose, did not even attempt a rounded critical evaluation. He comments *in extenso* only on Bierce's stories. Now, the stories do indeed provide a handle to some aspects of Bierce which a biographer can hardly ignore; but to create, for however logical a reason, the net impression that his literary importance springs chiefly from his stories is a capital distortion of the very subject one is trying to bring to focus. It is as if one should portray Thackeray in terms of his minor miscellanies in *Punch* with only a slighting incidental mention of *Vanity Fair* and *Pendennis*.

Of Bierce's eventual 'dramatic exit' into Mexico Mr. McWilliams remarks: 'Nothing he ever did was more fortunate so far as his fame is concerned.' True enough, from the point of view which tacitly belittles the writings while magnifying the writer. But what if one happens to be concerned with another kind of fame? The question then becomes: What did the dramatic exit accomplish toward making Bierce known in the sense of being pondered, inwardly digested, or simply read?

The answer thus far is, Next to nothing.

III

Bierce himself played into the hands of his detractors conscious and unconscious, hostile and friendly. At the low practical plane on which men achieve careers in letters and make themselves felt in their own day, he was one of the poorest managers who ever lived. In the period 1870–1900 there was but one possible way for such a writer to make his works count for a fraction of their worth. That way was by an unbroken association of decades with an established publishing house which could understand him, have faith in his long-range importance, and work and plan with him year in and year out for an indefinitely delayed reward. So far from benefiting by any such steadying continuity, Bierce published his little volumes of journalistic scraps here and there from London to San Francisco, at capricious intervals and in small editions which soon became minor collectors' items. His books were given to the world with the testy absentmindedness of a bored child throwing handfuls of pebbles into a pond, and with about as much effect. Some of them he owed to the quixotic caprices of friends and idolaters. In the end he gave himself up as hopeless in the rôle of a man of letters. He half reconciled himself to the thought that he had been, after all, nothing but a redoubtable journalist whose trade was, as he said, abuse.

Then, a tired, discouraged, half-forgotten old man, he was made the beneficiary (or the victim) of still another ill-conceived enterprise—this time a pretentious, ornate, forbiddingly monumental *Collected Works* into which his output of a lifetime was crammed with no selection and little arrangement, like remnants into a rag bag. This uncalled-for twelve-volume monstrosity reminds one of Bierce's comment on the absurdity of monuments to the unknown dead—'that is to say, monuments to perpetuate the memory of those who have left no memory.' He disappeared into Mexico. There or somewhere, in 1914 or another year, he died. The man and the works were at that time alike dead. By a romantic afterthought it was shortly (and dubiously) discovered that the man might be, after all, of the immortals. The works, which have an intrinsic quality suggesting indestructibleness, still await their resurrection to immortality.

By posthumous criticism, and also by the form of criticism known as publication, Bierce has been made a victim of the overspecialized professionalism which conditions most of the activities and institutions of our time. Everyone who has ever had a finger in publishing knows that it is always a burning question what a given author shall be published *as*. Did Bierce write some war stories? Very well, we will reprint them and capitalize on the renewed interest in the psychologic and other phenomena of war. Did he have a flair for the ghostly and the ghastly, was he at home among spinal chills and in the charnel house? Excellent: let us parade him as a neglected master of horror. So, very naturally, the baffled publisher reasons; and the no less baffled critic has always rather abetted than enlightened him. Bierce did work in these two veins, to be sure. He also did work in half a dozen other conventionally established categories. But no one of them is central to Bierce. Not all of them together contain him. To define him as a virtuoso of the short story or the sketch, an essayist, a satirist, a literary critic, a writer of reminiscences, or a practitioner of any other of the literary forms which we are accustomed to find sorted and packed in volumes for our convenience, is completely to miss his distinguishing quality and the source of his transcendence. Yet it is in these ways that he has always been defined.

Hardly a grain of intuition or of basic horse sense has been applied from beginning to end, by either Bierce himself or any other, to the problem of getting his manifest destiny realized and establishing him in his place among viable American authors. There is, to this day, but one method of finding out what Bierce is really worth and what his prolonged inaccessibility costs the national letters. It is a fearfully circuitous method—one physically denied to most and intellectually impossible to some hundreds of thousands who might, if they were permitted, discover Bierce with the thrill of stout Cortez. The first necessity is to be among the lucky few who possess Bierce in that formidable mausoleum, the *Collected Works*; or, failing this, one must be in a position to haunt an exceptionally well-stocked library. Then one must assimilate some 5000 pages of mingled prose and verse, genius and bathos, wheat and chaff, stuff certainly ephemeral and stuff possibly undying, not only tumbled together in confusion, but actually interpenetrating and almost inextricable. Finally one must, by an act of almost creative criticism which few can perform at all and none without a vast appropriation of time and tissue, winnow the whole immense bulk for oneself—in short, review Bierce in one's mind, not as he was published, but as he might be.

What Ambrose Bierce has always needed, then, what he needs to this hour and minute, is first to be seen, and then to be competently published, and then to be read. The third desideratum is automatic, granted the second. The capital difficulty is the first.

IV

Bierce would have hooted at the prospect of anyone's taking thought in the interest of his posthumous renown and laboring to ensure his eventually coming into, as the saying is, his own. He would have protested instantly that the dead have no 'own.' When he says: 'Respect for the wishes of the dead is a tender and beautiful sentiment, certainly,' he is careful to add: 'Unfortunately, it cannot be ascertained that they have any wishes.' In another context he observes:—

> Posthumous fame being what it is—if nothing can be said
> to be something—the desire to attain it is comic. It seems the
> invention of a humorist, this ambition to attach to your

name . . . something that you will not know you have attached to it. You labor for a result which you know that you
are to be forever unaware that you have brought about—for a
personal gratification which you know that you are eternally
forbidden to enjoy: if the gods ever laugh, do they not laugh at
that?

Let the gods laugh, and Bierce with them; but we have ourselves to
think of. As inheritors and beneficiaries of whatever in the past is
valuable, durable, we cannot leave him to his beloved oblivion, however
disposed we might otherwise be to take him at his reiterated word. A nation which does not eventually salvage the treasures which a Bierce leaves
accessibly buried would not deserve to breed men of genius. For a man of
genius—pure literary genius—is exactly what Ambrose Bierce was. It is
only a question of time, and perhaps of not much time, when we shall see
him emerge from the mists of his legend and appear not only as an
American writer of the very first stature, but also as a world figure.

What words hitherto written on this continent are likeliest to with-
stand the abrasions of time we need not pretend to know. Of things which
we can set beside the breath-taking thought of immortality without *ipso
facto* rendering them (or ourselves) ridiculous, I can think offhand of a
few: sixteen lines of Longfellow, bits of Poe; at least two pages of Holmes,
more of Thoreau, more still of Melville, conceivably two or three tales of
Hawthorne; some letters and various other passages of Abraham Lincoln;
the best aphorisms of Emerson and of Poor Richard. To these, after
twenty years of constant familiarity which began in skepticism and ended
in awe, I am obliged mentally to add a substantial amount of Ambrose
Bierce—how much, it is impossible to determine without actually
isolating it, but probably more than the English-speaking part of the New
World has yet had from any other one pen.

Contemplate any fragment from the best of Bierce: for instance, his
definition of applause as 'the echo of a platitude,' or of the forefinger as
'the finger commonly used in pointing out two malefactors,' or of an acquaintance as 'a person whom we know well enough to borrow from, but
not well enough to lend to,' or of achievement as 'the death of endeavor
and the birth of disgust.' Or take a pair of the prose epigrams: 'At sunset
our shadows reach the stars, yet we are no greater at death than at the
noon of life'; and this fine one: 'Every heart is the lair of a ferocious
animal. The greatest wrong that you can put upon a man is to provoke
him to let out his beast.' Or let it be one of the epigrams in verse:—

> Think not, O man, the world has any need
> That thou canst truly serve by word or deed.
> Serve thou thy better self, nor care to know
> How God makes righteousness and roses grow.

Or one of the several hundreds of fables, some in prose, some in rhyme:—

A Philosopher seeing a Fool beating his Donkey said: 'Abstain, my son, abstain, I implore. Those who resort to violence shall suffer from violence.'

'That,' said the Fool, diligently belaboring the animal, 'is what I am trying to teach this beast—which has kicked me.'

'Doubtless,' said the Philosopher to himself, as he walked away, 'the wisdom of fools is no deeper nor truer than ours, but they really do seem to have a more impressive way of imparting it.'

Because it is nearly impossible to imagine such *aperçus* as having had a personal author or a beginning, it is likewise hard to think of them as ceasing to be. They have a quality of intrinsic inevitableness—the quality of La Rochefoucauld's undying maxim that 'Hypocrisy is the homage which vice pays to virtue,' or of Joubert's that 'The man of imagination without learning has wings and no feet.' It is as if they had always been. Reading them, we say: These things were not written, they were discovered. Devoid of all betrayal of effort, all eccentricity either temporal or personal, they possess the limpidity of perfect style. They are quite as good in one language as in another, and in any language they seem to have written themselves. It is not even possible to detect that the ones written sixty years ago have either more or less of perennial timeliness than those written but thirty years ago. Look at them from what side you will, they present no facet to attrition; for their hardness is that of the black diamond.

V

It is a matter for some astonishment that no one has seized on the quasi-symbolical hint contained in the biographic accident of Bierce's sonship to a man named Marcus Aurelius. This name, in the illumination of subsequent events and the peculiar nature of Ambrose Bierce's distinction, seems like a prophecy uttered in the year 1799. The son, together with what he inherited from the Massachusetts Bay and Connecticut Bierces, got from somewhere a quality and a stature of mind such as put him actually in the lineage of the timeless classical moralists, aphorists, epigrammatists, and fabulists. Like them he repeatedly packed the whole force of his wit, the entire scope of his imagination, into a page, a *pensée*, a quatrain, an epithet.

It is a remarkable testimony to the ascendancy of a momentary fashion, a socio-literary habit, and the dictates laid down by the publishing trade for its own convenience, that critics will still seek in vain to localize Bierce's magnificence where it was always the most clouded—that is, in his longer works, and more especially his tales of soldiers, civilians, and ghosts. The age, it appears, wants its writers to be great by the ream, the romance, the tome, the shelfful. It can hardly be prevailed upon to look elsewhere for greatness. But we have to seek Bierce's by the anecdote, the paragraph, the retort courteous or discourteous, the single line, on pain of not finding it at all. The last thought to occur to us is that (as Joubert also said) what is exquisite is better than what is ample—and this in spite of the swarming reminders that, of all that has long survived, little is to be found in fiction and little of that little in the realistic novel. We are disconcerted and baffled by a writer whose longevity is his wit—'the salt with which,' Bierce said, 'the American humorist spoils his intellectual cookery by leaving it out.'

Bierce himself had the firmest possible grasp of these truisms, and all his thinking as a critic was done beyond the range of our modern illusion about the surpassing importance of novels. St. Peter's, he said, is a work of high art; then he asked, 'But is Rome a work of high art?' 'The only way to get unity of impression from a novel is to shut it up and look at the covers.' 'Novels are still produced in suspicious abundance and read with fatal acclaim, but the novel of to-day has no art broader and better than that of its individual sentences—the art of style. That would serve if it had style.' 'To their gift of genius the gods add no security against its misdirection. I wish they did. I wish they would enjoin its diffusion in the novel, as for so many centuries they did by forbidding the novel to be. And what more than they gave might we not have had from Virgil, Dante, Tasso, Camoëns, and Milton if they had not found the epic poem ready to their misguided hands?' 'The art of writing novels, such as it was, is long dead everywhere except in Russia, where it is new. Peace to its ashes—some of which have a large sale.' Bierce also expressed his literary philosophy in that most famous of all brief reviews (of course, of a realistic novel): 'The covers of this book are too far apart.' And he seldom missed an occasion to point out that current novels, though read and written about, go unjudged. 'Of the incalculable multitude written only a few have been read by competent judges, and of those judges few indeed have uttered judgment that is of record.'

The late Mrs. Mary Austin—a novelist—is reported by Mr. McWilliams as having found Bierce 'conscious of lack and failure in his own life. . . . What he really wanted would not come.' And she speaks of his 'alternate high confidence in himself and puzzled bewilderment over the failure of his genius.' Mrs. Austin, who was brilliantly wrong about many things, seems to have been dully right about Bierce's attitude toward himself. At least half the time he believed that he had wasted eminent gifts and made a blank failure of a life which might have counted if he had not frittered it away. But a man's notion of what he has accomplished may be one thing, his actual accomplishment another; and in the strange, perverse economy of genius the longest way round may be the shortest way home.

Bierce squandered himself, as it seemed, for year after year in the production of columns of witty trifles for the Hearst papers (which, by the

way, he used chiefly for the expression of views diametrically opposed to
everything young Mr. Hearst thought and was); and when it was all done
and the sands run out it was to be perceived, by those having eyes to see,
that he had submitted himself to the one form of compulsion most perfectly designed for his self-fulfillment. He had kept his independence of
mind. He had been saved in spite of himself from all manner of dif-
fuseness and from the consequences of the facility which was his without
the structural sense to make a salutary use of it. And he had wrought, as it
were in a trance, a greater body of consummate, hard-hammered,
supremely original opuscules than we owe to any other American and
perhaps to any other modern. It is idle, it is fantastic, to argue that such a
man did not, up to the measure of reasonable human possibility, get
himself expressed. Whatever he thought himself, whatever he may have
died thinking, he had not failed.

There were, indeed, times when he himself had more than an inkling
of the sense in which his ostensible waste was the only conservation, his
temporary failure the eventual success in which he instinctively believed.
Surely his own story, with that of the critics who would reduce him to
their standardized preconceptions and make him out anything on earth
but what he was, is told clear-sightedly enough in these lines 'For a Certain Critic':—

> The lark, ascending heavenward, loud and long
> Sings to the dawning day his wanton song.
> The moaning dove, attentive to the sound,
> Its hidden meaning hastens to expound:
> Explains its principles, design—in brief,
> Pronounces it a parable of grief!
> The bee, just pausing ere he daubs his thigh
> With pollen from a hollyhock near by,
> Declares he never heard in terms so just
> The labor problem thoughtfully discussed.
> The browsing ass looks up and clears his whistle
> To say: 'A monologue upon the thistle!'
> Meanwhile the lark, descending, folds his wing
> And innocently asks: 'What!—did I sing?'

VI

Time and the recurrences of history have strangely renewed the pertinence of a great deal that Bierce wrote in his lightest topical vein and
must have regarded at the time as ephemeral journalism needlessly well
written for its use. He had a mysterious knack of seizing on the eternally
recurrent aspects of things; and I do not see why we may not, with aptness
and in all sobriety, call that knack genius. ('These are the prerogatives of
genius: To know without having learned; to draw just conclusions from
unknown premises; to discern the soul of things.') A mind which has once

been even slightly steeped in Bierce is thereafter constantly visited by a curious sense of plagiarism in the events which make up any day's news, and remembered words of his may unexpectedly mildew the freshest thoughts of our day almost before they can be uttered.

On the morning when I sat down to begin these paragraphs a trivial item in the early news broadcast reported an impending strike by 1700 unionized drivers of funeral cars and hearses in Manhattan. ('Hearse, *n*. Death's babycarriage.') The advertised return of good times had emboldened the members of this worthy sodality to claim five dollars more a week for their services to society. I found myself suddenly challenged by that feeling of significant familiarity which we have—illusively—in dreams. It took only a second to identify its source across a gap of some years, and only a minute more to find it. It was Bierce's fable called 'A Prophet of Evil':—

> An Undertaker Who Was a Member of a Trust saw a Man Leaning on a Spade and asked him why he was not at work.
>
> 'Because,' said the Man Leaning on a Spade, 'I belong to the Gravediggers' National Extortion Society, and we have decided to limit the production of graves and get more money for the reduced output. We have a corner in graves and purpose working it to the best advantage.'
>
> 'My friend,' said the Undertaker Who Was a Member of the Trust, 'this is a most hateful and injurious scheme. If people can not be assured of graves I fear they will no longer die, and the best interests of civilization will wither like a frosted leaf.'
>
> And blowing his eyes upon his handkerchief, he walked away lamenting.

The last Presidential campaign reverberated with just such echoes. Here are two that have stuck in my memory:—

(1) One of the candidates announced a sudden decision to stump several thousand miles of itinerary that he had earlier conceded to his opponent. To the reader of Bierce this occurrence could not fail to bring back the fable of the Man Running for Office and overtaken by Lightning, which, as it 'crept past him inch by inch,' boasted: 'I can travel considerably faster than you,' 'Yes,' the Man Running for Office replied, 'but think how much longer I keep going.' (2) On the morning of November 4, a news broadcast reported that quaint quadrennial phenomenon of American politics, the defeated candidate's message of congratulation to the opponent whom, up to twenty-four hours earlier, he had been denouncing as a menace to our institutions—a message to the usual effect that, the voice of the people having been heard, it was the part of every good American to acquiesce faithfully in their decision. The words that inevitably flashed into my mind were, as usual, Bierce's:—

'To the will of the people we loyally bow!'
That's the minority shibboleth now.
O noble antagonists, answer me flat—
What would you do if you didn't do that?

Bierce's touch was just as unerring in comment on the ironies implicit in international affairs and racial relations. On the very morning when Mr. Landon announced his electioneering excursion to the West Coast, London was being agitated by the news of bloody Moslem-Hindu street riots in Bombay. Bierce's little editorial comment reaches us across half a century:—

Hearing a sound of strife, a Christian in the Orient asked his Dragoman the cause of it.
'The Buddhists are cutting Mohammedan throats,' the Dragoman replied with Oriental composure.
'I did not know,' remarked the Christian with scientific interest, 'that that would make so much noise.'
'The Mohammedans are cutting Buddhist throats,' added the Dragoman.
'It is astonishing,' mused the Christian 'how violent and how general are religious animosities.'
So saying, he visibly smugged and went off to telegraph for a brigade of cutthroats to protect Christian interests.

Thus, by a curious fatality, the world keeps putting its toes into bear traps which Bierce set decades ago. There is hardly an aspect of current domestic or international politics, aesthetics, industry, or science upon which he did not utter some word of a more telling finality than the new words which each occasion brings forth in floods. The whole moral history of Geneva and of Europe in the sinister years 1935–1936 is packed into the dialogue of his one terrible page called 'Moral Principle and Material Interest.' On the various economic quackeries of depression the last, most crushing word is still his:—

Philosopher.—I have been thinking of the pocopo.
Fool.—So have I; what is it?
Philosopher.—The pocopo is a small Brazilian animal, chiefly remarkable for singularity of diet. A pocopo eats nothing but other pocopos. As these are not easily obtained, the annual mortality from starvation is very great. As a result, there are fewer mouths to feed, and by consequence the race is rapidly multiplying.
Fool.—From whom had you this?
Philosopher.—A professor of political economy.
Fool.—Let us rise and uncover.

And the pious and fervid nationalists who insist to-day that God is on the side of their revived militarism, and that their aims are really dictated by the principles of Christian ethics, put themselves squarely in the trajectory of the epigram—a rabid pacifist-hater's utterance, by the way—which ends:—

> . . . Somewhat lamely the conception runs
> Of a brass-buttoned Jesus firing guns.

The same uncanny pertinence runs through a good half of Bierce's work, including much of it which, being specifically topical, can hardly have been expected to reach beyond its passing hour. There is, for example, a casual jingle called 'The Statesmen,' one of many written of another depression campaign in another century. It reads like a trenchant and accurate lampoon of the seven 1936 contenders for the Presidency and their haranguing partisans (harangue-outangs, Bierce once named their kind). It begins:—

> How blest the land that counts among
>   Her sons so many good and wise,
> To execute great feats of tongue
>   When troubles rise.

Then he sets the speakers one after another on their stumps—the men who shout with one voice: 'I—I alone—can show that black is white as grass.' Free silver is the panacea of one, free trade of another, freer banking laws of a third. ('Free board, clothes, lodging would from me win warm applause.') The single-taxer lifts up his voice, and after him the inflationist—'as many cures as addle-wits who know not what the ailment is.' From contemplation of the orators he falls to diagnosing the ills of the suffering Body Politic, whose wretched fate it is 'to be not altogether quick, nor very dead. You take your exercise in squirms, your rest in fainting fits between.' The complaint, he decides, is nothing but worms:

> Worm Capital, Worm Labor dwell
>   Within your maw and muscle's scope.
> Their quarrels make your life a hell,
>   Your death a hope.

And he ends this occasional trifle on a Butlerian touch well calculated to provoke rapacious envy in the best of our contemporary wits of the daily column and make their everlasting fortunes if they could contrive to duplicate it:—

> God send you convalesce! God send
>   You vermifuge.

It would, however, be a pity to leave the impression that Bierce's province was primarily political satire. I can think of scarce a phase of morals, religion, invention, or human relations which the reader of Bierce does not sooner or later see with a new starkness in the glare of his lightning flash. He even has, I discover, some petards to set under the grand shaman of psychoanalysis whose 250,000-word treatise I have moiled my way through in the interest of a publisher who needs one ounce of sense which he can understand on several pounds of ingenious hocus-pocus which he cannot. One of the most concentrated and high-powered of the petards is this: 'Thought and emotion dwell apart. When the heart goes into the head there is no dissension: only an eviction.'

And here is a last general word on the subject—a word which fits our day almost infinitely better than that for which it was written and will fit to-morrow better yet:—

> 'Whose deady body is that?'
> 'Credulity's.'
> 'By whom was he slain?'
> 'Credulity.'
> 'Ah, suicide.'
> 'No, surfeit. He dined at the table of Science, and
swallowed all that was set before him.'

VII

Bierce hated, in his time, some things which no longer seem so very hateful. He fought against ideas which now look impregnable and for ideas which the world has thrown on its scrap heap. Against labor and capital, democracy and monarchism, imperialistic war and pacifistic sentimentalism, he was equally implacable. Politically he was nearer to the complete Fascist, the out-and-out Hitlerian, than to anything else now extant; and yet he abominated tyranny. Sometimes, no doubt in weariness of spirit, he perpetrated humor which was jangling, in bad taste, and, worst of all, not very funny. His character contained indefensible (though not inexplicable) elements of arrogance, obstinacy, and the snob-baiter's snobbishness. Mr. H. L. Mencken, himself not exactly an apostle of optimistic sweetness and light, recoils from Bierce's 'appalling cynicism.' Perhaps the man's only quality which never knew a flaw was his courage.

This imbalance of attributes is inevitable material for the biographer. It is perhaps important to the critic, too, while an author is alive and his claim to attention an issue still being fought out. It may even be relevant to posthumous criticism of works composed on a scale great enough to contain the author whole, as novels and histories may. It has always been customary to discuss the work of Bierce in conjunction with his brilliant defects, and to find the defects in the writings by the simple process of ignoring those which do not contain them. But to-day, twenty-odd years after the probable time of his death, what do such excrescences matter to us as readers of that which we find intrinsically worth our time?

Bierce was always passionate in defense of two ideas: first, that a work of the imagination must be judged entirely apart from the personality which produced it; secondly, that an author, like a race horse or a discus thrower, has a reasonable claim to be rated by his best performances, not his worst or his average. These stipulations apply with unique force to his own characteristic works, precisely because they are so concentrated as to be nullified by the smallest flaw. If there is perfection in them, you may be sure that there is nothing else, for there is room for nothing else.

'The philosopher's profoundest conviction is that which he is most reluctant to express, lest he mislead.' 'Nothing is more logical than persecution. Religious tolerance is a kind of infidelity.' 'Experience is a revelation in the light of which we renounce the errors of youth for those of age.' 'In childhood we expect, in youth demand, in manhood hope, and in age beseech.' 'Adam probably regarded Eve as the woman of his choice, and exacted a certain gratitude for the distinction of his preference.' 'We are what we laugh at. The stupid person is a poor joke; the clever, a good one.'

> 'God keep thee, stranger; what is they name?'
> 'Wisdom. And thine?'
> 'Knowledge. How does it happen that we meet?'
> 'This is an intersection of our paths.'
> 'Will it ever be decreed that we travel always the same road?'
> 'We were well named if we knew.'

> Cried Age to Youth: 'Abate your speed!
> The distance hither's brief indeed.'
> But Youth pressed on without delay—
> The shout had reached but half the way.

In such things—and Bierce turned them out by hundreds—what matters or can ever matter but the justice of the perceptions, the impact of the truth or half-truth, the swift outflowing of suggestion, the sovereign way he had with words? What difference can it make whether the man behind the words was once, in his mortal clay, proud or humble, consistent or erratic, philanthropist or misanthrope, materialist or mystic, Catholic, Protestant, or pagan? Is there anything in the words themselves to disclose to you that he was a hedonist, a journalist, an adoptive Californian, a father, an ex-soldier who had been wounded and decorated for valor? Would they be any less incredible from an ascetic, a scholar, a Vermonter, a bachelor, a hunchback? Could you even tell by internal evidence within a century of when they were written? And if their author wrote so much as one paragraph which lives, how is it made in any single particular more or less living by the order or confusion of his life, or by the number of other paragraphs he may also have written which are now as dead as he?

In the worked-over river beds of his California in recent summers twenty-odd thousands of unprosperous hardy folk have camped and lived by the panning of gold. It does not occur to them to complain much about the quantity of sand and gravel that washes away as they rock their pans or sluice boxes. The issue to them is how many grains of gold remain when the last handful of waste has disappeared.

Ambrose Bierce's dross might have been, but was not, washed away in the critical process of editing his work for publication—a process unhappily never half performed. Subsequently his waste might have been sluiced away by public criticism and the composite taste of readers; but no sufficiently alert and disinterested consensus of criticism has yet been brought to bear, and, as I have noted, the work has been physically inaccessible to all but a trifling number.

The gold and the gravel, intermingled, remain *in situ* to this day, waiting for the greater critic called Time to do the work which the others have neglected. That the gold is there, of a purity and weight to stick to the pan, I have tried to indicate by a few random samples. Devoutly I believe that Time is going to prove, as I cannot, that it is not fools' gold.

The Old Northwest, the Midwest, and the Making of Three American Iconoclasts

David D. Anderson*

"An honest God is the noblest work of man."
—Robert Ingersoll, "The Gods," 1872

"Faith, n. Belief without evidence in what is told by one who
speaks without knowledge, of things without parallel."
—Ambrose Bierce, *The Devil's Dictionary*
(The Cynic's Word Book), 1906

"There is only one grade of men: they are all contemptible."
—E. W. Howe, *The Story of a Country Town*, 1883

I Origins

On December 23, 1837, in an address before the Ohio Historical and
Philosophical Society in Columbus, Ohio, Judge Timothy Walker of Cin-
cinnati recounted his own memories of the movement West from New
England in the first third of the nineteenth century. During those years,
while emigration threatened to depopulate some New England towns, it
contributed to a movement that saw more than one-third of the national
population move West in search of a new life. Walker said,

> I can well remember when, in Massachusetts, the rage for
> moving to Ohio was so great, that resort was had to
> counteracting fictions, in order to discourage it; and this
> region was represented as cold, sterile, sickly, and full of all
> sorts of monsters. The powerful engine of caricature was set in
> motion. I have a distinct recollection of a picture, which I saw
> in boyhood, prefixed to a penny, anti-moving-to-Ohio pam-
> phlet, in which a stout, ruddy, well-dressed man, on a sleek,
> fat horse, with a label, "I am going to Ohio," meets a pale, and
> ghastly skeleton of a man, scarcely half dressed, on the wreck
> of what was once a horse, already bespoken by the more politic

*Published by permission of the author. This is an original essay, written for this volume.

96

crows, with a label, "I have been to Ohio." But neither falsehood nor ridicule could deter the enterprising from seeking a new home. Hither they came in droves.[1]

Those who came West in the droves cited by Judge Walker in the early years of the nineteenth century sought two things: an open society and cheap land. They went West to grow with the new country, to work hard, and to prosper. Many of them, including Judge Walker and countless others, did so. At the same time they built the country, transforming the Old Northwest to the American Midwest in little more than half a century. Although, as the caricature suggests, it was difficult for destitute would-be emigrants to move West—land was cheap but not free, titles had to be proven, the expense of moving livestock, implements, and family West was considerable—many families little beyond destitution made the journey. The cartoon suggests, too, another fact about the movement West, a movement that often included other movements farther West: opportunity was often elusive, even beyond the emigrants' grasp. Many of them found instead the life that Ambrose Bierce, then editor of the sprightly San Francisco magazine *The Wasp*, described in 1883, forty-six years after Judge Walker remembered his youth and forty-one years after Bierce's own birth in Meigs County, Ohio, on June 24, 1842:

> With what anguish of mind I remember my childhood,
>   Recalled in the light of a knowledge since gained;
> The malarious farm, the west, fungus grown wildwood,
>   The chills then contracted that since have remained.
> The scum-covered duck pond, the pigstye close by it,
>   The ditch where the sour-smelling house drainage fell,
> The damp shaded dwelling, the foul barnyard nigh it. . . .[2]

The chills then contracted, in rural Ohio and Indiana before his Civil War service and subsequent emigration to California, remained with Bierce to the end, producing a man who has been called "Bitter Bierce," "Almighty God Bierce," and other names less printable. Those chills, frequently sketched by Bierce's biographers, were not merely the foundation that produced Bierce's later caustic writing; they were the foundation that produced a generation of rural iconoclasts who came out of the towns and countryside of the Old Northwest as it was becoming the Midwest, who challenged American orthodoxy, whether political, social, or theological, and who began a tradition of caustic self-criticism that is still with us.

The tradition that produced Bierce—the tradition that evolved in the rural Old Northwest in the years during which the frontier, the open society, and cheap land had passed beyond the Mississippi and the Midwest was becoming the American heartland—was compounded of the movement Westward in search of an elusive fulfillment and of concurrent intellectual, social, political, and theological ferment. That tradition also produced two of the most outspoken of Bierce's contemporary iconoclasts, Robert Green Ingersoll, born near Dresden, New York, on August 11, 1833, and Edgar Watson Howe, born near Treaty, Indiana, on May 3, 1853.

Two of the elements of that tradition were particularly important in shaping the adult lives of each of the three men, and these elements were equally instrumental in shaping the remarkably similar attitudes in their later work. Each of these was less the product of the movement West—in each case a series of moves—as of the movement's failed dream. The Ingersoll, Bierce, and Howe families were among those for whom success remained out of reach, and each family, after a succession of moves, was among those left to moulder in the backwater of national expansion.

Each of the three men was indelibly marked in his youth by paternal failure, and each was further marked by what was to him another dimension of paternal failure: the fundamental religious enthusiasm which each father had brought West with him and in which he took refuge. Each of the three absorbed the faith of the Westward movement in the opportunities available in a new, open society, and each sought a means—like Lincoln, in the new towns rather than on the farms—whereby he, unlike his father, might rise, in which his voice could be heard and perhaps his fortune made. And each carried with him a hatred for the religious repression of his youth.

Robert Ingersoll was born on August 11, 1833, in Dresden, New York, a backwater of the frontier that had passed on a generation earlier. He was the youngest of five children of the Reverend John Ingersoll, an ordained Congregational minister and a devout Calvinist, the head of a household that had become motherless shortly after Robert's birth. Robert's early history, from the age of three, was marked by his father's restless search. From his Eastern origins, he had already moved West, to New York; then, after Robert's birth, he moved from parsonage to parsonage in the new country to the West: to churches in Oberlin, Ashtabula, and other towns in Ohio's Western Reserve, in Kentucky, Indiana, Michigan, and Wisconsin, and finally in Marion and Greenville, Illinois. In the latter town Robert Ingersoll determined to make his break with the past. After scant formal education but a great deal of reading directed by his father and with a talent for oratory, he became a schoolmaster. He then decided to study law, recognizing, as did Lincoln twenty years before, that the law was the least uncertain of the many paths to success in the new, litigious society of the West.

Ambrose Bierce was, like Ingersoll, the youngest child of a large family, ten in all, and he was born in the course of family migration that had begun in Massachusetts, had gone to the Western Reserve in northern Ohio, and thence to the hills of southern Ohio, where, at a now-vanished settlement called Horse Cave, Ambrose was born on June 24, 1842. His father, Marcus Aurelius Bierce, a devout Calvinist overshadowed by a successful younger brother, then moved, with his overworked wife and slowly diminishing brood, to a farm near Circleville, Ohio, and thence to another near Warsaw, Indiana, and finally to one near Elkhart. Like Ingersoll, Ambrose Bierce had little formal education except for a year at Kentucky Military Institute, sponsored by his uncle. But he read widely at home, directed by his father. At 19, after a series of menial jobs in a saloon, a brickyard, a farm, and a printshop he enlisted in the Union Army.

Edgar Watson Howe, like the others, was born in the course of his family's migration, on May 3, 1853, during a brief stay at a farm near Treaty, Indiana. His father, Henry Howe, was a farmer and unordained Methodist preacher of vague Ohio or Pennsylvania origins; his mother, a widow with two children before her marriage to Henry, remains as faceless as those of Ingersoll and Bierce. She bore Henry Howe five children, of which Edgar was the eldest. The family moved on to a farm near Fairview, Missouri, when Edgar was three. There his father built and remained as preacher of the local Methodist church, rode the Methodist circuit, and farmed. Edgar's education was sporadic, and he worked on the family farm. At twelve he went to work in a print shop in Bethany, newly acquired by his father. When the shop and its ancillary newspaper were sold, Edgar remained there, still under the domination of his father. At fifteen, after his father had become involved in a local scandal, Edgar joined the army of wandering printers that roamed the byways and set the type in the small towns of the Midwest.

None of the families was destitute, or the moves farther West would have been impossible, but the dream of success that led to further moves continued to be elusive for each of the family heads. The Reverend John Ingersoll, in spite of a brief attempt at storekeeping, remained in the state of genteel poverty common to rural parsons; Marcus Bierce was never desperately poor, but often close to it; of the three, Henry Howe came closest to success in Missouri, but the sex scandal, whether based on fact or idle gossip, put it out of reach. Life for each of the sons was characterized by hard work, and each seized an early opportunity to strike out on his own. Ingersoll chose the law; Bierce, like Grant a generation earlier, the army, and then adventure and journalism in the West; Howe, the youngest, the role of townsman printer-editor. Each of them, before he was eighteen, had made a clear break with the past that had promised his father so much and delivered so little. In later years only Ingersoll spoke kindly of his father.

If the economic status of each family remained relatively stable in spite of continued search, so did the religious faith that each carried Westward. Both John Ingersoll and Marcus Bierce were men of the past, subscribing without reservation to a Calvinism undiluted since it had been carried across the Atlantic two centuries before and that had become anachronistic in the individualistic, democratic West. Henry Howe, conversely, preached open salvation, the free will and free grace gospel of Methodism welcomed in the hamlets and cabins, as well as the cane break camp meetings of the West. But in spite of doctrinal differences, each of the fathers impressed a common awareness on his son: the reality of sin and the omnipresence of a God of justice.

In spite of an age difference that extended over a generation, each of the three came from a background compounded of cheap land and the promise of opportunity in an open, dynamic society; of parental failure to seize those opportunities; of a contagious frontier faith in democracy, freedom, and individualism; of a faith in the central government as the instrument of progress. Each of them acquired a distaste for farming as a way of life or as a means of earning a living, and each knew that whatever opportunity still remained as the frontier moved beyond them would be found in the towns. None of the three ever forgot what was behind him, and none of them ever forgave. If Bierce, normally reticent, remembered most vividly the farm in Indiana, Ingersoll remembered the Sundays, the days controlled by his father:

> . . . When I was a boy Sunday was considered altogether too holy to be happy in. . . . Nobody said a pleasant word; nobody laughed; nobody smiled; the child that looked the sickest was regarded as the most pious. . . . Then we went to church. . . . [Father?] commenced at "firstly" and went on and on to about "twenty-thirdly." Then he made a few remarks by way of application; and then took a general view of the subject, and in about two hours reached the last chapter in Revelation. . . . Then came the catechism with the chief end of man. . . . [Father?] asked us if we knew that we all deserved to go to hell, and we all answered "Yes." Then we were asked if we should be willing to go to hell if it was God's will, and every little liar shouted "Yes." Then the same sermon was preached once more, commencing at the other end and going back. After that, we started for home, sad and solemn—overpowered with the wisdom displayed in the scheme of the atonement. When we got home, if we had been good boys, and the weather was warm, sometimes they would take us out to the graveyard to cheer us up a little. It did cheer me. When I looked at the sunken tombs and the leaning stones, and read the half-effaced inscriptions through the mass of silence and forgetfulness, it was a great comfort. The reflection came to my mind that the observance of the Sabbath could not last forever.[3]

Less facetiously Ingersoll described the specific incident that led to his rejection of the frontier Calvinism of his father. After listening to a horror-inspiring revivalistic sermon that may or may not have been preached by his father, he concluded:

For the first time I understood the dogma of eternal pain—appreciated "The glad tidings of great joy." For the first time my imagination grasped the height and depth of the Christian horror. Then I said, "It is a lie, and I hate your religion. If it is true, I hate your God."

From that day I have had no fear, no doubt. For me, on that day, the flames of hell were quenched. From that day I have passionately hated every orthodox creed. That Sermon did some good.[4]

Bierce, conversely, characteristically had little to say about his father or his own rejection of his parental and religious background, except by indirection. Apparently he returned to Indiana only twice, both times briefly, after his enlistment: after being seriously wounded in the head in 1863, he was invalided home for three months (this wound, according to his brother Albert, changed his entire personality), and, as neighbors remembered, for a short time several years after the war. According to his friend George Sterling, he referred to his family as "unwashed savages,"[5] and it is common knowledge that after his military service he gave up contact with all his family except Albert, who had preceded him to California and who secured for him a job in the San Francisco Mint. Ambrose was, according to Sterling, "fresh from the Civil War, a fierce propagandist."[6]

Although Sterling insists that Bierce had completed his memoirs, quoting him as saying that "I do not care to have them published while ——'s mother is alive. . . . But when they do see the light, he will come to my grave and howl,"[7] the manuscript, if it exists, is still undiscovered. Consequently, Bierce's biographers have depended on later, indirect statements for information about his developing convictions, assuming that, as Sterling insists, he had largely formed them in the war years, if not before. Later, Bierce's own family life was to be marked by misfortune, conflict, and tragedy.

Nevertheless, in spite of Bierce's indirection, certain facts are clear. He did reject further contact with his family and origins after his discharge from the army early in 1865; and, he certainly did not want to go back to the farm to dig in the soil. Nor did the war make a cynic of him, as his close friend and biographer, Adolphe de Castro, insisted.[8] Bierce's recollections of his wartime service, in the few bits of direct retrospective autobiography that he wrote, often suggest another view. Bierce had not merely come of age in the army, nor was it to direct his life and writing toward cynicism and bitterness; rather, he found a measure of meaning that he had not known before and was never to know again:

And this was, O so long ago! How they come back to me—dimly and brokenly, but with what a magic spell—those years of youth when I was soldiering. . . .

O days when all the world was beautiful and strange;

when unfamiliar constellations burned in the Southern mid-
nights, and the mocking-bird poured out his heart in the
moon-gilded magnolia. . . . Ah, Youth, there is no such
wizard as thou! Give me but one touch of thine artist hand
upon the dull canvas of the Present; gild for but one moment
the drear and somber scenes of to-day, and I will willingly surrender another life than the one I should have thrown away at
Shiloh.[9]

Indirection is no less dangerous for the biographer than for the critic,
but in the absence of more direct evidence other than Bierce's complete
and final break with his family and his origins, much has been made of
the attitudes that prevail in his work, and particularly the images of
violence done against parents ("My Favorite Murder" begins, "Having
murdered my mother under circumstances of unusual atrocity . . . ";[10]
"An Imperfect Conflagration" with the words "Early one June morning
in 1872 I murdered my father—an act which made a deep impression on
me at the time . . . ";[11] "A Bottomless Grave," "My name is John Bren-
walter. My father, a drunkard, . . ."[12]). Equally indirect is the attitude
toward organized religion and pious men evident in aphorisms:

Asked to describe the Deity, a donkey would represent
him with long ears and a tail. Man's conception is higher and
truer: he thinks of him as somewhat resembling a man.[13]

Equally barbed are the observations in verse:

The Lord's Prayer On A Coin
Upon this quarter-eagle's leveled face,
The Lord's Prayer, legibly inscribed, I trace.
"Our Father which"—the pronoun there is funny,
And shows the scribe to have addressed the money—
"Which art in Heaven"—an error this, no doubt:
The preposition should be striken out.
Needless to quote; I only have designed
To praise the frankness of the pious mind
Which thought it natural and right to join,
With rare significancy, prayer and coin.[14]

Whether Bierce could, like Ingersoll, metaphorically or factually
point to specific instances and experiences that led him to reject the faith
and the figure of his father, or whether it was a rejection that had evolved
with the emergence of his conscious memory, it is impossible to tell. The
evidence suggests, however, that it was the latter, that, like Ingersoll, he
had determined to break with both as he cast about for a means of earning
a living and achieving the success that the West had failed to deliver to his
father and family. Whether or not his brief stint in the print shop before
enlisting was a conscious choice of a career with opportunity for advancement, again, it is impossible to tell. It is clear, however, that the print

shop job, however menial and brief it must have been, was a social and perhaps economic advancement for him, and his enlistment papers show that he listed his occupation as printer. His first enlistment was in a ninety-day regiment; the second was for three years. His army career was reasonably distinguished, and, had he not been disappointed at the second lieutenant's commission tendered him at the end, he would have made the army his career. But, in San Francisco, at twenty-four, with little formal education or training, he began to write.

Edgar Watson Howe, eleven years younger than Bierce, made clear the sources of his iconoclasm both in *The Story of a Country Town* and in his memoirs. Of his father, he remembered:

> My father was a cross, dissatisfied man, and often whipped me, but conscience-whipping was worse. . . .
>
> I was brought up in my own father's family like a bound boy, for if he ever had any affection for me, I never knew it. He drove me to work early, and kept me steadily at it. One of my recollections is of his saying that I had been an expense to him until I was seven years old. . . .
>
> It always seemed to me father was unnecessarily harsh with all of us. Once I had a toothache, possibly one of the more stubborn of my first set. He knocked it out with a cold chisel and hammer. It was an efficient way, but nearly killed me, and he whipped me for crying. The whippings were not brutal, but painful and humiliating, and I scarcely escaped a day. . . . [15]

His memories of his father's religion and religious duties are equally clear and pointed:

> In addition to his circuit riding, every summer father held camp meetings, where collected people from a large territory. I always went with him when he selected the sites, and helped clean up the brush for the platforms and benches, and the covered wagons and tents in which the people lived five or six days.
>
> The first wickedness I ever heard of came with attendance on these camp meetings, for on their edges collected strange men who sold keg beer and whisky in bottles, and their patrons engaged in rough language and fighting. In our immediate neighborhood all were at least afraid of the church, but here I found a good many who were not. Being curious and active, I went everywhere, and heard men ridicule the services for which we were assembled.
>
> All the other children joined the church early, but I never did, nor was I invited to. This seems remarkable, but it is my recollection. I was always so much of an unbeliever in the religion of my father and his neighbors that they let me alone. [16]

At fourteen, Howe was at work in the print shop; within a year, he recalled, he was required to set two columns of brevier type a day, and he was embarked on a trade which, for generations of young Americans had become, in the tradition of Benjamin Franklin, both grammar school and university. At fifteen he moved to Gallatin, Missouri to work on the *North Missourian* and his break with the past was complete.

Ingersoll, Bierce, and Howe had each, well before his majority, broken with his father and his father's doctrine, and each carried with him a distaste for both so strong that not only were family ties virtually severed—in later years each of the three was relatively close only to one brother out of large families—but each had rejected as well his father's fundamentalist doctrine and his habit of failure, perhaps seen as the result of parental weakness (as Howe suggests in many instances). But each also carried with him a habit of hard work, a clear determination to rise, and a respect for the written and spoken language—characteristics that were to make them outspoken and often bitter spokesmen for the unorthodox in a country that, in the last quarter of the nineteenth century, was striving to become a prosperous, material, and yet sanctified nation. Ingersoll, Bierce, and Howe, products of an Old West as it became the increasingly stable Midwest, accepted the dream of success that dominated an America seeking a better life in that area in transition, and each of them achieved a measure of that success: in the law and public speaking, in small-town journalism, and in an eclectic writing career. But if the attitudes each acquired in his youth were responsible for that achievement in the open society their fathers had failed to find, they were also the substance of each man's best known, often scandalous work.

II Maturity

By the time each of the three had turned thirty, he was on the threshold of the successful career that he was to pursue for the rest of his life, and he had already begun to transmute the substance and effect of his youthful experience into the works that would bring him notoriety if not financial success. Ingersoll, after law practice in Illinois towns, had run unsuccessfully for Congress as a Democrat in 1860, had become a Republican in 1861, served until captured as Colonel of an Illinois cavalry regiment, and, paroled in 1863, had begun a political career in Illinois that was to take him nearly to the governor's office until he began to speak publicly on free thought.

By 1872 Bierce had completed his Civil War service as an infantry and staff officer, had served as custodian of captured property in Selma, Alabama, had traveled through the West with General William Hazen, worked briefly at the San Francisco Mint, and had begun to write political pieces for the *News-Letter* and draw anonymous, often vicious political cartoons. In 1868 he became editor of the *News-Letter* and in 1872 he published his first piece of fiction, "The Haunted Valley," in the

Overland Magazine. The same year he went to England and worked and wrote successfully for nearly four years. But in 1876 he returned to the San Francisco that seemed to be made for him and his talents, the city that was to be his intellectual and literary home in spite of continued restless wandering for the rest of his life.

Single-mindedly, Howe pursued small-town Midwestern journalism. At nineteen he was editor-publisher of the Golden, Colorado, *Globe*; in 1877, at twenty-four he purchased the failing newspaper in Atchison, Kansas, renamed it the *Globe*, and began to build it into what was to become, with William Allen White's Emporia, Kansas, *Gazette*, one of the two best-known small-town papers in America. He began to think, too, in terms of publishing a magazine. At the same time, however, he began to write thinly-disguised memoirs of his youth, and in 1883, after rejections by major publishers, he printed himself and began to distribute *The Story of a Country Town*, his first, his best, and his best-known work.

In 1872 Ingersoll wrote, presented, and published the work that was to preclude a successful political career, mark the beginning of a lucrative career as a public lecturer, and lead inevitably to the title of "The Great Agnostic" that was applied to him by friends and enemies alike, for different reasons, for the rest of his life. This was "The Gods," the first major barrage in a campaign against theology that was to become the dominant effort of his life.

"The Gods" is the result of Ingersoll's convictions on religion, science, God, and man that had been fixed all his adult life to that point. He had given an earlier anti-theological lecture, "Progress," in Pekin, Illinois, in 1860, but in the pursuit of his legal and political career, those convictions had largely been in abeyance. Whereas the earlier lecture had been reticent, its major target chattel slavery rather than theological tyranny, he had made the parallel between the two. In "The Gods" his target was unmistakable; the technique he employed was that of a legal brief, the result of his legal training and perfected argumentative skills. But the attitude and the bitterness were unchanged since his youth.

Like a curious blend of prosecutor and stump-pulpit evangelist, Ingersoll moves to the offensive in short, forceful, Anglo-Saxon sentences. First, his approach is barbed anthropological background, equating in his summary man's fear of the unknown with his creation of divine assistance:

> Each nation has created a god, and the god has always resembled his creators. He hated and loved what they hated and loved, and he was invariably found on the side of those in power. . . . All these gods demanded praise, flattery, and worship. . . . the smell of innocent blood has ever been considered a divine perfume. . . . the priests have always insisted upon being supported by the people. . . . [17]

He continues his general treatment with a description of these gods of the past as he sees that their priests have created them, but his implications are clear:

> Most of these gods were revengeful, savage, lustful, and ignorant. As they generally depended upon their priests for information, their ignorance can hardly excite our astonishment.
> . . . Some were so ignorant as to suppose that . . . to be governed by observation, reason, and experience was a most foul and damning sin. None of these gods could give a true account of the creation of this little earth. All were woefully deficient in geology and astronomy. As a rule, they were most miserable legislators, and as executives, they were far inferior to the average of American presidents.[18]

For Ingersoll, the diety of the Old Testament and the God of his Calvinist father, both of them the same, has been created by his priests, biblical and contemporary, in the same image:

> One of these gods, and the one who demands our love, our admiration, and our worship, if mere heartless ceremony is worship, gave to his chosen people for their guidance, the following laws of war: "When thou comest nigh unto a city to fight against it, *then proclaim peace unto it.* And it shall be if it make thee answer of peace, and open unto thee, then it shall be that all the people that is found therein shall be tributaries unto thee, and they shall serve thee. And if it will make no peace with thee, but will make war against thee, then thou shalt beseige it. And when the Lord thy God hath delivered it into thy hands, thou shalt smite every male thereof with the edge of the sword. . . . But of the cities of these people which the Lord thy God doth give thee for an inheritance, *thou shalt save nothing alive that breatheth."*[19]

And this, Ingersoll declaims, is our God, "And we are called upon to worship such a God; to get upon our knees and tell him that he is good, that he is merciful, that he is just, that he is love. We are asked to stifle every noble sentiment of the soul and to trample under foot all the sweet charities of the heart." But there is hope, Ingersoll proclaims, because there are those who are determined to be free: "Let the people hate, let the god threaten—we will educate them, and we will despise and defy him." Ultimately, we shall win:

> We are laying the foundations of the grand temple of the future—not the temple of the gods, but of all the people. . . . We are doing what we can to hasten the coming of the day when society shall cease producing millionaires and mendicants—gorged indolence and famished industry—truth in rags and superstition robed and crowned. We are looking for the time when the useful shall be the honorable; and when

Reason, throned upon the world's brain, shall be the King of
Kings, and the God of Gods.[20]

For Ingersoll, theology and religion were and would remain compounded of supersition, ignorance, and fear, the result of deficiencies in
human knowledge and reasoning power, both of which were abetted and
enforced by the rich, the powerful, and the vested interests, political,
economic, and theological, who sought to benefit by the religious faith
and fears of the masses. But just as religion had been created by human
beings for their own ends, so could it be destroyed, just as he had
destroyed its hold on himself, the fetters forged by his father, through his
own rational examination. He was to work toward its destruction to the
moment of his death.

For Bierce, however, religion was not primarily the exploited ignorance and superstition of the masses, to be routed by rational assault; it
was one dimension of the ultimate horror that is human life, the only
escape from which is death. Consequently, he believed that its scoun-
drelous effects would remain a convenient target as long as humanity, the
source of all scoundrelry, continued to live. Bierce's short pieces, his
essays, his verse, had attacked many manifestations of that scoundrelry in
London, in Washington, in San Francisco. Finally, however, in 1890, he
found the opportunity for a direct, pointed exposure of what he was convinced was the substance of religion.

The work which resulted, *The Monk and the Hangman's Daughter*,
had a curious inception. Bierce's then-friend Gustov Adolph Danziger—they later had a falling-out over sharing the credit for their collaboration—brought Bierce the manuscript of a story, "The Monk of
Berchtesgaden," written by Richard Voss and translated by Danziger
from its published version in a German magazine. A gothic horror story,
it was purportedly a medieval tale of a young monk who falls in love with
a hangman's daughter, goes mad as the result of confused emotions and
jealousy, and murders the girl. Bierce immediately saw its possibilities for
amplification as well as for exposure of religious duplicity, and agreed to
rewrite it. In a preface to a later edition, after his quarrel with Danziger,
Bierce pointed out that "In this version the work that came into my hands
from his has been greatly altered and extended." The resulting work, a
novella, provides much of the substance for Bierce's literary reputation.

If Ingersoll's "The Gods" is a rational indictment of religion, *The
Monk and the Hangman's Daughter* is an allegorical attack. The story
takes the young Franciscan monk, soon to be ordained, into the mountains near Berchtesgaden, to a monastery near a small city. On the way he
meets a young girl, the daughter of the hangman, and, like her father, an
outcast in the town and the church because of his admittedly necessary
profession. As he supports and defends her, both from the attacks by the
townspeople and the pursuit of a rich young wastrel, his sense of justice
and mercy becomes a love that his faith denies and his superior abhors.

The young monk is eventually sent alone high in the mountains to recuperate from a confusion-induced illness and to do penance for his sin. There he meets the girl again, exiled there as a dairy maid after her father's death, and a pastoral faith-masked love ensues. But a message tells the monk he is to be ordained and sent away, and his confused love leads him to resolve to leave the order and live in the mountains as a cowherder to protect and save the girl. The wastrel appears, he and the monk fight, the monk is injured, and, in a maddened state, he is convinced that he has been ordained by God a priest and that God has ordered him to save the girl for God and send her to heaven. In her hut, he prays to God to forgive her her love and stabs her to death. Happily he reports his ordination and the girl's salvation to his superior, but he is condemned to be hanged.

The novella is not merely an attack on Roman Catholicism, as its early critics insisted; it is to a great extent an allegorical depiction of the revival-induced, emotionally confused revivalist frenzy of the Midwestern frontier of his youth: the gentle young monk, the innocent caught between nature and dogma, is named Brother Ambrosius. As the small group of monks move through the mountains they might be moving through the Midwestern forests of Bierce's childhood:

> As we proceeded cautiously on our way giant trees barred our progress and dense foliage almost shut out the light of day, the darkness being deep and chill. The sound of our footfalls and of our voices, when we dared to speak, was returned to us. . . . we could hardly believe we were not accompanied by troops of invisible beings who mocked us. . . . Nor could our prayers and hymns give us peace; they only called forth other fowl and by their own echoes multiplied the dreadful noises that beset us. . . . [21]

When the monks and the townspeople celebrate a religious festival, the aftermath is not unlike the backwoods bacchanals that followed canebreak camp meetings in the rural Midwest. After the superior and the others leave, the young monk is left behind to clean up, and he witnesses the revels:

> The boys threw dry brushwood into the fire so that the flames illuminated the whole meadow and shone red upon the trees. Then they laid hands upon the village maidens and began to turn and swing them round and round. Holy saints! how they stamped and turned and threw their hats in the air, kicked up their heels, and lifted the girls from the ground. . . . They shouted and yelled as if all the evil spirits had them in possession. . . .
> Before long the madness of intoxication broke out; they attacked one another with fists and knives, and it looked as if they would do murder. . . . [22]

Later, again confined to his cell for penance by his superior after "defending the hangman's daughter against the statements of an honest Christian girl," Brother Ambrosius reflects,

> I am troubled about Benedicta. If not confined to my cell I should go toward the Galgenberg: perhaps I should meet her. I grieve for her as if she were my sister.
>
> Belonging to the Lord, I have no right to love anything but him who died upon the cross for our sins—all other love is evil. O blessed Saints in Heaven! what if it be that this feeling which I have accepted as a sign and token that I am charged with the salvation of Benedicta's soul is but an earthly love? Pray for me, O dear Franciscus, that I may have the light, lest I stray into that road which leads down to Hell. Light and strength, beloved Saint, that I may know the right path, and walk therein forever![23]

Brother Ambrosius has faith, but if it is not rooted in the ignorance, superstition, and fear denounced by Ingersoll, it has its origins in a denial of the natural world that surrounds him, and his psychological destruction becomes inevitable. All that is left are madness, murder, and the final scene:

> I descended the mountain by precipitous paths, but the Lord guided my steps so that I neither stumbled nor fell into the abyss. At the dawning of the day I arrived at the monastery, rang the bell and waited until the gate was opened. The brother porter evidently thought me a fiend, for he raised a howl that aroused the whole monastery. I went straight to the room of the Superior, stood before him in my blood-stained garments, and, telling him for what deed the Lord had chosen me, informed him that I was now an ordained priest. At this they seized me, put me into the tower, and, holding court upon me, condemned me to death as if I were a murderer. O, the fools, the poor demented fools![24]

Bierce leaves us to speculate on the nature of Brother Ambrosius's crime; was it murder or love, a sin of the flesh or the spirit? Only the mad Ambrosius knows that the crime perpetrated on the innocent Benedicta was not his, that the guilt belonged to the morally blind father superior, his monks, and his people.

For Bierce as for Ingersoll, religion is based upon the propagation of duplicity, self-deception, and madness, a confusion of misplaced and misdirected love and hate, guilt and innocence. To Bierce it was as well a confusion of sexual and religious frenzy, the motivating energy of the frontier revival. But neither the energy nor the frenzy it produced was new; religious-induced sexuality was as common in the middle ages as the frontier Midwest and, he was convinced, in the respectable congregations and parsonages of the nation.

Whereas Ingersoll had phrased his assault on religious orthodoxy in rational discourse and Bierce in allegory, Howe chose for *The Story of a Country Town*, perhaps without consciously doing so in the long evenings of writing on his kitchen table, a form that William Dean Howells called "a very remarkable piece of realism" and Mark Twain "a history."[25] Admittedly autobiography transmuted into fiction, it was the first of what, with Edgar Lee Masters's *Spoon River Anthology*, Sherwood Anderson's *Winesburg, Ohio*, and Sinclair Lewis's *Main Street*, was, in the eyes of Eastern critics, to constitute by 1920 what they saw as a literary genre.

For Howe, however, *The Story of a Country Town* was none of these; it was, as he insisted in pre-publication arguments, not "A Story of a Country Town" but "*The* Story";[26] it was the story of those who had gone West to grow up with the country and had found themselves isolated in the backwater of expansion, there to find not fulfillment or success but the humdrum pathos of small-town living and dying.

The novel—or perhaps more accurately, the non-fiction novel as it would be called if it were written today—is largely the chronicle of life in the town. The plot, a love triangle that leads to tragedy, is superimposed on or intruded into the life of the town as seen through the eyes of the young narrator, a life compounded of mediocrity and spite, of meanness and pettiness, of the puritanical religiosity that has made of the townspeople, in the unsophisticated view of the young narrator, "a virtuous community."

Permeating the book and the town—actually two, Fairview and Twin Mounds, Missouri—are an atmosphere of gloom and a sense of impending doom, the combined result of the nature of the setting, the melodramatic plot, and the undercurrent of revivalist religion. The three produce confused, hard-working men and over-burdened, unhappy women, all of them finding what comfort they can in the hope if not belief that beyond the grave they will find the fulfillment that has eluded them in the West that had promised so much and proffered so little—except beyond the geographical or metaphysical horizon.

The book is narrated by Ned Wedlock, the son of the local preacher, who has come West with his family to grow up with the country and who does so in the course of the narration, becoming a printer-editor, and eventually finding an almost ethereal love and the only satisfying relationship between man and woman in the novel or the town. The love triangle is that of Ned's friend and uncle, Jo Deering, a few years older than Ned, who loves a new minister's daughter and proves his worth by learning to become a miller and constructing a mill and a house virtually single-handedly. Then, after their marriage, Jo is driven to jealous madness when he learns that his wife had, at sixteen, been in love with the town's remittance man—wastrel. The marriage is destroyed, and Jo murders his wife's suitor. Arrested for murder, he commits suicide in jail, and his wife, still in love with him, dies of a broken heart. They are buried together in the town churchyard.

The plots are, however, unimportant; the substance of the book lies in Ned's observations in the town, each an opportunity for Howe to comment on the nature of life and of individual human lives in the frontier backwaters of Fairview and Twin Mounds. Of the backwater and the westward movement, he observes,

> In the dusty tramp of civilization westward—which seems to have always been justified by a tradition that men grow up by reason of it—our section was not a favorite, and remained new and unsettled after counties and states farther west had grown old. Everyone who came there seemed favorably impressed with the steady fertility of the soil, and expressed surprise that the lands were not all occupied; but no one in the great outside world talked about it, and no one wrote about it, so that those who were looking for homes went to the west or the north, where others were going.
>
> There were cheap lands farther on, where people raised a crop one year, and were supported by charity the next; where towns sprang up on credit, and farms were opened with borrowed money. . . . where no sooner was one stranger's money exhausted than another arrived to take his place. . . . where bankruptcy caught them all at last. . . . [27]

Nevertheless, there were those who did remain:

> . . . when anyone stopped in our neighborhood, he was too poor and tired to follow the others.
>
> I became early impressed with the fact that our people seemed to be miserable and discontented, and frequently wondered that they did not load their effects on wagons again, and move away from a place which made all the men surly and rough, and the women pale and fretful. . . . [28]

Despair, gloom, his father's faith, and his father dominate his earliest memories:

> When I think of the years I lived in Fairview, I imagine that the sun was never bright there (although I am certain that it was), and I cannot relieve my mind of the impression that the cold changing shadow of the gray church has spread . . . and enveloped all the houses where the people lived . . . the shadow is denser around the house where I lived than anywhere else. . . . [29]

His father's faith had two important components:

> My father's religion would have been unsatisfactory without a hell.
>
> It was a part of his hope for the future that worldly men who scoffed at his piety would be punished, and this was as much a part of his expectation as that those who were faithful to the end would be rewarded. Everybody saved, to my father's thinking, was as bad as nobody saved. . . . [30]

That which he most desired seldom came to pass; that
which he dreaded, frequently, but no matter; he gave thanks
to the Lord because it was best to do so, and asked no questions. . . . [31]

This was the father, pious, grim, and determined, who remained a
confused God-image in young Ned's memory; this was the father, too,
who in a last, desperate bid for some measure of fulfillment, eloped one
night with the equally pious widow, Mrs. Tremaine, only to find infatua-
tion turned to guilt and hate and himself condemned to wander alone in
torment until ignoble death and a frightening eternity were to overtake
him.

The Reverend John Westlock's religion, like that denounced by Ingersoll and allegorized by Bierce, is compounded of fear and unhappiness;
Howe's atmosphere of gloom is almost as gothic as Bierce's, whether that
of threatening nature or the threat of impending damnation. Love is
synonymous with guilt, and it is denied by temporal life in the town. Nor
is there a place for it in the life promised in the hereafter in return for
privation and acceptance in the here and now. And of all the sins that
must be avoided under pain of eternal damnation, the greatest is love.

Of the three iconoclasts, Ingersoll was dead before the end of the
nineteenth century and Bierce disappeared in Mexico late in 1913. Only
Howe lived to see the frontier backwater of his youth incorporated into
the American mainstream, dying at 84 in Atchison, Kansas. Each of the
three had come out of an Old Western frontier that had its roots in the
early years of the nineteenth century; each had experienced the impact of
that frontier and the privation that it left in its wake; and each had known
the religious harshness that had made the new Midwestern backwater
bearable. At the same time each formed attitudes that he carried to
adulthood, that provided the substance of his writing and his reputation,
and that he carried to his grave. In his maturity each of the three struck
powerful blows at the pious cant, the hypocrisy, the intellectual enslave-
ment that he saw as a theology of hate. In the process, each of them
gained a measure of the success that the Old Northwestern frontier had
promised and withheld from his father as that area became the American
Midwest. And, together with resulting notoriety, "the Great Agnostic,"
"Bitter Bierce," and "the Sage of Potato Hill" have found remarkably
similar places in the unfolding American myth of the past.

Notes

1. Timothy Walker quoted in Daniel J. Ryan, *History of Ohio*, 3 (New York: 1912), p.
3.

2. From Bierce's column in *The Wasp*, November 3, 1883, quoted in Robert A. Wiggins, *Ambrose Bierce* (Minneapolis: 1964), p. 8.

3. Robert G. Ingersoll, *The Works of Robert G. Ingersoll*, 1 (New York: 1907), pp.
377–79.

4. Robert G. Ingersoll, "Why I Am An Agnostic," *The Works of Robert G. Ingersoll*, 4 (New York: 1907), p. 17.

5. George Sterling, quoted in Carey McWilliams, *Ambrose Bierce* (New York: 1929), p. 26.

6. George Sterling, "The Shadow Maker," *The American Mercury*, 6 (September 1925), 10.

7. *Ibid.*, p. 19.

8. Adolphe de Castro, *Portrait of Ambrose Bierce* (New York: 1929), p. 13.

9. Ambrose Bierce, "On a Mountain," in *The Collected Works of Ambrose Bierce*, 1 (New York: 1909), p. 269.

10. Ambrose Bierce, "My Favorite Murder," *The Collected Works of Ambrose Bierce*, 8 (New York: 1911), p. 147.

11. Ambrose Bierce, "An Imperfect Conflagration," *Ibid.*, p. 171.

12. Ambrose Bierce, "A Bottomless Grave," *Ibid.*, p. 9.

13. Ambrose Bierce, "Epigrams," *Ibid.*, pp. 356–57.

14. Ambrose Bierce, "The Lord's Prayer on a Coin," *The Collected Works of Ambrose Bierce*, 4 (New York: 1910), p. 206.

15. E. W. Howe, *Plain People* (New York: 1924), pp. 10–12.

16. *Ibid.*, pp. 6–7.

17. Robert G. Ingersoll, "The Gods," *The Works of Robert G. Ingersoll*, 1 (New York: 1907), p. 7.

18. *Ibid.*, pp. 8–9.

19. *Ibid.*, pp. 12–13.

20. *Ibid.*, pp. 89–90.

21. Ambrose Bierce, in collaboration with G. R. Danziger, *The Monk and the Hangman's Daughter*, in *The Collected Works of Ambrose Bierce* (New York: 1946), pp. 667–68.

22. *Ibid.*, p. 684.

23. *Ibid.*, p. 690.

24. *Ibid.*, p. 724.

25. E. A. Howe, *The Story of A Country Town*, Claude M. Simpson, ed. (Cambridge, Massachusetts: 1961), pp. ix, xii.

26. Calder M. Pickett, *Ed Howe: Country Town Philosopher* (Lawrence, Kansas: 1968), p. 67.

27. Howe, *The Story of A Country Town*, pp. 7–8.

28. *Ibid.*, p. 8.

29. *Ibid.*, p. 15.

30. *Ibid.*, p. 16.

31. *Ibid.*, p. 17.

Ambrose Bierce

Jay Martin*

Ambrose Bierce was born in 1842 in the backwoods settlement of Horse Creek Cave in Meigs County, Ohio, the tenth child of parents whom he later characterized as "unwashed savages." His childhood and adolescence were unhappy. He told Walter Neale that his first real love affair occurred at the age of fifteen, with "a woman of broad culture . . . well past seventy . . . [but] still physically attractive, even at her great age." At the age of nineteen, he was the second man in his county to enlist in the Ninth Indiana Volunteer Infantry, and the only American writer of importance to fight in the Union Army. While directing the advance of his brigade's skirmish line against an intrenched Confederate force at Kenesaw Mountain, Bierce, his commander reported, "was shot in the head by a musket ball which caused a very dangerous and complicated wound, the ball remaining within the head from which it was removed sometime afterwards." He returned from battle to learn that the young girl he wanted to marry was no longer interested in him.

In these far from humorous facts lies the background to Bierce's humor. For what his youth formed in him was a particular understanding of the world. In *The Phenomenological Approach to Psychiatry*, J. H. Van den Berg argues that "man seldom sees objects, things as such, he sees *significations* which things assume for him." For Ambrose Bierce, it was not simply that by the end of the war he had learned to suspect such cherished nineteenth-century genteel ideals as the sanctity of the family, the pastoral associations which surrounded childhood, the belief in the purity of womanhood, or the assumption that war was noble and conducted by commanders untouched by vainglory or personal ambition. It was not simply that he had learned to despise social ideals of any sort, and to have "a conscience uncorrupted by religion, a judgment undimmed by politics and patriotism, a heart untainted by friendships and sentiments unsoured by animosities." More than this, the world, as he perceived it, took on a threatening aspect; like the musket ball, it attacked his head, his reason. The terrain of reality which he plotted—he was a topographic of-

*Reprinted by permission of the author, the editor, and the publisher, copyright © 1973, Rutgers University, the State University of New Jersey. From *The Comic Imagination in American Literature*, ed. Louis D. Rubin, Jr. (New Brunswick: Rutgers University Press, 1973), pp. 195–205.

114

ficer—he saw filled with traps. Where others saw a handsome prospect, he saw danger lurking and always assumed that beneath pleasing appearances was a threatening reality. He was convinced, in short, that reality was delusory. By emphasizing mind he attempted to preserve mind, always threatened by physical obliteration or mental deception; he defended the mind, and in doing so, took as his major theme the *growth of reflection*, the compulsion to scrutinize and observe.

This might have been a tragic theme, for reflection leads to a deeper and deeper penetration of delusion and at last to the conviction that all is delusion—that, ultimately, as Bierce said in a late letter, "nothing matters." Reality, Bierce did conclude in *The Devil's Dictionary*, was "the dream of a mad philosopher," the logical product of irrational minds, and therefore absurd—"the nucleus of a vacuum." But he treated this conviction comically, and employed humor to expose the absurdities of his deluded contemporaries and the institutions delusions created and perpetuated. In short, he preserved his own mind by ridiculing the crazed world that questioned his sense and sensibility.

His humor, this is to say, was destructive, essentially a counterattack. In his *Vorschule der Asthetik*, the philosopher Jean Paul has distinguished four constituents of humor, all of which are present in Bierce's writings. Humor, he says, obliterates distinctions, tending to identify the great and small, the pathetic and ludicrous, the beautiful and the horrible. Associated with this characteristic is that of "inverse effect": what seems to be good is damnable, or vice-versa. Both are often made convincing by what Jean Paul calls "humoristic subjectivity," which draws the reader into the subjective vision of the author through direct address. Finally, there is the humor of the grotesque and deformed. As an instrument of mind, humor, then, overturns forms, makes codes unstable, and questions the truth of accepted conventions. This aspect of humor is crucial for an understanding of Bierce's writing. In an important essay, "To Train a Writer," Bierce himself set down the knowledge which a humorous writer should possess. In addition to acquaintance with rhetoric and classical literature, Bierce said, "it would be needful that he know and have an ever-present consciousness that this is a world of fools and rogues, blind with superstition, tormented with envy, consumed with vanity, selfish, false, cruel, cursed with illusions—frothing mad! . . . He must be a sinner and in turn a saint, a hero, a wretch." Bierce was the chief product of his own school, and his humor the consequence of his education.

Certainly, Bierce's humor resembles that of other American writers. Poe's emphasis on the grotesque, Melville's inclination to treat conventions ambivalently, Twain's tendency to take a burlesque or "satanic" view of society, and, in the twentieth century, H. L. Mencken's satires on the "booboisie," or Nathanael West's and Henry Miller's very different attacks upon convention—with all of these writers Bierce has affinities. More largely, he shares with them all a sense of the growing abyss in

America between the ideal symmetry of intelligence and the riotous chaos of a materialist and self-deceiving social life—a theme which not only humorists, but other American writers, chiefly Henry James and Scott Fitzgerald, pursued. Perhaps most important of all, with regard to the American-ness of his humor, Bierce early made the pragmatist's discovery that truth was instrumental, and did not consist in a set of principles. "Time was," Bierce wrote, ". . . when the moral character of every thought and word and deed was determined by reference to a set of infinitely precious 'principles'—infallible criteria—moral solvents . . . warranted . . . to disclose the gold in every proposition submitted to its tenets: I have no longer the advantage of their service, but must judge everything on its own merits—each case as it comes up." In almost every case his judgment was—*guilty*.

But Bierce was also, perhaps, the only American comic writer who deliberately attempted to write in a major tradition of European humor. He took his basic moral values from the example of antiquity. "To say of a man that he is like his contemporaries is to say that he is a scoundrel without excuse," Bierce observed. "The virtues are accessible to all. Athens was vicious, yet Socrates was virtuous. Rome was corrupt, but Marcus Aurelius was not corrupt. To offset Nero the gods gave Seneca." Bierce was convinced that the feather of truth in the midst of delusion was permanent and culture-free. Certainly, this was his assumption when he commented to Nellie Sickler in 1901: "The only originality that you or any modern can hope for is originality of expression—style. No one can think a new thought (that is worth thinking) or feel a new emotion." That conviction led him to give careful study to style. His first literary mentor, James Watkins, a veteran of New York and London journalism, had instructed him in 1868 to read Voltaire, Swift, and Thackeray's sketches in *Punch*. Not long after, Bierce sailed for London, where he came under the influence of Tom Hood the younger and wrote columns for the humorous weeklies *Fun* and *Figaro*. Bierce's contemporaries were aware of his conscious attempts to place himself in classic satiric traditions, and frequently compared him to Rabelais, Heine, Swift, and Pope. Perhaps in the end it is most just to say, as Watkins observed to Bierce in 1874, that with the methods of the great satirists and epigrammatists Bierce fused "real" "American thought" and so produced "the net result of its processes phrased with . . . wit and point and epigram."

But ultimately, Bierce is uniquely himself, a writer his contemporaries and subsequent critics have found difficult to classify. Unlike other Americans, his basic comic mode consisted in attack. Invective, a kind of secular curse, is probably the oldest form of satiric writing and consists, in its essence, of a direct assault whose purpose is to obliterate its object through abuse. Bierce described himself and his philosophy of criticism in an *Examiner* column of 1889: "Knaves and vulgarians, imposters, sycophants, the various unworthy and the specifically detestable, no sooner draw his eye than he is on them with bitter abuse." One of the knaves who caught his eye was the English wit Oscar Wilde. After remarking "the limpid and spiritless vacuity of this intellectual jellyfish," Bierce continues:

> And so, with a knowledge that would equip an idiot to dispute with a cast-iron dog, an eloquence to qualify him for the duties of caller on a hog-ranch and an imagination adequate to the conception of a tom-cat, when fired by contemplation of a fiddle-string, this consummate and starlike youth, missing everywhere his heaven-appointed functions and offices, wanders about, posing as a statue of himself, and, like the sun-smitten image of Memnon, emitting meaningless murmurs in the blaze of women's eyes.

Even more primitive in its fury is his invective against a local "hoodlum":

> Chuck him overboard! Let him suffocate in slimes and stenches, the riddances of sewers and the wash of slums. Give his carcass to the crabs utterly, and let the restless shrimp embed its body in his eye-socket, or wave its delicate antennae from his pale nostril. Let globes and tangles of eels replace his bowels, and the muscular squid lay coils of clammy tentacle about the legs of him. Over with him!

Invective always lurked about the edges of whatever comic forms Bierce employed and might break out at any time. His own conclusion about his temperament was apt: "I am not a poet, but an abuser."

Very far from savage invective is the civilized wit of the epigram, a form which Bierce also practiced frequently. The influence on Bierce of La Rochefoucauld's *Maximes* was reinforced by the convention in western humor of "familiar sayings," a mode which ultimately derived in America from Protestant proverbialism and was practiced by John Phoenix, Josh Billings, and Bill Nye. Mark Twain's epigraphs for *Pudd'nhead Wilson's New Calendar* are similar to, but generally less good than Bierce's definitions in *The Devil's Dictionary* or the epigrams which may be found, glowing with congealed fury, all through Bierce's work. Bierce defined *Alone* as "in bad company"; *Positive* as "mistaken at the top of one's voice"; a *Bride* as "a woman with a fine prospect of happiness behind her"; a *Handkerchief* as "a small square of silk or linen used at funerals to conceal a lack of tears"; *Love* as "a temporary insanity curable by marriage"; and *Year* as "a period of 365 disappointments." His writing so often glittered with such epigrams that in twelve volumes of collected work he could afford to omit such quips as these: "To forgive is to err, to be human is divine"; "If men and women could read one another's secret thoughts we might shorten our vocabulary by the length of the world 'virtue,' " and "for the study of the good and the bad in woman, two women are a needless expense." Obviously, though very different in form, invective and the epigram have in Bierce's writing the same function—to attack, to expose, and thus to destroy folly. Bierce answered a critic in 1868 by asserting: "We lash the Evil-disposed only and commend the Good alone"; but he discerned little good and toward evil was unsparing: "In a civilization, in which everything should work as it ought, a man after committing an essentially mean act would make his will, bid his weeping creditors a long farewell, pick up a handsaw, and go out and disembowel himself by rasping it transversely across his abdomen."

The satiric tendency in Bierce is clearly in the vituperative tradition of Archilochus and Juvenal, and contrasts strikingly with the more genial tone of the Horatian wit which characterized American humor until the second half of the twentieth century. Aware of the conflict between the two traditions, Bierce mocked a reviewer who criticized him for indelicate humor:

> O, certainly [humor] should be "delicate." Every man of correct literary taste will tell you it should be "delicate"; and so will every scoundrel who fears it. . . . A man who is exposed to satire must not be made unhappy—O dear, no! He must find it very good reading. . . . Don't mangle the man, like that coarse Juvenal, and that horrid Swift, but touch him up neatly, like Horace or a modern magazinist.

But during Bierce's career, American comic forms and conventions operated entirely in the spirit of Horace. The tall tale, the humorous anecdote, literary burlesque, the literary hoax, the deadpan comedy of western oral narrative, parody, and the comic debate were wit forms which had prevailed in eighteenth-century English and American literature and were, in the post-Civil-War period, Americanized by Mark Twain, Artemus Ward, and Bret Harte. Such forms all tend to show a *distance* between the writer and the object of his satire, a self-effacement of the author usually achieved through the use of a naive narrator, and a general acceptance of the fact that, after all, human error is inevitable and understandable.

Ambrose Bierce never acknowledged—and, in fact, explicitly denied—that error could be tolerated. But he was, of necessity, a writer for newspapers and popular magazines, and was confined by the conventions of literary journalism to forms which were familiar to his audience. Thus, at the heart of his work is a deep, unmediated conflict between his urge to attack, to utterly destroy the object of his humor, and the assumptions of the forms available to him, that wit should function as a gentle corrective of error. While his tone is always exacerbated and personal, defending the integrity of the head and assailing the excesses of the heart, the comic forms which he perforce used allowed for the heart's folly or the head's defeats. This is to say that there is a conflict in Bierce's work between attitudes which should produce wit and forms which must offer humor. "Nearly all Americans are humorous," he said; "if any are born witty heaven help them to emigrate! . . . Humor is tolerant, tender; its ridicule caresses. Wit stabs, begs pardon—and turns the weapon in the wound." This conflict creates the primary tension in Bierce's style: the war between, on the one hand, his language—a language so savage that it is almost out of control, in which invective leads to vituperation and vituperation to frenzy; and, on the other hand, the forms he employs, whose tendency is to blunt, to efface, and to tolerate weakness. Indeed, the inert geniality of his forms becomes, itself, a prod which drives his diction to still greater fury, his images into more grotesque deformations. At times, he is willing, almost impelled, to allow his language to destroy the very forms which seek to hold them in check. For this reason, Bierce was never able to work in long forms. He hated the novel, and spoke of the work of Howells and James as "the offspring of mental incapacity wet-nursed by a conspiracy." But Bierce was incapable of controlling his language in the long, loose novel form. Even his longest stories are seldom more than a few pages, and his *Fantastic Fables* usually but a few lines long. All of his work is held together by the will, which knows that any opportunity for disruption, any flaw in the iron control, any lapse in logic, will allow the savage power of his language to break through the walls of form for a rampage of vituperative devastation.

Bierce's war with language has a direct and striking effect on the nature of action in his fiction. Even the characters in it are remarkably sparing in speech; in many of his tales no character speaks a single word. In "The Affair at Coulter's Notch," for instance, Captain Coulter obeys orders to bomb enemy forces near a plantation house without remonstrance, even though, as we later discover, the house is his own, and he knows he will kill his family inside it. In "The Coup de Grâce," Downing Madwell kills a wounded friend out of mercy, is seen doing so by an officer, and is led off to execution, without speaking. "A Son of the Gods" is a war story in which, as Bierce himself writes, "Not a word is spoken." In "One of the Missing," Jerome Searing dies of stroke through self-induced hysteria without uttering a sound. The painful apotheosis of this method occurs in "Chickamauga," where a child who turns out to be a deaf mute sees the aftermath of a battle which he cannot hear. At the end, finding the body of his mother, blown apart by a shell, he stands, "motionless, with quivering lips." Bierce silences words, as if language itself, released from the mind, could be emitted only as a scream.

This war of savage language against genial forms, of structural restraint against colloquial looseness, marks all of Bierce's writing and distinguishes him from his humorous contemporaries. He deals with their subjects and employs their forms, but the differences are apparent. His ridicule is unmitigated and thorough. He begins with Adam and Eve:

> Little's the good to sit and grieve
> Because the serpent tempted Eve.
> Better to wipe your eyes and take
> A club and go out and kill a snake.

> But if you prefer, as I suspect,
> To philosophize, why, then, reflect:
> If the cunning rascal on the limb
> Hadn't tempted her, she'd have tempted him.

He turns to civilization, conscious that the defects which produced the Fall are enlarged in institutions. Local government:

> Somebody has attempted to rob the safe in the office of the City and County Treasurer. This is rushing matters; the impatient scoundrel ought to try his hand at being a Supervisor first. From Supervisor to thief the transaction is natural and easy.

Social morality:

> Tombstone, Arizona, is said to have Three-score liquor saloons and only one Bible, yet the run on the sixty Saloons is greater than the struggle to get at the one Bible.

He perceived a society which, indeed, had written a new Bible, whose commandments Bierce mockingly records in "The New Decalogue";

> Have but one God: they knees were sore
> If bent in prayer to three or four.
>
> Adore no images save those
> The coinage of thy country shows.
>
> Take not the name in vain. Direct
> Thy swearing unto some effect.
>
> Thy hand from Sunday work be held—
> Work not at all unless compelled.
>
> Honor thy parents, and perchance
> Their wills thy fortunes may advance.
>
> Kill not—death liberates thy foe
> From persecution's constant woe.
>
> Kiss not thy neighbor's wife. Of course
> There's no objection to divorce.
>
> To steal were folly, for 'tis plain
> In cheating there is greater gain.
>
> Bear not false witness. Shake your head
> And say that you have "heard it said."
>
> Who stays to covert ne'er will catch
> An opportunity to snatch.

Of social institutions, Bierce writes—

Concerning marriage:

> Of two kinds of temporary insanity, one ends in suicide,
> the other in marriage.

Concerning commerce and religion:

> I saw the devil. He was working free—
> A customs-house he builded by the sea.
> "Why do you do this?" The devil raised his head:
> "Of churches I have built enough," he said.

Bierce attacked individuals as fiercely as institutions. Of a powerful railroad entrepreneur he remarked:

> [Collis P.] Huntington is not altogether bad. Though severe he is merciful. He tempers invective with falsehood. He says ugly things of his enemy, but he has the tenderness to be careful that they are mostly lies. . . . Mr. Huntington's ignorance is chronic and incurable. The number of things he does not know is undiminished by Time: the accuracy with which he does not know them is unaffected by reflection.

All about him, in short, Bierce saw and castigated evil. Yet, he was convinced that real improvement in man or his institutions was impossible. Human beings, quite simply, found happiness in evil; impossible to correct, they are merely "worthy of extermination." It was his considered opinion, he told Nellie Sickler not long before his death, that "you cannot make the world better—nobody can. In the 'business of uplift' by conscious and associated effort, the uplifters are simply pulled down to the level of the thing that they are raising." Bierce attacked evil not to correct it, but to protect himself against it, as if only his accurate observation of evil—his exposure of irrationality—could save his mind from it. This omnivorous growth in Bierce of observation and reflection paralyzed his sense of correction and contented him with the preservation of his mind's symmetry.

In his representation of family life he is at his most violent. He had suffered deeply both as a child and as a parent, and in a series of sketches called *The Parenticide Club*, he imitates in overt action the kind of psychic tensions in family life that alienist psychoanalysts would later describe. Again, this is to say, Bierce thrust through the delusions of civilization to expose the irrational hatreds which even such sacred institutions of civilization as the family were created to control and conceal. "My Favorite Murder" begins: "Having murdered my mother under circumstances of singular atrocity, I was arrested and put upon my trial, which lasted seven years." "Oil of Dog" is the next tale and begins with this jocular introduction: "My name is Boffer Bings. I was born of honest parents in one of the humbler walks of life, my father being a manufacturer of dog oil and my mother having a small studio in the shadow of the village church, where she disposed of unwelcome babes. In my boyhood I was trained to habits of industry; I not only assisted my father in procuring dogs for his vats, but was frequently employed by my mother to carry away the debris of her work in the studio." Equally as casual is the narrator of "An Imperfect Conflagration": "Early one June morning in 1872, I murdered my father—an act which made a deep impression on me at the time."

By inversely mingling innocence with crime, the beautiful with the horrible, the reputable with the profane, Bierce saw all aspects of the world as reprehensible, insanely grotesque. The only imaginable relief from such a deformed world was in the symmetry of death. Bierce anticipated André Breton and other surrealists when he remarked to a friend as they overlooked a midwinter fair: "Wouldn't it be fun to turn loose a machine gun into that crowd?" After a disordered childhood and adolescence Bierce had learned his principles of personal order through his military experience, in which, for the soldier, life is perfectly symmetrical—its aims are well defined and are to be achieved by clarity and precision of action. Symmetry and death, the two dominant features of a soldier's experience, he thus came to associate, while social life, as he perceived it, was marked by the continuous danger of asymmetry and self-deception, a death in life. Bierce needed to live his death in order to control his life. His last piece of humor, not inappropriately, then, consisted in his suicidal disappearance at the age of seventy-two into Revolutionary Mexico, where no subsequent trace of his end has ever been found.

The Forms of Burlesque in
The Devil's Dictionary

James Milton Highsmith[*]

DICTIONARY, *n*. A malevolent literary device for cramping the growth of a language and making it hard and inelastic. This dictionary, however, is a most useful work—*The Devil's Dictionary*.

Ambrose Gwinnett Bierce was known in California as "the wickedest man in San Francisco" and in London as "Bitter Bierce." He not only enjoyed this reputation but encouraged it by a calculated reticence and by a mordant wit in his notorious newspaper columns. Mark Twain and Bret Harte had been writing for the *Californian* in San Francisco for a few years when Bierce got his first newspaper job in 1867 on the *News-Letter* in the same city. This appointment began a career in journalism that lasted until his strange and controversial disappearance in Mexico in 1913.

The various satiric forms which Bierce explored in his journalism have not been appreciated as have his successful short stories, such as "An Occurrence at Owl Creek Bridge," "Chickamauga," and his other psychological and macabre productions that consciously opposed the smiling aspects of life presented by Miss Nancy Howells, as he called William Dean Howells.[1] Nowhere was Bierce's love of satire more evident than in the burlesque definitions that he created from 1875 until 1906.[2] Though he used several titles for his columns defining words, he preferred "The Devil's Dictionary." However, the first publication of the collected definitions (from A to L) in book form by Doubleday, Page and Company in 1906 employed the title *The Cynic's Word Book*. Bierce commented in this way on the bowdlerized title: "Here in the East, the Devil is a sacred personage (the Fourth Person of the Trinity, as an Irishman might say) and his name must not be taken in vain."[3]

An examination of Bierce's forms of burlesque in *The Devil's Dictionary* offers a more reliable evaluation of his achievement than does his content. He never developed a system of thought, and he was capable of changing his attitudes with great facility from idealism to cynicism, from

[*]Reprinted with permission of the editor, *Satire Newsletter* (Oneonta, New York), 7, No. 2 (Spring 1970), 115–27.

philanthropy to misanthropy. With time, furthermore, he ceased to hope that the world would take cognizance of his ideas, although he occasionally suggested ironical remedies for the American failure to perceive the genius of his satire. For example, he proposed the introduction of "an improvement in punctuation—the snigger point, or note of cachinnation: It is written thus ‿ and presents, as nearly as may be, a smiling mouth. It is to be appended, with the full stop, to every jocular or ironical sentence . . . thus: "Mr. Edward Bok is the noblest work of God ‿ !' "[4] Bierce, nevertheless, did not appear to be composing his burlesque for moral effects. Neither did he seem to have principally in mind the other usual reasons for creating satire—for the sake of fun alone; or for a means of criticizing contemporary romantic fiction in behalf of realism, as Walter Blair claims for the literary comedians;[5] or as a means of learning literary craftsmanship by imitating acknowledged models, as Franklin Rogers states for Twain.[6] Rather, Bierce's definitions suggest that he was interested in exploring the nature of the forms themselves and making them more functional in terms of the material at hand.

Bierce turned his attentions more and more toward form, with equal amounts of contumely for the public and courage for experimentation. Besides, for the modern writer with a conservative predisposition, form was the only avenue of creativity left. As Bierce expressed it, "Nothing new is to be learned in any of the great arts—the ancients looted the whole field. . . . originality strikes and dazzles only when displayed within the limiting lines of form."[7] We are even reminded of Oscar Wilde's aestheticism by Bierce's claim, "In literature, as in all art, manner is everything and matter nothing; I mean that matter, however important, has nothing to do with the *art* of literature; that is a thing apart" (X, 63).

To develop and explore satiric forms, Bierce applied his experiences in journalism as well as his own cherished ideal of a witty and polished style. Writing for newspapers in London and in America trained him in succinctness and in arranging material for maximum clarity and effectiveness. Certainly such a background was congruent with his own preference for neo-classical wit and polish in style. Wit, he explained over and over in his essays, should replace humor in satire, for it has the distinct and incisive shape of a poniard and is not sentimental and amorphous: "Humor is tolerant, tender; its ridicule caresses. Wit stabs, begs pardon—and turns the weapon in the wound."[8] He also viewed polish as prerequisite for literature, because the power of expression "is not a gift, but a gift and an accomplishment. It comes not altogether by nature, but is achieved by hard, technical study."[9]

Because of his interest in the aesthetic nature of form, it is not surprising to find in his burlesque something other than a mere imitation of a vogue that had been in the air for at least half a century. The definitions in *The Devil's Dictionary* suggest, in fact, that our diabolical lexicographer may have aimed at refining satiric forms for American humor.

Certainly we can see an effort to sharpen and differentiate the various forms of burlesque—mock-heroic, parody, Hudibrastic, and travesty. Many of the entries are, of course, the happy results of mixtures and are not pure examples of any single form.[10]

Bierce's manipulation of burlesque indicates a passing familiarity with the historical development of traditional forms as well as an interest in adjusting them to his own personality and values. Although he was not the scholar of literature that he liked to imagine, he had been exposed to the European heritage of burlesque before initiating his own burlesque definitions. For example, James T. Watkins, editor of the *News-Letter*, which gave Bierce his first job in journalism, encouraged satire along the lines of Swift, Voltaire, and Thackeray—but before this he had been reading intensively such stylists as Gibbon, Burke, Landor, and Pope.[11] And soon afterwards, from 1872 to 1875, Bierce immersed himself in the literary and journalistic activities of Fleet Street. Among his London friends, incidentally, was William Schwenck Gilbert.[12]

Since to some extent Bierce was writing within a historical tradition, it might not be amiss to approach his burlesque with the formal terms ordinarily applied to earlier achievements in burlesque.[13]

What Bierce achieved with the four forms of burlesque (mock-heroic, parody, Hudibrastic, and travesty) can be clearly ascertained by comparing examples of them with his definitions that do not employ such forms, as the long and amorphous essay defining INADMISSABLE, or even the quatrain defining DEAD:

> Done with the work of breathing; done
> With all the world; the mad race run
> Through to the end; the golden goal
> Attained and found to be a hole!

Here there is no imitation of high (or even low) matter or manner, no satiric incongruity between content and form. There is merely unabated, metrical cynicism, and the final effect of the definition is unimpressive.

But when we come to his entries that show a manipulation of burlesque forms, what a different result! Here, we feel, is a satirist who, with great aplomb, has created definitions distinctively his own.

Bierce enjoyed all four forms of burlesque. As might be expected, he was especially effective with high burlesque, since its emphasis on style was congenial to his ideas of wit and polish. To create mock-heroic definitions, he did not draw on the epic machinery of Homer or Virgil. *His* culture came to a focus in the panegyric, the polemic, the evangelical harangue, and even the epitaph. Such forms, as bombastic as epics sometimes are, were for Bierce deplorable modern attempts to fashion forms that would emulate the serious and significant achievements of the ancients. But in effect, such attempts merely acknowledge the general diminution of the grand in modern times.

The devil would indeed be pleased with the mock-heroic definition of ABDOMEN, which treats this organ in the incongruously high manner of a panegyric:

> The temple of the god Stomach, in whose worship, with sacrificial rights [*sic*], all true men engage. From women this ancient faith commands but a stammering assent. They sometimes minister at the altar in a half-hearted and ineffective way, but true reverence for the one deity that men really adore they know not. . . .

By his ironical sublimation of a purely physical matter, our lexicographer reminds us of how arbitrarily we elevate and define our values and beliefs, which are often in reality not so sublime after all. By the definition's implications, actual gluttony is contrasted with pretended sacrosanctity, but the cynicism implied does not disturb us, because of our pleasure with the exaggerated and ironical laudation of the "rights."

Bierce sometimes allowed his formal and elaborate eulogies to assume the form of the poetic apostrophe—in the definition of EXCESS, for example, we read,

> Hail, high Excess—especially in wine.
> To thee in worship do I bend the knee
> Who preaches abstemiousness unto me—
> My skull thy pulpit, as my paunch thy shrine.
> Present on precept, aye, and line on line,
> Could ne'er persuade so sweetly to agree
> With reason as thy touch, exact and free,
> Upon my forehead and along my spine. . . .

Whether such a grand form can disguise the fact of a hangover is disputable. Anyway, we enjoy the exaggeration for itself, as we do in similar apostrophic eruptions in the definitions of DELUSION, GRAPE, and LEAD.

Other definitions that might be thought of as mock-heroic satirize the general style of the polemic while never imitating a specific model as would parody. In such definitions as FLY-SPECK, K, and ZENITH, Bierce condemned the whole tribe of scholars by imitating their serious, elaborate, and monotonous style. Apparently, he considered scholarly polemics to be deplorably recognizable by classifications (such as of the forms of burlesque), analogies, digressions, Latinate terms (e.g., *Musca Maledicta* for house-fly in FLY-SPECK), acknowledgments to sources and to etymologies and to other scholars and their hypotheses, and, above all, a pedantic objectivity. The point of the satire is usually the contrast between the form of the polemic and its inconsequential or ridiculous subject matter. Note, for example, how Bierce achieved this contrast in his definition of ZENITH:

A point in the heavens directly overhead to a standing man or a growing cabbage. A man in bed or a cabbage in the pot is not considered as having a zenith, though from this view of the matter there was once a considerable dissent among the learned, some holding that the posture of the body was immaterial. These were called Horizontalists, their opponents Verticalists. The Horizontalist heresy was finally extinguished by Zanobus, the philosopher-king of Abara, a zealous Verticalist. Entering an assembly of philosophers who were debating the matter, he cast a severed human head at the feet of his opponents and asked them to determine its zenith, explaining that its body was hanging by the heels outside. Observing that it was the head of their leader, the Horizontalists hastened to profess themselves converted to whatever opinion the Crown might be pleased to hold, and Horizontalism took its place among *fides defuncti.*

Bierce achieved unity in this definition by consistent and ironical use of the imagery of cabbages and heads and by logical development of his definition from this basis. The unity is nonetheless remarkable when we recognize the possible presence of quite different influences: from Western humor, the deadpan tradition; from eighteenth-century satire, the mock-scholarly history or etymology; and from San Franciscans, who taught Mark Twain the comic or inappropriate use of technical or foreign terms.

Bierce implied that bombastic delivery of trivial matters is not limited to the machinery of panegyrics or of scholarship. He was also aware of the style of high-powered addresses by pretentious evangelists—witness the definition of

LETTUCE, *n.* An herb of the genus *Lactuca*, "Wherewith," says that pious gastronome, Hengist Pelly, "God has been pleased to reward the good and punish the wicked. For by his inner light the righteous man has discerned a manner of compounding for it a dressing to the appetency whereof a multitude of gustible condiments conspire, being reconciled and ameliorated with profusion of oil, the entire comestible making glad the heart of the godly and causing his face to shine. But the person of spiritual unworth is successfully tempted of the Adversary to eat of Lettuce with destitution of oil, mustard, egg, salt and garlic, and with a rascal bath of vinegar polluted with sugar. Wherefore the person of spiritual unworth suffers an intestinal pang of strange complexity and raises the song."

Such definitions may be far from the studied elegance of "The Rape of the Lock," and the devices of the epic are absent, but the spirit and principles behind the definition are similar to Pope's—to manipulate and exaggerate a general form way out of proportion to the subject so that the resulting contrast satirizes form or content or both, as here we laugh at the rabid manner and absurd matter of an evangelist.

Besides his mock-heroic treatments of panegyries, polemics, and evangelical harangues, we may include even his ironical epitaphs as exemplifying those definitions whose high and serious forms offer satiric contrast with low content. In such definitions as EPITAPH, PIE, and CEMETERY, we find a variety of rhyme and meter for what Bierce's civilization has often considered a noble form of expression. But the definition of INSCRIPTION includes one of his most delightful manipulations of the genre of tombstone literature.

> "The clay that rests beneath this stone
> As Silas Wood was widely known.
> Now, lying here, I ask what good
> It was to me to be S. Wood.
> O Man, let not ambition trouble you,
> Is the advice of Silas W."

Bierce, like other San Franciscans, was especially prolific with parodies, which also capitalize on the effect of a contrast of a grand sytle with a trivial content. But these forms are less general than those of the mock-heroic. Not a genre but a *particular* author's work or work's style is imitated in a parody, and the reader is expected to recognize satiric adumbrations of the original. As David Worcester explains it, "We do not find a parody printed side by side with its original. It is the reader's part to supply knowledge of the model. He must hold up the model, and the author will furnish him with a distorted reflection of it" (p. 42). Like the parodies by other San Franciscans, those by Bierce often indicate an awareness of English or European models. But he never seemed to consider his parodies a matter of apprenticeship to the styles of the masters, as perhaps Twain and Bret Harte came to view their burlesques of novels. When Bierce created a parody, it had the air of being a true historical judgment or even an act of justice on a so-called masterpiece, though under the guise of irony. Fortunately, this self-seriousness does not impede the *esprit* of *The Devil's Dictionary*, which is itself a parody of Webster's dictionary and reflects a rather general interest in words and word-making at this point of American literary culture.

A fine example of a parody of the distinctive style of the Bible emerges in the definition of

ABNORMAL, *adj.* Not conforming to standard. In matters of thought and conduct, to be independent is to be abnormal, to be abnormal is to be detested. Wherefore the lexicographer adviseth a striving toward a straiter resemblance to the Average Man than he hath to himself. Whoso attaineth thereto shall have peace, the prospect of death and the hope of Hell.

The style of the definition is mock-serious, as Bierce imitates stylistic devices and the heavily didactic tone sometimes found in Biblical passages of admonition. The high style, furthermore, is in direct contrast with the ignoble advice to conform. And by the resulting incongruity, Bierce maliciously laughs at two of our common failings, our grand bravado and our timid conformity, which are capable of appearing in the same person at the same time. Furthermore, as the definition progresses, the gap between style and subject widens, until the tone of the style becomes almost rabid and the advice to conform grows despicably bigoted and is ultimately sent to Hell. Other definitions parody Biblical stylistic devices and join them to contemptible subject matter—see, for example, ICONOCLAST and especially DECALOGUE, which Bierce illustrates with such couplets as these:

> Thou shalt no God but me adore:
> 'Twere too expensive to have more. . . .
>
> Take not God's name in vain; select
> A time when it will have effect.
>
> Work not on Sabbath days at all,
> But go to see the teams play ball. . . .
>
> Don't steal; thou'lt never thus compete
> Successfully in business. Cheat.

Thus unmercifully are we shown the expedient reality that has often underlain such pontifical thou-shalt-nots.

A delightful parody of a particular poem is in the definition of elegy:

> ELEGY, n. A composition in verse, in which, without employing any of the methods of humor, the writer aims to produce in the reader's mind the dampest kind of dejection. The most famous English example begins somewhat like this:
> > The cur foretells the knell of parting day;
> > The loafing herd winds slowly o'er the lea;
> > The wise man homeward plods; I only stay
> > To fiddle-faddle in a minor key.

By concluding his quatrain bathetically, Bierce points explicitly to the flaws of "Elegy Written in a Country Churchyard" as he saw them—the fiddle-faddling or pointless ambling through depressing thoughts in dreary and soporific verse. And in his definition of WEATHER, the trochaics of "Locksley Hall" are brilliantly debunked by Bierce's attaching them to a trivial or low content, weather-forecasting, that is deflated at the same time:

> Once I dipt into the future far as human eye could see,
> And I saw the Chief Forecaster, dead as any one can be—
> Dead and damned and shut in Hades as a liar from his birth,
> With a record of unreason seldom paralleled on earth. . . .

The poetic rhythms of Tennyson or Gray or the Bible were not the only victims of Bierce's parodies. He also selected for subtle exaggeration the style, tone, and inherent attitudes of the Declaration of Independence in his definition of INTRODUCTION, a malevolent social ritual (according to the definer) that robs us of privacy and hurls us into the midst of enemies, real or potential. Therefore, the Declaration of Independence should be reworded in this way to suit the reality:

> We hold these truths to be self-evident: that all men are created equal; that they are endowed by their Creator with certain inalienable rights; that among these are life, and the right to make that of another miserable by thrusting upon him an incalculable quantity of acquaintances; liberty, particularly the liberty to introduce persons to one another without first ascertaining if they are not already acquainted as enemies; and the pursuit of another's happiness with a running pack of strangers.

With parody of either prose or poetry, then, as with mock-heroic, form is obviously elevated out of proportion to the low nature of the content, and the resulting contrast can satirize both form and content. With the forms of low burlesque, Hudibrastic and travesty, satire usually focuses upon a content that is itself inherently noble but is irreverently given an inappropriately low form.

In Bierce's definition of FEMALE he employed a Hudibrastic doggerel of unremitting iambic tetrameter that whisks us, not along a narrative line, but through little dramatic vignettes, the general treatment of which adds little credit to the idea of femininity. And at the same time the rhyming couplets outrageously juxtapose objects and ideas that are normally unassociated with each other but which might be paradoxically related, such as snails and males, advice and dice, strife and wife:

> The Maker, at Creation's birth,
> With living things had stocked the earth.
> From elephants to bats and snails,
> They were all good, for all were males.
> But when the Devil came and saw
> He said: "By Thine eternal law
> Of growth, maturity, decay,
> These all must quickly pass away
> And leave untenanted the earth
> Unless Thou dost establish birth"—
> Then tucked his head beneath his wing
> To laugh—he had no sleeve—the thing
> With deviltry did so accord,
> That he'd suggested to the Lord.
> The Master pondered this advice,
> Then shook and threw the fateful dice
> Wherewith all matters here below
> Are ordered, and observed the throw;

> Then bent His head in awful state,
> Confirming the decree of Fate. . . .
> That night earth rang with sounds of strife—
> Ten million males had each a wife; . . .

Bierce similarly deflated the general subject matter of art connoisseurs in his definition of ART, the tribe of office-holders in DEPUTY, sermonizing in HOMILETICS, pork-barrel politics in TARIFF, professional augurs in INAUSPICIOUSLY, the fine points of theological argumentation in INFRALAPSARIAN, the world of fashion in LORD, and the electoral college in MAN. He experimented tirelessly with metrics and rhymes in these Hudibrastics seeking maximum satiric effectiveness, and he implied that there might be more than a little similarity between the contrived low and pedestrian treatment and the subject so treated. The definition of ABRACADABRA experiments with a doggerel of a diverse rhyme and meter (though predominantly anapestic with a varying number of feet per line). Such a rollicking movement discredits the general idea of human wisdom:

> By *Abracadabra* we signify
>   An infinite number of things.
> 'Tis the answer to What? and How? and Why?
> And Whence? and Whither?—a word whereby
>   The Truth (with the comfort it brings)
> Is open to all who grope in night,
> Crying for Wisdom's holy light. . . .
>
> Of an ancient man the tale is told
> That he lived to be ten centuries old, . . .
> Philosophers gathered from far and near
> To sit at his feet and ear and hear,
>   Though he was never heard
>   To utter a word
>   But "*Abracadabra, abracadab,*
>   *Abracada, abracad,*
> *Abraca, abrac, abra, ab!*"
>   'Twas all he had,
> 'Twas all they wanted to hear, and each
> Made copious notes of the mystical speech,
>   Which they published next—
>   A trickle of text
> In a meadow of commentary. . . .
>
>   He's dead,
>   As I said,
> And the books of the sages have perished,
> But his wisdom is sacredly cherished.
> In *Abracadabra* it solemnly rings,
> Like an ancient bell that forever swings.
>   O, I love to hear
>   That word make clear
> Humanity's General Sense of Things.

The anapestic rapidity of the definition resembles less the pace of a stately sage than that of a scampering, mischievous imp. And such treatment is appropriate for Bierce's attitudes toward men who affect wisdom and attempt to explain life in downright misleading oversimplifications. Incidentally, he signed several other definitions (which happen not to be Hudibrastic in form) with the pseudonym Judibras, perhaps a gesture of significant whimsy.

An implied similarity between a degrading or jocular treatment and a subject inherently noble is characteristic of travesty, though here the subject is more particular (specific authors, people, books) and not as general as *females* or *human wisdom*. In his satiric thrusts Bierce was not above deflating names revered in the history of Western culture: he presented Heinrich Schliemann as obsessed with the paltriest kind of scholarship, and Aristophanes and Wagner as tin-pan-alley co-composers of an opera for frogs, in his definition of

> FROG, *n*. A reptile with edible legs. The first mention of frogs in profane literature is in Homer's narrative of the war between them and the mice. Skeptical persons have doubted Homer's authorship of the work, but the learned, ingenious and industrious Dr. Schliemann has set the question forever at rest by uncovering the bones of the slain frogs. . . . The frog is a diligent songster, having a good voice but no ear. The libretto of his favorite opera, as written by Aristophanes, is brief, simple and effective—"brekekexkoäx"; the music is apparently by that eminent composer, Richard Wagner. . . .

By treating Wagner, Aristophanes, and Schliemann in a low manner through directing them into make-believe ridiculous activities, the definition perhaps suggests that these noble men did occasionally allow their hobbies to ride them. A similar conclusion is suggested for Plato in the definition of SOUL, for Zeno in CALLOUS, for Locke and Kant in UNDERSTANDING, and for Calvin in FRYING-PAN, which, we are told, was an artifact

> invented by Calvin, and by him used in cooking span-long infants that had died without baptism; and observing one day the horrible torment of a tramp who had incautiously pulled a fried babe from the waste-dump and devoured it, it occurred to the great divine to rob death of its terrors by introducing the frying-pan into every household in Geneva. Thence it spread to all corners of the world, and has been of invaluable assistance in the propagation of his sombre faith.

In a group of travesties that cite the celebrated figures of myth and religion, we are reminded of Lucian's treatment of the gods and their votaries as ever so human in their attitudes and activities. In ZEAL (defined as "A certain nervous disorder afflicting the young and inexperienced. A passion that goeth before a sprawl.") as in OPTIMIST, the

Almighty is somewhat lowered by having merely to recognize and deal with the fools who espouse his cause. Also in the Lucian manner is the definition of CLIO, who loses her dignity, as Bierce presents her presiding over history in a manner recalling a temperance lecture; the definition of NECTAR, in which we see Juno getting drunk on Kentucky rye; and the definition of GRACES,

> who attended upon Venus, serving without salary. They were at no expense for board and clothing, for they ate nothing to speak of and dressed according to the weather, wearing whatever breeze happened to be blowing.

And in defining WRATH Bierce implied that the figures of Greek and Hebraic legends are perhaps more similar in their ill-tempers than in their amicability.

For the subjects of his travesties, Bierce did not rest with particular figures of myth and cultural history. He was apt at zeroing in on his own renowned contemporaries, whom he loved to depict in unbecoming and inconsistent postures. Choosing one's contemporaries may limit the effectiveness of a travesty, of course, if their significance becomes obscured with time. But Bierce's subjects usually had the prestige (whether actual or self-imagined) that made them fit targets for satiric assault. In defining WALL-STREET, for example, Bierce saw a peculiar irony in Carnegie's deploring the capitalism by which he had made his fortunes. But an even keener travesty (in the definition of DIARY) attempts to deflate the ideas of William Randolph Hearst about himself that were too grandoise to fit into our cosmology:

> Hearst kept a diary wherein were writ
> All that he had of wisdom and of wit.
> So the Recording Angel, when Hearst died,
> Erased all entries of his own and cried:
> "I'll judge you by your diary." Said Hearst:
> "Thank you; 'twill show you I am Saint the First"—
> Straightway producing, jubilant and proud,
> That record from a pocket in his shroud.
> The Angel slowly turned the pages o'er,
> Each stupid line of which he knew before,
> Glooming and gleaming as by turns he hit
> On shallow sentiment and stolen wit;
> Then gravely closed the book and gave it back.
> "My friend, you've wandered from your proper track:
> You'd never be content this side the tomb—
> For big ideas Heaven has little room,
> And Hell's not latitude for making mirth,"
> He said, and kicked the fellow back to earth.

Bierce never tired of lampooning Hearst, the monarch of the San Francisco *Examiner* and for approximately twenty years Bierce's employer who continued sending him paychecks even when he resigned, which was with some frequency.[14] Bierce, incidentally, said that his service for the Hearst enterprises was dedicated to the people who needed him most, "the millions of readers to whom Mr. Hearst is a misleading light."[15] In travestying contemporary personages Bierce showed a devilish catholicity of taste by including Madame Blavatsky (cited in the definition of THEOSOPHY as the "greatest and fattest of recent Theosophists") and William Dean Howells (shown in the definition of SPOOKER hard at work writing about the activities of genteel spooks).

Whether he was treating a high subject ignominiously or a low subject grandly, Bierce was aware of the importance of form, its wit and polish, as this sampling of definitions suggests. If he was diabolical, it was in the sense of Blake's devil, who did not rest with the establishment and its dictates. Bitterness and cynicism are certainly present, but with what diabolical pleasure we other devils enjoy the style! Perhaps it is time, then, to recognize, in *The Devil's Dictionary's* experimentation with the forms of burlesque, a contribution to American letters. As Bierce claimed in his definition of DICTIONARY, his lexicon is a most useful work.

Notes

1. Quoted in Paul Fatout, *Ambrose Bierce: The Devil's Lexicographer* (Norman, Oklahoma, 1951), p. 131, from Bierce's columns in the *Californian*, vol. I, nos. 2 and 3 (February and March, 1880).

2. The date 1875 was established only recently by Ernest Jerome Hopkins, whose research uncovered 851 definitions beyond the thousand or so included in Bierce's own authorized publication of his collected works. See Ernest Jerome Hopkins, "Bierce, the Caustic Columnist," introduction to *The Enlarged Devil's Dictionary by Ambrose Bierce* (Garden City, N.Y., 1967). pp. xi–xxiv. Apparently, Bierce forgot about many of his earlier items, for is collection was prefaced with the statement that he began the exercise of definitions in 1881.

3. Letter from Ambrose Bierce to George Sterling, May 6, 1906, in *The Letters of Ambrose Bierce*, ed. Bertha Clark Pope (New York, 1967), p. 120.

4. Ambrose Bierce, "For Brevity and Clarity," in *The Collected Works* (New York and Washington, 1909–1912), XII (*Ante-penultimata*, 1912), 387. All references to Bierce's works will be from this edition of twelve volumes which he supervised. *The Devil's Dictionary* constitutes volume VII (1911).

5. Walter Blair, *Native American Humor* (1800–1900) (New York, 1937), pp. 102–124; also "Burlesques in Nineteenth-Century American Humor," *American Literature*, II (1937), 247.

6. Franklin P. Rogers, *Mark Twain's Burlesque Patterns* (Dallas, 1960), pp. 10–23.

7. Ambrose Bierce, "On Literary Criticism," X (*The Opinionator*, 1911), 43.

8. Ambrose Bierce, "Wit and Humor," X, 61.

9. Ambrose Bierce, "Matter of Manner," X, 61.

10. For the purpose of brevity, I am limiting my investigation to the forms of burlesque and ignoring other forms of satire, such as those of rhetoric and irony, though these certainly deserve attention. Several scholars have investigated Bierce's rhetoric, in terms of his development of the "zigzag sentence," the crescendo, the non-sequitur, the epigram, and the devices of bathos and juxtaposition. See, for example, Wilson Follett's appraisal in two articles—

"Ambrose Bierce, an Analysis of the Perverse Wit That Shaped His Work," *Bookman*, LX-VIII (November 1928), 284–289, and "America's Neglected Satirist," *Dial*, LXV (July 18, 1918), 49–52. Bierce's use of the forms of irony, particularly the irony of the various *eidola* of mock lexicographers in *The Devil's Dictionary*, should be investigated in a separate study.

11. Fatout, p. 79.

12. Hopkins, p. xviii.

13. See David Worcester's *The Art of Satire* (Cambridge, Mass., 1940) and especially Richmond P. Bond's first chapter, "The Nature of Burlesque," in his *English Burlesque Poetry* (Cambridge, Mass., 1932).

14. Robert A. Wiggins, *Ambrose Bierce* (Minneapolis, University of Minnesota Pamphlets of American Writers, No. 37, 1964), p. 19.

15. "A Thumbnail Sketch," XII (*In Motley*, 1912), 307.

The Heart Has Its Reasons: Ambrose Bierce's Successful Failure at Philosophy

Lawrence I. Berkove*

The short stories of Ambrose Bierce reflect an author who was almost a philosopher. Indeed, he was sometimes called "philosopher" as a respectful compliment, but his admirers were nearer the mark than they knew. To an unusual degree, Bierce strove his whole life long to discipline himself to reason logically. More than that, he struggled to create a rational and logically consistent system of values for himself out of his selective but intense reading in philosophy and his own reflections. "The test of truth is Reason, not Faith; for to the court of Reason must be submitted even the claims of Faith."[1] But he failed. Or, rather, he failed to put together a philosophy to which he could assent wholeheartedly. For his deepest values were not rational but humanitarian. The same Civil War which burned away his patriotic fervor, his religious faith, and his youthful idealism and turned him into a skeptic, also burned into him an ineradicable compassion for man, whom he saw ever afterward as a victim: of Nature, of war, and of himself. Bierce was never at peace after the Civil War, for a civil war see-sawed within him. His head and heart clashed for mastery. This inner civil war fused in his psyche with the outer, and the poignant stories of conflict that he subsequently wrote have since reflected two battlefields.

It is justifiable to intend "philosophy" in its formal sense when speaking of a philosophical dimension to his writings. Bierce read formal philosophy and frequently referred to it in his newspaper columns. Partly from such external evidence but mostly on the basis of internal patterns which closely resemble certain philosophical positions, it is possible to assess the degree of importance particular philosophies had in Bierce's stories. Shortly, I will discuss his use of these sources in more detail but for the moment I will only name them. From classical times: The Eleatics, the Cynics, and the later Stoics. From modern times: the French and English skeptics of the Enlightenment. Undoubtedly, there are other

---

*This article is part of a fuller study of Bierce's fiction in Lawrence I. Berkove's *Ambrose Bierce: A Braver Man Than Anybody Knew* (Ann Arbor: Ardis, 1981). Reprinted here by permission of the author.

significant philosophical influences in his work—Plato perhaps—but the ones I've mentioned are the most prominent. Though he took these philosophies seriously and responded to them, he did not adopt them. He was too much a man of his times not to be profoundly aware of the limits of human reason and distrustful of the human mind.

This distrust can be found in his ambivalent attitude toward war. He was able to hate it intellectually, but not emotionally. Whenever he recalled the sense of adventure, the unsullied idealism, the heroism, and the pure youthful surge of his war years, a sentimental indulgence came over him, and the sharp memories of carnage and tragedy gave way a little to nostalgia.

> There steals upon my sense the ghost of an odor from pines that canopy the ambuscade. I feel upon my cheek the morning mist that shrouds the hostile camp unaware of its doom, and my blood stirs at the ringing shot of the solitary sentinel.[2]

There is a remarkable juxtaposition in this passage of these two radically different reactions. Bierce was aware of their presence in him, and of their contradictory natures. He never managed to reconcile them; he fostered the values of reason and endeavored to suppress those of emotion. "Thought and emotion dwell apart," he said. "When the heart goes into the head there is no dissension; only an eviction."[3] He called his fond memories of his war years "illusions" and thought much the same of almost every happy memory or pleasurable sensation: youth, life, truth, and love.

> I dreamed of a constant love and spoke
> In my sleep, they say, of an iron yoke.[4]

As he grew older, the realm of illusion seemed larger to him, and its moral deception more enraging. Writing about the intellectual prerequisites of a writer, he once said:

> And it would be needful that he [a writer] know and have an ever present consciousness that this is a world of fools and rogues, blind with superstition, tormented with envy, consumed with vanity, selfish, false, cruel, cursed with illusions—frothing mad![5]

From his war years on, Bierce increasingly distrusted not only his emotions, but his memory and his senses as well. In his opinion, they were inferior mental faculties that only registered impressions and, pander-like, indulged the "low, enjoying power." "Perception," he once said, "is not the same thing as discernment."[6] To discern the truth about life, to know the viciousness with which he felt the world of nature and man to be infused, Bierce relied upon reason. Slowly and painfully, literally at the cost of blood, sweat, and tears, Bierce put together a reasonable philosophy of life to which he tried to adhere with all his might.

Bierce's passion for reason and his subsequent idealization of it grew out of his conclusion that man must adapt himself to life instead of futilely trying to impose himself—and an artificial concept of order—upon it. In both war and peace, he had observed that the laws of strategy and the laws of nature operated remorselessly, but that through reason the wise man might learn them and save himself from at least some of their adverse effects. Reason was a hard taskmaster, but it is plain from the forthright and controversial articles of his early journalistic career that Bierce applied himself assiduously and conscientiously to his lessons.

In these articles, Bierce is frequently found to be championing unpopular opinions in the name of reason. While on the *Argonaut*, for example, he defended both the Chinese and the Negroes against their detractors—almost the whole of the San Francisco community—and "reasonably" disputed some of the main charges against them.[7] In 1889, dissenting from the popular feeling that some military action should be taken against Germany for its hostility toward American interests in Samoa, Bierce coolly noted that America was militarily unprepared.

> We have a grievance, apparently, but it is not true in military affairs that he is thrice armed who has a just quarrel.
> To fight without hope is not soldierly; it is the act of a fool. A general who should bring on a decisive engagement with all the advantages on the side of the enemy would be dismissed, and should be shot.

He proceeds bluntly to the point that by extending its interests into foreign lands, America is asking for trouble.

> A nation is like an individual; when angry it is blind to the plainest considerations and most conspicuous facts. It forgets the values and relations of things; its whole intellectual world is suffused with a false light. The wildest and maddest fancies find acceptance, the soberest dictates of common sense are ignored. It is against this condition of things that the American people should be warned.[8]

The moral for the country, as for a man, is that it must not allow its heart to go into its head.

In a widely misinterpreted passage, Bierce even went so far as to advocate the imitation of Christ, but for intellectual reasons only. He once revealed his "ultimate and determining test of right" as the example of Christ. "What, under the circumstances, would Christ have done?" But his explanation of his position reveals a set of values which are rational rather than Christian:

> He [Christ] taught nothing new in goodness, for all goodness was ages old before he came; but with an intuition that never failed he applied to life and conduct the entire law of righteousness. I have before described him a lightning moral calculator; to his luminous intelligence the statement of the problem conveyed the solution—he could not hesitate, he could not err.[9]

The disparity between an orthodox Christian view of Christ and Bierce's is here clearly seen as the difference between a God who makes and represents laws and an incredibly fast and accurate computer-like mind which applies laws already made. In the long run, therefore, a man who imitates Christ is simply availing himself of ready-made rational decisions.

Further examples of Bierce's admiration of reason can be found in abundance in the journalism of his entire career, but despite this abundance, his deepest values were other than purely rational ones. Especially in his San Francisco *Examiner* columns of 1887–1893, the period during which he wrote his best short stories, an occasional article appears and, not infrequently, a story also which by implication undercuts the rule of reason he usually advocated. From the prominence given to reason in these stories, and from the variety of positions he takes in them on the issue of reason, we can recognize a probing of his own system for loopholes and a resentment at his own conclusions. Many of his so-called pronouncements are really hypotheses, well-turned assertions waiting further and fuller testing. Such a pronouncement is his sardonic remark, "All are lunatics, but he who can analyze his delusion is called a philosopher."[10] The idea behind this epigram is analyzed at some length in the 1891 story, "Parker Adderson, Philosopher," which deals with a condemned spy who at first, at least, regards his imminent execution with philosophical serenity. Other statements, such as the following quatrain, also seem turned inward, ironic comments on his struggle to settle his own conflicting thoughts on the ultimate value of reason:

> The sea-bird speeding from the realm of night
> Dashes to death against the beacon-light.
> Learn from its evil fate, ambitious soul,
> The ministry of light is guide, not goal.[11]

Reason for its own sake kills the spirit, Bierce seems to say. It must have a directing purpose. But if one rejects revelation, as Bierce certainly did, where does one find purpose?

Bierce looked to Nature for purpose. Not Wordsworth's Nature, but the scientist's Nature. Man must follow the Nature revealed to him by his reason, learn its laws and obey them. If he is wise enough, Bierce thought, man can learn from observation; if not, he will have to learn from experience. Life itself will tell man what he needs to know and pass judgment on his decisions. When man makes the wrong decision, he suffers and dies. But man, through reason, can learn what is to be. If he would be happy, let him desire that end.

Towards this grim-sounding philosophy of life Bierce was pushed by his reason, aided and abetted by a thoughtful reading of a variety of philosophers and writers who inclined toward reason and empiricism. First among these influences were the Cynics. Bierce has often been called a cynic, in the popular, loose sense of the term. This is an exaggeration. But that he was aware of Cyncism as a philosophy and respected it, there is no doubt. His famous *The Devil's Dictionary* was first published as the *Cynic's Word Book* and in it is the definition of a cynic as "a blackguard whose faulty vision sees things as they are, not as they ought to be." More to the point, however, is the emphasis of the Cynics upon the exposure of illusion; their distinction between natural and artificial values; their emphasis upon self discipline and virtuous action; and their readiness to set themselves apart from the community in order to be fearlessly critical of it.[12] Bierce would not have encouraged others to think him a Cynic if there had not been some accuracy to the charge.

Much more influential upon his personal philosophy and his literature was Stoicism. It would be an exaggeration to describe him as a Stoic but perhaps more than any other single philosophy it left its mark upon him.

Bierce's first contact with Stoicism might well date to his boyhood. A book on Stoicism was published in 1855 by his eminent uncle, Lucius Verus Bierce, whom Ambrose knew and admired, and it is possible that he knew about the book. In any case, however, that Bierce read the Stoics and read them carefully, is a matter of record. Not only have various critics noticed Bierce's resemblance to the Stoics[13] but Bierce himself readily admitted it. In 1893, for example, he wrote:

> I am for preserving the ancient, primitive distinction between right and wrong. The virtues of Socrates, the wisdom of Aristotle, the examples of Marcus Aurelius and Jesus Christ are enough to engage my admiration and rebuke my life. From my fog-scourged and plague-smitten morass I lift reverent eyes to the shining summits of eternal truth, where they stand; I strain my senses to catch the law they deliver.[14]

Later in his life, he recommended for the training of a writer "the ancients: Plato, Aristotle, Marcus Aurelius, Seneca and the lot—custodians of most of what is worth knowing," and especially praised Epictetus who, he said, teaches "how to be a worthy guest at the table of the gods."[15] In an 1899 letter of consolation to a friend, Bierce enlarges on this last statement:

> When I'm in trouble and distress I read Epictetus, and can warmly recommend that plan to you. It does not cure, but it helps one's endurance of the ill. I go to Epictetus with my mental malady—and misfortunes themselves are nothing except in so far as they affect us mentally. For we of our class do not suffer hunger and cold, and the like, from our failures and mischances—only dejection. And dejection is unreasonable.[16]

It is no accident that common to both the later Stoics and Bierce is a positing of a "God" of natural processes and an impersonal and painful universe of which man is definitely not the center; an ascription to reason of man's hope of survival; and the notion that through the correct use of reason a sort of happiness is possible for man. Yet, although Bierce was pushed toward these conclusions by both his reason and his reading, he balked at embracing them totally. Some idea of his resistance to the inexorable force of his reason can be gained by examining what appears to be a major debt to the Stoic philosophers Epictetus and Marcus Aurelius. For example, in Epictetus Bierce would have found this observation:

> What disturbs men's minds is not events but their judgments on events. For instance, death is nothing dreadful, or else Socrates would have thought it so. No, the only dreadful thing about it is men's judgment that it is dreadful.[17]

It is tempting to conjecture whether this might not have been the nucleus of his story, "Parker Adderson, Philosopher." In that story, a curious exchange of contradictory opinions takes place. At the beginning, the captured Union spy, Parker Adderson, appears not to be afraid of death while his captor, a Confederate general, says that it is "horrible." By the end of the story, however, the general appears to be at ease about death whereas Adderson has become panic-stricken. The story, therefore, is ambivalent, and appears to support both Epictetus' position—and its opposite.

The resemblance of another reflection of Epictetus to "The Affair at Coulter's Notch" is almost too great for coincidence.

> Never say of anything, "I lost it," but say, "I gave it back." Has your child died? It was given back. Has your wife died? She was given back. Has your estate been taken from you? Was not this also given back? But you say, "He who took it from me is wicked." What does it matter to you through whom the Giver asked it back? As long as He gives it you, take care of it, but not as your own; treat it as passers-by treat an inn.[18]

In the story, Coulter, a Union artillery officer from the South, is ordered by a vindictive general to shell what the general knows to be Coulter's own home. Coulter obeys. Later, with advancing Union officers who bivouac that night in the shattered dwelling, he finds the bodies of his wife and child killed by his own shelling.

The same ambiguous relation exists between the tale, "The Mocking-Bird: A Story of a Soldier Who Had a Dream," and one of Marcus Aurelius' meditations:

> Return to thy sober senses and call thyself back; and when thou hast roused thyself from sleep and hast perceived that they were only dreams which troubled thee, now in thy waking hours look at these (the things about thee) as thou didst look at those (the dreams).[19]

In this story, Private Grayrock, a Union sentinel, awakens from a dream of losing touch with his brother, only to discover that a Confederate he had fired at earlier—and killed—was his brother.

Strikingly similar to another of Marcus Aurelius' meditations, "Death is a cessation of the impressions through the senses, and of the pulling of the strings which move the appetites, and of the discursive movements of the thoughts, and of the service to the flesh,"[20] is "An Occurrence at Owl Creek Bridge." The entire story arises out of the hallucinations that occur in the unconscious mind of a man who is being hanged, a man who "was as one already dead." Although his death occurs, in reality, in the fraction of a second it takes the knot of the noose to break his neck, to his mind—and the reader's—his life continues (speciously) for what seems hours.

A recent interpretation of "An Occurrence at Owl Creek" has also argued that the story has an Eleatic dimension, that it can be understood as a philosophical commentary on the paradox of Zeno's arrow. According to the critic, "Bierce pairs unanswerable philosophical logic [i.e. that the man's death will never occur] with the implacable logic of natural law."[21] In this case, therefore, an empirical refutation of Zeno's paradox is advanced.

The odd thing about all of the foregoing resemblances between the sayings of the Stoics and Bierce's stories is that while the stories seem to dramatize the sayings, they do so as if in protest against them. The sayings of the Stoics appeal mainly to the intellect; Bierce's stories, however, appeal contradictorily both to the emotions and the intellect, and the emotional appeal is the more powerful. If the stories are seeded at the core with the Stoic counsel of resignation, inviolate in its validity and unaffected by the stories' pathos or the reader's passion, this counsel is not what Bierce conveys to the reader. Rather, it is a freshly aroused sympathy for one's fellow man based on a sharpened awareness of man's demonstrated limitations and the invincible and pitiless violence of life. Pure reason, after all, is inhuman and Bierce does not lash ignorance where it is excusable—a mortal consequence of being imperfect.

This distinction takes us to the heart of Bierce's stories. In the best of them, he *explores* reason. Is man a rational creature? he asks himself. How effective is man's ability to use reason? Is there a higher standard of value than reason?

Not even in his declining years, when he became slightly more resigned to life, did he wholly acquiesce to the rule of reason. For to Bierce, the greatest good was a feeling above reason; it was happiness.

> To local standards of right and wrong he [a writer] should be civilly indifferent. In the virtues, so-called, he should discern only the rough notes of a general expediency; in fixed moral principles only time-saving pre-decisions of cases not yet before the court of conscience. Happiness should disclose itself to his enlarging intelligence as the end and purpose of life; art and love as the only means of happiness.[22]

Of civilization, which he regarded as the greatest and most enduring product of reason, he said: "It has accomplished everything, but it has not made humanity any happier. Happiness is the only thing worth having. . . ."[23] Even in the last year of his life, he restated this belief, albeit somewhat gloomily:

> Nothing else is of any value—just happiness. The difference between a good person and a bad one is that one finds happiness in goodness, the other in badness; but, consciously or unconsciously happiness is all they seek, or can seek. Even self-sacrifice is a species of indulgence. And at the end of it all we see is that nothing matters.[24]

This longing for happiness, however, was present even in his earlier years. In the autobiographical battle memoirs he wrote in the eighties (e.g. "On a Mountain," "What I Saw of Shiloh," and "Four Days in Dixie") there is also an undisguised nostalgia for the happiness and thrill of his youth. For Bierce, the feeling of happiness was a real fact; that it was induced by illusion or ignorance, another fact. Yet such is life, and such are the respective merits of wisdom and happiness, Bierce would say, that the wise man faced with the choice between the two would choose happiness, though by that choice he forfeited his wisdom. This, at least, is the moral of "Haïta the Shepherd," one of the original *Tales of Soldiers and Civilians*, the 1891 collection of stories upon which his fame chiefly rests. In this parable, a pure and pleasant shepherd lad is tantalized and confused by the abrupt appearances and disappearances of a maiden of surpassing beauty. Finally, a holy hermit tells the boy who she is and why she vanishes whenever he tries to become better acquainted or to learn how to keep her:

> ". . . Know, then, that her name, which she would not even permit thee to inquire, is Happiness. Thou saidst the truth to her, that she is capricious for she imposeth conditions that man can not fulfill, and delinquency is punished by desertion. She cometh only when unsought, and will not be questioned. One manifestation of curiosity, one sign of doubt, one expression of misgiving, and she is away! How long didst thou have her at any time before she fled?"
> "Only a single instant," answered Haïta, blushing with shame at the confession. "Each time I drove her away in one moment."
> "Unfortunate youth!" said the holy hermit, "but for thine indiscretion thou mightst have had her for two."[25]

In the irony of that single word, "indiscretion," is the implication that there is a judiciousness above reason.

Happiness is not a theme in Bierce's stories. In fact, it is conspicuous by its absence. None of his major protagonists are happy, or seek for happiness. In Bierce's deadly universe, they fight for sanity or survival; Pyrrhic victories are their utmost achievement; happiness is a luxury beyond consideration. Bierce's own experiences with happiness convinced him that it was at best ephemeral and not infrequently a prelude to disaster.

Moreover, as Haïta discovered, happiness could not be deliberately achieved. Though Bierce personally longed for it, he did not deceive himself about its opposition to reason. With Swift, Bierce might have said that it was "a perpetual possession of being well-deceived."

Bierce's early awareness of the futility of hoping for happiness or of expecting pure reason, and his realization that the imperfect creature man was, in truth, imperfectible, led him to be skeptical of reason, happiness, man, and himself. In 1878 he wrote that when he came to California in 1866 he had "a cast-iron conviction about everything from the self-evident to the unknowable, both inclusive."[26] In 1888, he wrote that he had memorized the following passage from Bacon: "He that has justly considered matters, the causes which bring them about, and the consequences which flow from them, is denied a choice and remains always a skeptic."[27] But Bierce did not have to go to Bacon for his skepticism, for years earlier, under the tutelage of the editor James Watkins, he had studied the great skeptics of literature and had incorporated their philosophies into his own.

An important start in the difficult undertaking of identifying and assessing the influence of such writers on Bierce was made by Harry Lynn Sheller in his dissertation on Bierce's satire. Among his findings is that Bierce's debt to the English and French writers of the Enlightenment is quite substantial. He claims that it goes beyond occasional literary allusions and imitations, and extends to a basic similarity in ideals, attitude, and philosophy of life between Bierce and some of the leading spirits of the age, chiefly Swift and Voltaire.[28] Sheller says that "Bierce cannot be accused of imitation." Instead, he finds that Bierce was inspired by the examples and ideas of his predecessors to develop his own thought and satiric patterns in a way consistent with his original genius and his integrity.[29] Thus, in order to fully exploit Sheller's conclusion, it is necessary to go beyond the similarities between Bierce and other authors, and to examine also that aspect of his satire in particular and his art in general which reacted to stimulus in a wholly original and creative way. I have already indicated such a reaction in my discussion of Bierce's love-hate relationship with the Stoics. To some extent, a similar relationship exists between Bierce and the writers of the Enlightenment, with this difference: that while he was not completely comfortable with their conclusions, he was at home with their tool of skepticism. This he made his own and henceforth used it distinctively for his own purposes.

The tag name, "The Age of Reason," is a misleading label for the eighteenth century because it implies only a favorable attitude toward reason. The major contributions of such writers as Swift, Voltaire, and La Rochefoucauld, however, consist of their attacks on reason, their use of skepticism and empiricism to awaken men from their rosy dreams of what reason might accomplish and remind them of their limitations and of reason's. It was these demonstrations, this use of the analytic power of reason to check the synthetic, that appealed to Bierce. He already had an accelerator; he needed a brake.

As Sheller observed, Bierce was not an imitator. He was not an eighteenth century anachronism writing at the end of the nineteenth century; his use of skepticism was masterful but modern. An interesting comparison and contrast of Bierce to certain Enlightenment authors might be made, for example, with the theme of how man's love for woman leads him to folly. The most famous eighteenth century treatment of this theme is probably Pope's mock epic, *The Rape of the Lock*. The humorous opening lines establish the tone of the poem, and immediately alert the reader to be skeptical of what he reads:

> What dire offence from amorous causes springs,
> What mighty contests rise from trivial things,
> I sing . . .   (Canto I, ll. 1–3)

There is no tragedy in this poem because the subject is too slight for tragedy, because the characters are toy-like types that cannot feel or know real sorrow, and because the reader is in on the joke. Throughout the poem Pope invests the reader with the cloak of skepticism, and gently points out the reasonable moral to him after having saved him from the indignity of laughing foolishness to scorn, only to find out later that he had laughed at himself.

Earlier, Swift had treated the same subject with a sharper humor. In his *Tale of a Tub*, violence and warfare are attributed to so slight a cause as a frustrated love affair. A certain prince, Swift says, was inflamed by the eyes of a female, but "she was removed into an enemy's country" before he could enjoy her.

> Having to no purpose used all peaceable Endeavours, the collected part of the *Semen*, raised and enflamed, became adust, converted to Choler, turned head upon the spinal Duct, and ascended to the Brain. The very same Principle that influences a *Bully* to break the Windows of a Whore, who has jilted him, naturally stirs up a Great Prince to raise mighty Armies, and dream of nothing but Sieges, Battles, and Victories.[30]

In Swift, skepticism is not invoked to save the reader from embarrassment but to jolt him into seeing himself for what he is: a creature more subject to the rule of passion than he would like to think. After reading Swift, one cannot take without salt the dictum that man is a rational being.

Bierce's treatment of the theme occurs in his story, "Killed at Resaca." In it, Lt. Herman Brayle distinguishes himself among his comrades in the Union Army by his apparent indifference to death. It is widely interpreted as courage. One day, the lieutenant outdoes himself in gallantry, and conspicuously gallops across the battlefield in fulfillment of a command, though he had been ordered to take a safer route. He is killed, of course, but not before his example inspires a hundred Union soldiers to leave their shelters and rush to their own needless deaths on the battlefield. A fellow officer finds among his effects "an ordinary love letter," in which Lt. Brayle's sweetheart indirectly insinuates that he is a coward. "These were the words which on that sunny afternoon, in a distant region, had slain a hundred men. Is woman weak?"

If the story had ended at this point, it could have been described as an exercise in irony and a lesson in skepticism. Courage in battle is seen to be, in the case of Brayle, a death-wish inspired by an amorous cause, a trivial thing when put into perspective. In the case of the foolhardy Union soldiers, their courage was just an indulgence of emotion—a thoughtless sympathy. None of these deaths was necessary; in a very real sense, Brayle and the others were victims of their own loss of reason, of obeying their feelings instead of their minds. Thus far, Bierce parallels Swift. But there are differences.

For one, Brayle and the others are the victims, and not the offensive and offending bullies and princes of whom Swift wrote, and they do die. Moreover, Brayle is not a stereotype character or a straw man. Handsome, intelligent, and admirable in character, he has been informed with personality and is believable. In addition to these differences from Pope and Swift, Bierce adds another important one as he continues the story for a few more paragraphs. Brayle's fellow officer, the narrator, carries the love letter to its sender, a woman of fascinating beauty and charm. She reads it with some embarrassment but no apparent remorse, then casts it into a fire in revulsion when she sees a blood-stain on it. "How did he die?" she asks. The officer turn his glance full on her before answering.

> The light of the burning letter was reflected in her eyes and touched her cheek with a tinge of crimson like the stain upon its page. I had never seen anything as beautiful as this detestable creature.
> "He was bitten by a snake," I replied.[31]

With this ending Bierce turns skepticism upon itself and pushes what had been merely irony to a tragic insight. In those last lines, Bierce confirms and intensifies our verdict against the woman, and recruits our sympathy for the lieutenant. We put out of mind our first and uncharitable conclusion that Brayle is merely infatuated and revise our opinion of the matter. No longer is Brayle a victim of his immature feelings, he is now a victim of an unworthy and heartless but fatally attractive charmer. By developing character in the sweetheart, by changing her from an abstract woman into a live woman of great beauty, Bierce leads us to see her from the narrator's point of view, to apprehend with him her fatal power, and out of compassion for Brayle to reject the lesson just taught us by our skepticism. But this is a trap, for to try to justify Brayle on sentimental instead of reasonable grounds is to imply that had we been in his place, we too might very well have acted unreasonably. And thus Bierce implicates us in the tragedy, for Brayle's tragedy is ours, too; though in theory reason can save us, in practice it is beyond our grasp and we are ruled by our emotions. The story, therefore, does not resolve the issue of love for a woman leading a man to folly. On the contrary, it adds complexity to the issue. And by turning skepticism against itself, Bierce frustrates our hope for an easy and simple solution to the dilemmas of life.

This tool of skepticism put into his hands by writers of the Enlightenment enabled Bierce to analyze not only his memories and impressions, but the ideas of those writers as well. Thus reason and skepticism both came under his scrutiny. Though conjecture, it is likely that just as he reacted against some of the maxims of the Stoics, so did he react against some of the notions of the French and English skeptics and put their claims to the test. La Rochefoucauld, for example, widely acknowledged to have had an indisputable influence on Bierce through his maxims,[32] would easily have attracted Bierce's attention with such observations as the following: "Vanity, a sense of shame, and above all temperament often make up the valour of men and the virtue of women."[33] The pertinence of this maxim to "Killed at Resaca" is self-evident. While it cannot be proved that this maxim, specifically, was the seed of the story, its appropriateness to the story, and its pertinence to Bierce's themes of fear, valor, and emotion make it at least worthy of consideration as having seminal value.

> Intrepidity is unusual strength of soul which raises it above the troubles, disorders, and emotions that might be stirred up in it by the sight of great danger. This is the fortitude by which heroes keep their inner peace and preserve clear use of their reason in the most terrible and overwhelming crises.[34]

Again, the striking relevance of this observation to Bierce's war stories, especially "The Affair at Coulter's Notch," and "A Horseman in the Sky," must be noted. Again, however, since the heroes of those stories lose their inner peace because of their intrepidity, these same stories might both be taken to be commentaries, not necessarily acquiescent, on this maxim.

In this survey of Bierce's philosophical position, I have not aimed at a complete chronicling of his intellectual indebtedness nor have I insisted on claiming direct influences of particular statements on Bierce's stories. But that there is a considerable and complex philosophical dimension to Bierce's stories I hope has been demonstrated.

By now it should be evident how and why Bierce failed to be consistently philosophical. But that bitter struggle was not fruitless for out of it came some incomparable stories—a remarkable success of literature. Further, there is a consistency to these stories of conflict; at their deepest level but one they reflect failure. The failure, for one, of human reason to persuade itself that it has found fulfillment and purpose in human existence. The failure of idealism to convince experience that it is not an illusion, and often a deadly delusion. The failure of skepticism to keep from turning on itself and becoming pyrrhonism.

In the final analysis, Bierce used literature to communicate compassion—the one honest and positive value he had left when philosophy failed. The desperate situations in which he placed his protagonists represent, allegorically, the insoluble dilemmas with which he grappled. Though his problems were philosophical, his concern was man. In his tragic vision that man never won, that death was man's inevitable portion and Pyrrhic victory his utmost reward, Bierce sublimed his compassion for human existence.

Notes

1. Bierce, Ambrose, "Epigrams," Vol. VIII of the *Collected Works*, (New York: Neale, 1909–1912), p. 361.

2. "What I Remember of Shiloh," *Works*, I, p. 268.

3. *Works*, VIII, p. 352.

4. San Francisco *Examiner*, 31 July 1887, p. 4.

5. "To Train a Writer," *Works*, X, p. 77. Originally published in the *Examiner* in 1899.

6. *Examiner*, 15 May 1887, p. 4.

7. The *Argonaut* 2, No. 9 (March 9, 1878), p. 9. A liberal attitude toward the Chinese is also present in "The Haunted Valley," which appeared in *The Overland Monthly* in July, 1871. In *The Wasp* of March 24, 1882, Bierce aligned himself with the abolitionist sentiment toward blacks. In various columns of the *Examiner*, Bierce consistently defended the Jews and Mormons against what he saw to be irrational prejudice.

8. *Examiner*, 3 February 1889, p. 4.

9. *Examiner*, 28 June 1891, p. 6.

10. *Works*, VIII, p. 369.

11. *Works*, VIII, p. 374.

12. Kidd, I. G., "Cynics," Vol. 2 of *Encyclopedia of Philosophy*, ed. Paul Edwards, (New York: Crowell Collier and Macmillan Inc., 1967), pp. 284–285.

13. Typical of the early reviews are two pieces by Wilson Follett which make only incidental reference to a Stoic element in Bierce: "Bierce in His Brilliant Obscurity," *New York Times Book Review*, 11 October 1936, pp. 2 and 32; and "Ambrose, Son of Marcus Aurelius," *Atlantic Monthly*, 160, No. 1 (July 1937), 32–42. Other critics have also alluded to it briefly without developing the idea further.

14. Bierce, "Actors and Acting," *Works*, IX, pp. 176–177. Originally published in the *Examiner* in 1893.

15. "To Train a Writer," *Works*, X, p. 76.

16. Bierce, Letter to Percival Pollard, 8 January 1899. Quoted by permission of the Berg Collection, New York Public Library.

17. Epictetus, item no. 5, "The Manual of Epictetus," *The Stoic and Epicurean Philosophers*, ed. Whitney J. Oates (New York: Modern Library, 1957), p. 469.

18. Epictetus, item no. 11, p. 470.

19. Marcus Aurelius, meditation no. 31, "Meditations, Book VI," *The Stoic and Epicurean Philosophers*, p. 530.

20. Marcus Aurelius, meditation no. 28.

21. Logan, F. J., "The Wry Seriousness of 'Owl Creek Bridge,' " *American Literary Realism* 10, No. 2 (Spring 1977), p. 110.

22. Bierce, "To Train a Writer," *Works*, X, p. 77.

23. "The Social Unrest," *Cosmopolitan* XLI, No. 3 (July, 1906), p. 301. This article was a transcript of a debate between Bierce, Morris Hillquit, and Robert Hunter. Hillquit and Hunter leaned toward Socialism in varying degrees; Bierce opposed their views.

24. Bierce, Letter to Nellie (Vore) Sickler, 17 April 1913, [Carey McWilliams, ed.], "A Collection of Bierce Letters," *University of California Chronicle* XXXIV, No. 1 (January, 1932), p. 47.

25. *Works*, III, pp. 306–307.

26. Quoted by Harry Lynn Sheller, "The Satire of Ambrose Bierce: Its Objects, Forms, Devices, and Possible Origins," Diss. Univ. of Southern California 1945, p. 417, from *The Argonaut*, 9 March 1878.

27. *Examiner*, 4 March 1888, p. 4.

28. Sheller, pp. 438–440, 443–444.

29. Sheller, p. 448.

30. Swift, Jonathan, *A Tale of A Tub* (Oxford: Basil Blackwell 1957), p. 104.

31. *Works*, II, p. 104. Like many other authors, Bierce occasionally gives his characters names that suggest significant traits about them. The resemblance of Brayle to Braille may be a clue to Bierce's characterization of Brayle as a man of feeling instead of sight.

32. Among the many critics who have remarked the likelihood of an influence of La Rochefoucauld upon Bierce are Wilson Follett (see note 13); Vernon Watkins, quoted in Carey McWilliams, *Ambrose Bierce: A Biography* (New York: A. and C. Boni, 1929; rpt. with new introduction Archon, 1967), pp. 84–85; McWilliams himself (*Biography*, p. 126); and Sheller, passim.

33. La Rochefoucauld, maxim no. 200, *Maxims*, trans. w. intro. by L. W. Tancock (Baltimore, Penguin 1959), p. 62.

34. La Rochefoucauld, maxim no. 217, p. 62.

Ambrose Bierce and Realism

Howard W. Bahr*

Ambrose Bierce, a writer who paradoxically enough owns a certain sort of fame because of his obscure position in American letters, has a strange fascination for those readers, especially undergraduate students, who are suddenly brought into contact with and "discover" Ambrose Bierce. Yet peculiarly enough, too, scholars and critics very seldom go beyond this discovery stage; they scout around the coast of the Bierce island (I hesitate to ascribe to him the magnitude of a continent), but rarely do they penetrate the periphery for any intensive exploration and cartography. Like the blind men in the famous fable of the blind men and the elephant, one scholar stumbles against the macabre tales of Bierce and exclaims, " 'Tis plain to me that Ambrose Bierce is very much like Poe," while another—equally as blind—happens to grasp Bierce's satirical caudal appendage and exclaims, "Why no, it is obvious that Bierce is very like Jonathan Swift." Thus the blind men continue to mislead those who choose to remain blind.

While again it may be an exaggeration of Bierce's importance to employ this elephant figure as an analogy, nevertheless his work, when viewed in its entirety, has enough varied aspects to make it a patent misrepresentation to generalize by putting him arbitrarily into any one category, whether it be that of Poe imitator, Swiftian satirist, or one of the advance guards of realism in America. The chief purpose of this study has been to examine his work, using as a point of survey the consideration of realism as it is exhibited in his tales and as he discusses it in his critical works; however, since I have approached this investigation with no predisposition, the result has been that I have occasionally strayed from the narrow confines of the topic of the realism in Bierce in order to determine if possible how exactly to classify him as a writer. Yet the very nature of the method which Bierce employed in assembling the material for the twelve volumes of his *Collected Works*, as well as the final form in which this work appears, has made the latter and more important phase of my problem rather difficult to cope with.[1] That is, since a large amount of his critical pronouncements was of an occasional nature, called forth by some particular writing or writer, and since, also, we can never be

*Reprinted by permission of the editor, *Southern Quarterly* (University of Southern Mississippi), 1 (1963), 309–31.

quite certain whether any given pronouncement is a true statement of his belief or merely a weapon to use in the attack on one of his many enemies, we must approach with caution any particular opinion which he expounds.

Regardless of the motive behind any isolated statement, one thing is fairly certain: Bierce did not consider himself a realistic writer, that is, as belonging to any "school" of writing. His own definition of realism bears this out and shows his contempt for those who strove to get close to the grass roots in their writing:

> REALISM, n. The art of depicting nature as it is seen by toads. The charm suffusing a landscape painted by a mole or a story written by a measuring worm.[2]

His way of defining reality shows the same contempt for those who attempt to present things as they "really"—which Bierce defines as "apparently"—are:

> REALITY, n. The dream of a mad philosopher. That which would remain in the cupel if one should assay a phantom. The nucleus of a vacuum.[3]

If we take this latter definition at its face value, it would seem that Bierce was almost positing a philosophic principle that nothing is actually real, that existence is an illusion—things only appear to be. Furthermore, his stories tend to bear out this point of view, for some of his situations depend entirely upon how things appear to an individual at some particular moment of heightened sensibility or excitement. For example, a stuffed snake with shoe button eyes appears to be a real living snake, exerting its hypnotic power, to a man whose imagination gives a completely different interpretation of the impression conveyed to him by his visual sense;[4] the corpse of an enemy soldier, viewed in a forest at night, appears to a hypersensitive sentry to be approaching him with baleful intent;[5] the muzzle of a rifle appears to be as large as a cavern to the soldier buried under the debris of a fallen building in such a helpless position that he must look directly at the ominous opening.[6]

In spite of this apparent belief in the illusive nature of all phenomema, Bierce believed that there is something which is real: Truth. Truth is what happens, whether it appears to be a mere coincidence or not. There is an order to the laws of the universe, for what we call accident, according to Bierce, is "an inevitable occurrence due to the action of immutable natural laws"[7] which are above man's ability to comprehend and explain in terms of predictability, possibility, or probability. That this is one of Bierce's basic beliefs, particularly as it applies to literature, is evident in the following statement:

> Probability? Nothing is so improbable as what is true. It is the unexpected that occurs; but that is not saying enough; it is also the unlikely—one might almost say the impossible. . . . Con-

sidered from a viewpoint a little anterior in time, it was almost unlikely that any event which has occurred would occur—any event worth telling in a story. Everything being so unearthly improbable, I wonder that novelists of the Howells school have the audacity to relate anything at all.[8]

Bierce was quite vehement in denouncing this concern of Howells and his school for the adherence to the "rule of probability" in writing fiction:

Among the laws which Cato Howells has given his little senate, and which his little senators would impose on the rest of us, is an inhibitory statute against a breach of this "probability"— and to them nothing is probable outside the narrow domain of the commonplace man's most commonplace experience.[9]

To Howells and those who attempted to fuse—and confuse—realism and probability, Bierce has an answer, an answer consistent with his own doctrine of appearance and truth:

Fiction has nothing to say to probability; the capable writer gives it not a moment's attention, except to make what is related *seem* probable in the reading—*seem* true.[10]

Thus it would appear that for Bierce there was no need for the writer of fiction to be confined and constrained by any narrow bounds of probability and possibility, just as long as he made what he related seem probable or possible to the reader "in the reading." The latter part of his statement indicated that there is an obligation imposed upon the reader as well as upon the writer, for not only must there be a 'willing suspension of disbelief' while the reader allows the story to penetrate and permeate his imagination, but there must also be an active effort on the part of the reader to give the story a fair chance to make this appeal: the reader must allow the proper time and place for his reading. Bierce illustrates this in one of his stories, "The Suitable Surroundings," in which the writer of ghost stories berates an acquaintance for reading one of his tales while riding to work on the street car. Bierce has his writer explain the duties of the reader which correspond to his privileges:

An author has rights which the reader is bound to respect. . . . The right to the reader's undivided attention. To deny him this is immoral. . . . I can move you to tears or laughter under almost any circumstance. But for my ghost story to be effective you must be made to feel fear—at least a strong sense of the supernatural—and that is a difficult matter. I have a right to expect that if you read me at all you will give me a chance; that you will make yourself accessible to the emotion that I try to inspire.[11]

The appeal of a story, then, should be to the thinking and emotional faculties of the individual, not merely to his sentiments. It was on this

very score that Bierce found fault with the short story as it was being written by his contemporaries: it did not provoke either thought or emotion,
but was designed to "stir up from the shallows of the readers' understanding the sediment which they are pleased to call sentiment."[12]

The importance which Bierce places upon the imaginative faculty
clearly indicates that in this area he approaches very close to the Romantic point of view. On this basis it is not too presumptuous to say that his
doctrine more nearly resembles that of the Romantic writers, if we judge
him from his critical statements rather than from his own performance in
fiction. He says not only that a writer need not, but that he must not, be
tied down by the laws of probability and possibility. The artistic writer
who relates the impossible has, as Bierce puts it,

> but passed over the line into the realm of romance, the
> kingdom of Scott, Defoe, Hawthorne, Beckford, and the
> authors of the *Arabian Nights*—the land of the poets, the home
> of all that is good and lasting in the literature of the imag-
> ination. Do these little fellows, the so-called realists, ever think
> of the goodly company which they deny themselves by confin-
> ing themselves to their clumsy feet and pursuing their stupid
> noses through the barren hinterland, while just beyond the
> Delectable Mountains lies in light the Valley of Dreams, with
> its tall immortals poppy-crowned?[13]

At first glance it would appear that Bierce here is aligning himself completely with the Romantic point of view, but there are at least two am-
biguities in this passage which militate against classifying him with the
true Romantics. In the first place, we note that he does not say "all the
good and lasting in *literature*," but instead, "in the literature of the *imagination*." Does this mean that literature of the imagination is but one
aspect of literature as a whole, or does it imply that literature of the imagination is of a higher order than other types? In the second place, the term
"so-called" realists is confusing. Does he mean that the writers who call
themselves realists are reprehensible for not adhering to the precepts of
true realism in their work, or does he intend to imply that the basic ideas
of the whole school only constitute a so-called realism, that there may be a
true realism which is fundamentally sound as an aesthetic doctrine? The
answers to these questions—questions which are not mere quibbles but
which form the real crux of the problem of attempting to classifying
Bierce's work—have been attempted by several students of Bierce.
McWilliams, for example, does a neat bit of tight-rope walking and
decides that "his inspiration was romantic, but his method was almost
modern in its realism at times. . . ."[14] What he means by "modern" and
the qualifying "at times" takes most of the edge from his evaluation,
although in another context he does at least give a fair explanation of the
term "romantic" as he applies it to Bierce: "his conception of 'art' as a
world of romantic strangeness and bizarre sensation. . . ."[15] He speaks of

Bierce's "romantic stories, that is, strange stories. . . ."[16] Thus at least we know what he means when he says that Bierce is "a romantic who wrote like a realist"[17] provided that we know what he means by realist.

Whether or not the emphasis on strangeness and the bizarre which McWilliams has noted constitutes a romantic inspiration, it must be granted that Bierce shows a decided interest in the strange and unusual situation and a marked concern for the bizarre sensation. The problem which now confronts us is that of attempting to determine what his purpose is in presenting such materials and how he utilizes them in his stories. The question of purpose is foremost in any attempt at classification of Bierce's work. For example, he employs some of the materials of the "local color" school of the mining district of the West, as well as some of the effects of the "tall tales" story tellers. Yet the way in which he presents some brief moment in the life of a man who has returned to a deserted mining camp,[18] tells the story of the ghastly horse who wins a race by frightening the other horse out of its wits,[19] or relates the tale of the curried cow who excels in the art of kicking[20] is often conditioned and modified by some other purpose than that of merely telling a story. Bierce was always consciously a satirist, as well as a master of irony, and these two elements of satire and irony are usually found even in his most bizarre and strange stories. The curried cow, for example, who has lamed and maimed all the marriageable men in the surrounding territory, is finally mastered through the ingenuity and deception of a country preacher, but in the end she turns upon the woman who has "married alive"[21] that gentleman of the cloth in order to have someone to carry on the farm work, the chief duty being that of currying the cow. The "Oil of Dog" story,[22] a horrible tale in its basic elements, tells of the father and mother of a boy who engage in their respective professions of manufacturing dog oil (included as a basic ingredient of all prescriptions written by the local doctors) and disposing of unwanted babies, enterprises in which the son is a necessary assistant. A merger is effected after the boy drops one of the human corpses in the dog oil vat and the resulting product is found to be of superior quality. Consequently, the parents begin making dog oil of travellers, neighbors, and the committee of citizens who come to protest against the decimation of the local population, and they finally end up by making dog oil of each other.

Yet this story, gruesome as its details may be, is not designed primarily to startle and shock the readers' sensibilities, for after the initial shock, so well achieved by Bierce's excellent use of understatement and matter-of-fact presentation, we know that we are not supposed to accept the story as the account of something which actually could have happened.[23] There is *truth* in the story, however, for Bierce believed that mankind in general is predatory, rapacious, and susceptible to the consuming desire to pursue some personal end regardless of the cost. Consequently, the story attempts to present this idea in a striking yet unusual manner. There is a great deal more than this in the story, however, and a complete analysis of its component parts requires a thorough and comprehensive knowledge of Bierce and his work. For example, the rather strange product, oil of dog, appears to the casual reader of Bierce to be nothing but an instance of his unusual way of thinking, yet the reason for his use of such a detail becomes clear when we realize that he was an ardent dog-hater as well as a hater and exposer of quackery of all kinds. Thus a situation in which oil of dog is prescribed by all physicians provides the opportunity for Bierce to express his dislike of dogs and his disgust for what he considered as man's slavery to that animal, as well as a chance to strike out at the way in which physicians and druggists turned to profit the gullibility of the trusting public, dog oil here representing the quack element in medicine.[24]

While the foregoing discussion may not have a direct bearing on our topic, it does serve to show that some of Bierce's "strangeness" in particular tales is not so strange when we consider what he was attempting to do and when we have a greater comprehension of Bierce's work and modes of thought. He was more than just a teller of tales; he was an observer and critic of humanity. He attempted to show man as he appeared to be to him, and Bierce was not very often pleased with the spectacle. Thus, in order to determine whether his writing is or is not realism, it is not entirely out of place to examine his views on man and his natural environment, for the way that an observer perceives and interprets will determine the manner in which he records and communicates his ideas to others. In the short essay "Natura Benigna" we find a clear exposition of Bierce's views on man and nature:

> What a fine world it is, to be sure—a darling little world "so suited to the needs of man." A globe of liquid fire, straining within a shell relatively no thicker than that of an egg—a shell constantly cracking and in momentary danger of going to pieces. Three-fourths of this delectable field of human activity are covered with an element in which we cannot breathe and which swallows us by myriads. . . . Of the other one-fourth more than one-half is uninhabitable by reason of climate. On the remaining one-eighth we pass a comfortless and precarious existence in disputed occupancy with countless ministers of death and pain—pass it fighting for it, tooth and nail, a hopeless battle in which we are foredoomed to defeat. Everywhere death, terror, lamentation, and laughter more terrible than tears—the fury and despair of a race hanging on to life by the tips of its fingers! And the prize for which we strive, "to have and to hold"—what is it? A thing that is neither enjoyed while had, nor missed when lost. So worthless it is, so unsatisfying, so inadequate to purpose, so false to hope and at its best so brief, that for consolation and compensation we set up fanatic faiths of an aftertime in a better world from which no confirming whisper has ever reached across the void.[25]

If we accept this completely pessimistic picture of man and his universe as the true expression of Bierce's belief, we might well ask what purpose he had in writing. The wrong answer to this question, the one usually given by those who have insufficient acquaintance with the work of Bierce, is that he was a complete and confirmed misanthrope who derived sadistic pleasure from presenting both man in general and individual men in particular in as lurid a light as possible.[26] This, say such critics, is the reason for the realistic effects in his writing—to make man appear as vividly base and depraved as his artistic talent enabled him. Such a view is not altogether incomprehensible, for on the surface it does appear that Bierce's satire was not designed to correct evils and injustices in man and in his relationships to his fellowmen. As a matter of fact, Bierce was greatly opposed to "reform literature." In a letter to one of his pupils—he had a considerable following of aspiring writers who looked to him for advice and instructions—he said that "men holding Tolstoi's views are not properly literary men (that is to say, artists) at all. They are missionaries."[27] In another letter to the same person he indicated that he believed that reform was impossible in "a world which is the habitat of a wrongheaded and wronghearted race of irreclaimable savages."[28] Any attempt to publicize a program of reform through literature met with his hearty disapproval, for as he wrote to the poet George Sterling,

> Yes, I was sorry to whack [Jack] London, for whom, in his character as an author I have high admiration, and in that of publicist and reformer a deep contempt.[20]

This belief in the irredeemable nature of mankind in the aggregate seems to have been basic with Bierce, for he had no real sympathy for the masses, regardless of the causes of their brutalization. In another letter he stated:

> I have no love to waste on the irreclaimable mass of brutality that we know as "mankind." Compassion, yes—I am sincerely sorry that they are brutes.[30]

Thus far it would appear that the weight of the evidence is on the side of those who assign to Bierce the rôle of complete misanthrope, and there is even more evidence to show that he was more actively misogamistic and misogynistic, in spite of the claim of Walter Neale that Bierce had some forty *affaires d'amour*, which, according to Neale's standards, was a rather meagre performance in view of the countless opportunities which presented themselves to Bierce.[31] Yet if we read further in Bierce we get a truer perspective of his ideas on the possibility for the regeneration of mankind. Perhaps the clearest statement of this is found in a letter to Sterling:

> Why don't you study humanity as you do the suns—not from the viewpoint of time, but from that of eternity. The Middle

Ages were yesterday, Rome and Greece the day before. The individual man is nothing, as a single star is nothing. If the earth were to take fire you would smile to think how little it mattered to the scheme of the universe; all the wailing of the egoist mob would not affect you. Then why do you squirm at the minute catastrophe of a few thousand or million pismires crushed under the wheels of evolution. Must the new heavens and the new earth of prophecy and science come in *your* little instant of life in order that you may not go howling and damning with Jack London up and down the earth that we happen to have?[32]

We see, then, that what Bierce objected to was the anthropocentric conception of the universe of the egoistic reformers who wanted amelioration of the social, political, and economic evils for themselves here and now. It would appear that Bierce believed in gradual reformation of mankind through the slow and orderly processes of evolution and not through the efforts of rabble-rousing left wingers. Thus the writers whose guiding principle was "realism with a purpose" were anathema to Bierce and not to be considered as literary artists. Moreover, he felt that since in the total scheme of the universe man occupied such a small place, we should not be concerned about the misery of a few brutes.

With such a cosmological outlook, it is not surprising that Bierce could never concern himself with the writing of a long work dealing realistically with any of the problems of humanity in the mass, nor could he concern himself with an extended portrayal of the struggles of an individual against an inimical environment. Consequently, he believed that the novel was not a true art form and that the materials of the so-called realistic novel were not conducive to the production of either good art or an interesting story. He was particularly violent in his denunciation of the "reporter school of writing":

> The master of this school of literature is Mr. Howells. Destitute of that supreme and almost sufficient literary endownment, imagination, he does, not what he would, but what he can—takes notes with his eyes and ears and "writes them up" as does any other reporter. He can tell nothing but something like what he has seen or heard, and in his personal progress through the rectangular streets and between the trim hedges of Philistia . . . he has seen and heard nothing worth telling.[33]

The chief objection which Bierce had to the "reporters," in addition to the fact that they were Philistines, was that they lacked imagination: the materials for a story which passed through their hands came out exactly as they went in, without the significant adaptation and illumination which are the hallmark of the artist. Thus, said Bierce,

> these storywriters of the Reporter School hold that what is not interesting in life becomes interesting in letters—the acts,

> thoughts, feelings of commonplace people, the lives and loves
> of noodles, nobodies, ignoramuses and millionaires; of the
> village vulgarian, the rural maiden whose spiritual grace is not
> incompatible with the habit of falling over her own feet. . . .[34]

Apparently, Bierce believed that most of the writers of the realistic (reporter) school, having no imagination, and hence nothing interesting to write, thought that they were doing something fine and artistic if they presented a few stumbling louts (and millionaires) engaged in the uninteresting and unimaginative activity of doing nothing more than stumbling.[35] More than once he attacked Howells, who, said Bierce, was supremely interested in "propagating the Realistic faith which his poverty of imagination has compelled him to adopt. . . ."[36]

This same lack of imagination, along with the reportorial attempt to record what one hears, was responsible for what to Bierce was one of the most heinous of crimes perpetrated by the realists in the name of literature: the use of slang and the misuse of dialect. His epigram on a writer—it might be possible to identify the specific individual if one went deeply enough into the matter of the original date and circumstances of its composition—shows his disgust for those who purposely mutilated and mishandled language to achieve an effect:

> A Fabulist of wide repute
> Whose laugh was loud and wit was mute—
> Whose grammar had the grace of guess,
> And language an initial S—. . . .[37]

Opposed to dialect in principle, Bierce nevertheless thought that there were certain circumstances under which its use was permissible: "To be allowable in either verse or prose it must be the mother speech, not only of the character using it, but of the writer himself. . . ."[38] Yet the writer must exercise restraint in the use of dialect, and characters who speak in dialect must be played down and subordinated:

> If the exigencies of the narrative demand the introduction of
> an unlettered hind whose speech would naturally be "racy of
> the soil" he must needs come in and sport the tangles of his
> tongue. But he is to be got rid of as promptly as
> possible—preferably by death. The making of an entire story
> out of the lives and loves and lingoes of him and his co-
> pithecans—that is effrontery.[39]

As for Mary Wilkins Freeman, Mary Murfree, Hamlin Garland, and other such "offenders against sweetness and sense," Bierce was convinced "that it were better if instead of writing things 'racy of the soil' they would till it."[40]

Such writers not only offended by the language of their characters, but committed the consummate outrage of building their stories around low and ignorant characters. Mary Murfree was depicted by Bierce as sitting "in perpetual session on the Delectable Mountains, with a lapful of little clay-eaters and snuff-rubbers" while she "sweats great beads of blood to build the lofty crime and endow it with enough galvanic vitality to stand alone while she reaches for more mud for a new creation."[41] The chief fault with such writers, Bierce believed, was that they chose the wrong sort of characters who spoke the wrong sort of language:

> They seem to think, and indubitably do think, that the lives and adventures, the virtues and vices, joys and sorrows of the illiterate are more interesting than those prone to grammar and ablution.[42]

But an even more serious offense, Bierce believed, was the use of "the lame locution of the merely ignorant—the language of the letterless—that is not dialect. . . ."[43] Yet he would allow a small amount of this, but only enough to give *vraisemblance* in prose fiction or to add humor to verse.[44] Such language—"English of the cornfield and the slum"—he believed could be humorous and amusing if used in moderation, but it was to be avoided in serious or sentimental composition.[45]

Bierce's own practice follows his theory, for in his stories there is very little dialect or language of the ignorant and unlettered. In fact, he was so sparing in his use of dialect or regional speech that the reader is almost shocked when he comes upon such a passage as we find in "The Story of a Conscience" in which a Confederate spy uses what purports to be the dialect of the Tennessee Cumberland Mountains region.[46] The dialect does not ring true, but the shock is dissipated when the reader discovers that it is the intent of the writer to make the specious speech of the individual one of the means by which his spy status is brought to light.

In some of his newspaper work, however, Bierce employed what at first glance appears to be language of the unlettered. This is particularly true of the "Little Johnny" series which ran in the *Examiner*, yet a closer scrutiny of these articles shows that they are consonant with his critical dicta. In the first place, Bierce here was attempting to write humorous sketches, a type of writing in which unlettered language is allowable according to his principles. Moreover, Bierce relaxed his artistic standards for his newspaper work, for he had no illusions about the type of writing which the newspapers and popular magazines demanded. As he expressed his attitude to one of his correspondents, "If I have to write rot, I prefer to do it for the newspapers, which make no false pretenses and are frankly rotten. . . ."[47] However, Bierce evidently thought rather highly of his "Little Johnny" writing, for he included some of these sketches in his collected works. Consequently they deserve a somewhat closer examination, for Bierce intended these twelve volumes to contain only the work which he wished to be preserved.

This closer examination reveals that these sketches were not actually either dialect or the recorded language of the ignorant, but rather the attempt to transcribe in juvenile spelling the English language as it is used and spelled—quite often phonetically—by an American boy of the period. Yet they are more than that, for even in their crude guise they exhibit the sharp and trenchant wit which is the Bierce trademark. The "mitionary" who escaped from the cannibal king of the "sand which" islands by the ingenious expedient of offering his cork leg as the first installment of the dinner at which he was to be the *piece de resistance* and was "so thankfule to Heven for his profidenshial escape that he left the Church and has ever since led a blameless life as a pollitishian" is a fair sample from the satirist who was at work behind the disguise of the contributor, "Little Johnny."[48]

Opposed as he was to the misuse of dialect, Bierce's criterion for its use was, as we have seen, that of *vraisemblance*. He found, however, that the writers of the reportorial school exceeded these demands and that they transgressed further by attempting to erect synthetic authentication for their dialogue.

> Are we given dialogue? It is not enough to report what was said, but the record must be authenticated by enumeration of the inanimate objects—commonly articles of furniture—which were privileged to be present at the conversation. And each dialogian must make certain and uncertain movements of the limbs or eyes before and after saying his say. All this in such prodigal excess of the slender allusions required, when required at all, for *vraisemblance* as abundantly to prove its insertion for its own sake.[49]

Here again, Bierce usually followed his own theory in practice, for he not only avoided the use of dialect in his stories, but he also kept dialogue itself at a minimum. An examination of his stories shows that in most of them very few words are spoken by the characters, particularly by the main characters. In "The Man and the Snake," for example, not a word is spoken until the very end of the story. The "man" never speaks a word except for a few words in his own mind.[50] In "Chickamauga" not a word is uttered, for the only true character in the story is a deaf mute child.[51] While these are extreme cases, nevertheless they show Bierce's tendency to keep dialogue at a minimum. Apparently his concept of the short story—and for him there could be no other kind—was that it should be mainly the account of an individual reacting psychologically to a situation, not a record of several individuals whose chief reaction to anything and everything is a spontaneous and excessive overflow of indigenous vocalization.

From what we have already noticed both in Bierce's theory and in his practice, it is fairly obvious that he had a definite conception of what literature should be. Likewise, we can discover from his own work that apparently his writing was conditioned by the fundamental belief that the writer is nothing if he is not an artist:

> Literature . . . is an art;—it is not a form of benevolence. It
> has nothing to do with "reform," and when used as a means of
> reform suffers accordingly and justly.[52]

Here again we see the emphasis which Bierce placed on the artistic basis
of writing, along with his opposition to the reform writers which we have
previously noted. It is necessary, however, that we attempt to determine
what Bierce considered to be the function of the artist and the method of
carrying out this function.

The primary requirement of an artist, according to Bierce, is that he
produce something interesting, and it was this very concern with "the
interesting" which led Bierce to choose unusual characters and situations: "The exceptional—even 'abnormal'—person seems to me the more
interesting. . . ."[53]

This concern for the exceptional and abnormal may be one of the
contributing causes for his belief that a true work of literary art, whether
poetry or prose, must be compressed, compact, and of narrow scope.
Consequently, his interest lay not in group experience, but in the experience of the individual, and even that for only a short period of time.
As Bertha Pope expressed it, "His unit of time is the minute, not the
month."[54] Quite often this minute is the last moment of life for the individual in the story, as for example in "An Occurrence at Owl Creek
Bridge,"[55] "One of the Missing,"[56] "The Death of Halpin Frayser,"[57]—a
"moment" in which a great deal seems to take place. This concern with
death, often death under bizarre circumstances, has led some critics of
Bierce to speak of his morbid interest in the macabre, but such criticism is
unjustifiable when we remember that of all experiences which men
undergo in life, only two are common to all men—that moment when
they enter life and that instant when they depart from it. Consequently,
Bierce's representation of man's struggle against death, presented in
realistic terms, could very easily arise from an impulse other than that of
wanting to shock the reader's sensibilities with horrible details. The fact
that many people refuse to think about death, even death in a nonviolent
form, may be partly responsible for this type of misreading of Bierce.
George Sterling, who knew Bierce as well perhaps as anyone knew him
and whose subsequent suicide proved that death had no great terrors for
him, sums up this aspect of Bierce's work fairly well:

> There was a ray [in Bierce's writing technique] that touched
> man only in his hour of pain, of terror, of death—a ray that
> revealed what we hesitate to behold and which leaves the
> weaker beholders ungrateful for the vision accorded.[58]

Thus it is the fact alone that Bierce so often dealt with the moment of suffering, terror, and death, and not his lack of artistic taste, that has turned
those readers who always want something cheerful against him. That he

was a pessimist as far as contemporary humanity was concerned almost goes without saying, but his choice of the moment of suffering, terror, and death in the experience of the characters in his stories does not arise, as some would claim, from any diabolical strain of misanthropy in his nature which danced in unholy glee when humanity was placed on the rack. Yet he does display some of the clinician's interest in observing the reaction of individual men under momentary stresses and in bizarre situations and in recording these reactions in a restrained, straightforward manner. Samuel Loveman, one of the many young writers whom Bierce attempted to sponsor, points out rather clearly this characteristic of Bierce's writing:

> In Bierce, the evocation of horror becomes for the first time, not so much the prescription or perversion of Poe or Maupassant, but an atmosphere definite and uncannily precise. Words so simple that one would be prone to ascribe them to the limitations of a literary hack take on an unholy terror. . . .[59]

Pattee also has called attention to Bierce's reserve and directness,[60] but he has little else either of truth or of value in his short paragraph on Bierce.[61] In this same context Pattee charges Bierce with lack of sincerity, a charge which anyone who knew Bierce or his work would be quick to refute. He was so sincere, in fact, and so much a perfectionist that he was intolerant of any sham and deception among his fellow artists, even to the point of "merciless cruelty," as Sterling put it.[62] Sterling is not always reliable as a commentator on Bierce, for we have evidence that he and Bierce were constantly quarreling, but we have Bierce's own statement as corroboration of this point. In a letter to Sterling he states:

> All my life I have been hated and slandered by all manner of persons except good and intelligent ones; . . . I knew in the beginning what I had to expect. . . . And the same malevolence that has surrounded my life will surround my memory if I am remembered. Just run over in your mind the names of men who have told the truth about their unworthy fellows and about human nature "as it was given them to see it." They are the bogie-men of history. None of them has escaped vilification. Can poor little I hope for anything better?[63]

That Bierce conceived of his mission as that of telling the truth about mankind and human nature as it was given him to see it is evident; that he saw also that he would be misunderstood, slandered, and hated is equally manifest. To discover how well his prophecy has been fulfilled it is only necessary to read the work of his several biographers, none of whom, with the exception of Neale, seems to have any other guiding purpose than that of belittling or slandering Bierce and his work or, as in the case of Danziger,[64] to use Bierce as an instrument for his own self-inflation—a kind of plum for a Jack Horner performance.

Bierce's realism, if we can call it that, has its origin in his artistic purpose of presenting man and human nature as they appear to him, to tell the truth about what he has observed. His quarrel with the "so-called realists" stems largely from their break with literary tradition and their demand for a distinctive regional literature—literature of America, the West, the South, or whatever region is to be exploited in letters. Bierce claimed that there was no place for "geography" in literature,[65] and he spoke derisively of Hamlin Garland's "cornfed enthusiasm" with which he hailed the dawn of a new era of literature dominated by Western man.[66] As Bierce expressed it:

> It is all very fine to be a child o' natur' with a home in the settin' sun, but when the child o' natur' with a knack at scribbing pays rent to Phoebus by renouncing the incomparable advantage of strict subjection to literary law he pays too dearly.[67]

This one sentence contains the germ of almost all of Bierce's literary creed, for here he attacks the dialect writers, the "geography" school, and those who disregard the tradition of literary law, the immutable laws of the art which have come down through Aristotle, Longinus, and other critics and producers of the world's literature. Bierce's reverence for the past is in a way an argument against those who, supported by a misuse of the doctrine of evolution, maintain that the new is always better than the old and that the past has nothing of value to offer to the present and to the future. In this regard, Bierce states his belief quite succinctly in this bit of verse:

> The years go on, the old comes back
>   To mock the new—beneath the sun
>   Is nothing new; ideas run
> Recurrent in an endless track.[68]

Bierce would not object to anyone calling attention to the fact that in this quatrain he was "running in the track" of Tennyson. If good tracks have been laid in the past, why not utilize them now? There is no virtue in laying a new track in a desert merely because it is a new track. Bierce believed that there was a right way of doing things, a way determined by all the wisdom and experience of the past. In this respect he might be called a classicist, for he believed very much as did Dr. Johnson that there must be certain fixed principles which are immutable and not to be tampered with. His little volume *Write It Right* is in this very vein.[69] This booklet is in the main a list of "do's" and "don't's" for the writer and contains strictures against grammatical and semantical departures from traditional usage.

Bierce's strict adherence to what he considered the laws of literature, laws which are more comparable to aristocratic than to democratic principles, along with his sense of artistic integrity, would allow him to make no compromise for himself nor to condone those infractions of the laws in other writers. Most of his attacks, both in prose and in verse, against his contemporary writers were interpreted as mere malicious spitefulness of a sadistic misanthrope or, as Pattee says, of a journalist whom "adverse criticism of his work turned . . . into something like a literary anarchist who criticized with bitterness all things established."[70] Actually, it appears that Bierce was only living up to his principles and attempting to keep pure the literary stream. It probably cost him a considerable amount of money to remain true to his literary ideals, for he refused to write the type of story demanded by the popular magazines even when there was no sale for the kind of short story he was writing. To one editor, a Mr. Davis connected with the *Metropolitan Magazine*, who wanted Bierce to supply some stories, he replied:

> I know how to write a story for magazine readers for whom literature is too good, but I will not do so so long as stealing is more honorable and interesting.[71]

This same uncompromising spirit is evident in his letter to Sterling, written in 1903, in which he said, "Publishers want nothing of me but novels—and I'll die first."[72]

True to his faith, Bierce never wrote a novel, a fact which has led to the rather prevalent belief that he was not capable of writing one.[73] Psychologically speaking, this may be true, for Bierce did not believe that the novel was a true literary form and, consequently, he could not bring himself to prostitute his art by making such an attempt; but to say that such a careful and conscious craftsman as Bierce could not write a novel—if not an excellent one, at least as good as those turned out by his scribbling contemporaries—is begging the question. His nearest approach to the novel is *The Monk and the Hangman's Daughter*, a well written and fairly well received long short story or novelette, but as there is considerable dispute as to just how large a part Bierce had in the adaptation and revision of this German story which Danziger translated into English, no conclusions as to artistic technique drawn from the examination of this story are justifiable.

There are several reasons why Bierce was opposed to the novel, but perhaps the most significant one was his belief that the novel is too diffuse: it covers too much time, brings in too many characters, and requires too much exposition and explanation. Danziger quotes a letter from Bierce which bears this out:

> All "explanation" is unspeakably tedious and is to be cut as short as possible. Far better to have nothing to explain—to *show* everything that occurs, in the very act of occurring.[74]

This statement points up what might be called Bierce's realistic technique: to show what happens in the act of happening, with enough selected details to give a certain *vraisemblance*. Since multiplicity of detail destroys the illusion, Bierce objected strenuously to the attempts of the "realist" to show everything in minute detail. "It is of the nature of realism," said Bierce, "never to stop till it gets to the bottom."[75] For him, art was not a composite of accumulated details and minutiae, a fact which is clearly brought out in the following statement:

> Where is the sense of all these devices for producing an "illu-sion." Illusion, indeed! When you look at art do you wish to persuade yourself that it is only Nature?[76]

It is evident, then, that Bierce believed that art is something more than a mere realistic presentation of natural details, for "only in its non-essentials is art a true copy of nature."[77] Here again we are reminded of the neo-classical attitude toward art of Dr. Johnson.

From this examination of Bierce's critical statements, from a brief look at some of his stories as a means of checking the application of his theories, and from comments by his contemporaries and by literary critics, we are led to what should be the culmination of our study, the attempt to answer the question, what is Bierce—realist, romanticist, or classicist? The answer that I propose is that there was only one kind of "ist" that he desired and attempted to be: *artist*. If the requirements of his art demanded realistic techniques, he employed them; if his interest pointed, as it often did, in the direction of the bizarre and the unusual, he was not adverse to the use of the romantic point of view. Above all, however, and at all times, he attempted to adhere to the "immutable laws of literature" with the catholic rigidity of the classicist, even though he attempted just as assiduously to interpret life realistically as it was given him to see it.

Let us come, then, full circle to our point of departure, Bierce's own definition of realism as "the art of depicting nature as it is seen by toads." Perhaps to his contemporaries and to those who will make the final evaluation of his work, Bierce, too, is a toad. But does not the toad have a long classical tradition and a jewel in his head as well as an over-abundance of venom in his mouth? Or was Bierce's jewel only a shell frag-ment, a corroding memento of his Civil War experiences, which made him what he was, as his brother Albert claimed, "Bitter Bierce"?

Notes

1. Bierce, at the end of his writing career, attempted to bring together what he con-sidered the best and most representative examples of his work in all fields. A great deal of this had appeared in newspapers and periodicals. Some of his writing he considered too insignifi-cant to be included in his "works," while a fair proportion of what he did include was rewrit-ten for the collection. Some of his early journalistic work is extremely hard to come by, a situation due in no small degree to the destruction of both newspaper and periodical files in San Francisco during the earthquake and fire.

2. Ambrose Bierce, *The Collected Works of Ambrose Bierce* (New York and

Washington: The Neale Publishing Company, 1909–12), *The Devil's Dictionary*, VII, 276.

   3. *Ibid.*, pp. 276–277.

   4. *Works*, II, *In the Midst of Life*, "The Man and the Snake," 311–323.

   5. *Works*, III, *Can Such Things Be?* "A Tough Tissue," 106–120.

   6. *Works*, II, *In the Midst of Life*, "One of the Missing," 71–92.

   7. *Works*, VII, *The Devil's Dictionary*, 17.

   8. *Works*, X, *The Opinionator*, "The Short Story," 247.

   9. *Ibid.*, p. 243.

  10. *Ibid.*, p. 247.

  11. Works, II, *In the Midst of Life*, "The Suitable Surroundings," 355.

  12. *Works*, X, *The Opinionator*, "The Short Story," 239.

  13. *Ibid.*, p. 248.

  14. Carey McWilliams, *Ambrose Bierce: A Biography* (New York: A. and C. Boni, 1929), p. 235.

  15. *Ibid.*, p. 307.

  16. *Ibid.*

  17. *Ibid.*, p. 235.

  18. *Works*, II, *In the Midst of Life*, "A Holy Terror," 324–349.

  19. *Works*, VIII, *Negligible Tales, On with the Dance, Epigrams*, "The Race at Left Bower," 104–109.

  20. *Ibid.*, "Curried Cow," pp. 76–88.

  21. The number of times and the manner in which Bierce used this term seem to indicate that it was actually equivalent to "buried alive" and to point out his basically misogamistic nature.

  22. *Works*, VIII, *Negligible Tales*, etc., "Oil of Dog," 163–70.

  23. The two opening sentences of this tale serve as an excellent example of the realistic effect Bierce could achieve by understatement: "My name is Boffer Bings. I was born of honest parents in one of the humbler walks of life, my father being a manufacturer of dog oil and my mother having a small studio in the shadow of the village church, where she disposed of unwelcome babes."

  24. If is of interest to note here that Bierce uses "oil of dog" in another instance to illustrate the quackery of religion. In a sketch called "The Broom of the Temple" he presents a situation in which several individuals are considering what can be done to avert a national catastrophe: "The advice of the fourth was that the column of the capitol be rubbed with oil of dog" (*Works*, VI, *Fantastic Fables*, 175).

  25. *Works*, XI, *Antepenultima*, "Natura Benigna," 148–149. As an epitome of man's relationship to an inimical natural environment, this excerpt is a close approach to the naturalism of such writers as Stephen Crane. Indeed, the following passage from Crane's "The Blue Hotel" appears to have been derived from the Bierce passage quoted above: "One viewed the existence of man then as a marvel, and conceded a glamor of wonder to these lice which were caused to cling to a whirling, fire-smote, ice-locked, disease-stricken, space-lost bulb" (*The Red Badge of Courage and Other Writings* [Boston: Houghton Mifflin Company, 1960], p. 273).

  26. See, for example, Ambrose Bierce, *The Collected Writings of Ambrose Bierce* (New York: The Citiadel Press, 1946), Introduction by Clifton Fadiman, *passim*.

  27. Bertha Clark Pope, *The Letters of Ambrose Bierce, with a Memoir by George Sterling* (San Francisco: The Book Club of California, 1922), p. 5.

  28. *Ibid.*, p. 34.

29. *Ibid.*, p. 113.

30. *Ibid.*, p. 4.

31. Walter Neale, *Life of Ambrose Bierce* (New York: W. Neale, 1929), p. 129.

32. Pope, *op. cit.*, pp. 149–150.

33. *Works*, X, *The Opinionator*, "The Short Story," 240.

34. *Ibid.*, p. 242.

35. Neale, *op. cit.*, pp. 236–237. Neale says, "Louts, their antics, their mental (?) [*sic*] processes, their immoral code, disgusted him [Bierce] as much when he encountered them in books as they did when he shudderingly passed them in the street. Kitty the housemaid was all right in his room, making his bed, . . . but she had no place in his drawing room—nor in his literature."

36. *Works*, X, *The Opinionator*, "On Literary Criticism," 30.

37. *Works*, VI, *The Monk and the Hangman's Daughter* [and] *Fantastic Fables*, "A Pair of Opposites," 378.

38. *Works*, XI, *Antepenultima*, "Writers of Dialect," 173.

39. *Ibid.*, p. 174.

40. *Ibid.*

41. *Ibid.*, p. 176.

42. *Ibid.*, p. 177.

43. *Ibid.*, p. 178.

44. *Ibid.*

45. *Ibid.*, p. 181.

46. *Works*, II, *In the Midst of Life*, "The Story of a Conscience," 165–177.

47. *Letters*, p. 102.

48. *Works*, XII, *In Motley*. The section called "The King of Beasts" contains a number of "Little Johnny" articles.

49. *Works*, X, *The Opinionator*, "The Short Story," 243.

50. *Works*, II, *In the Midst of Life*, "The Man and the Snake," 311–323.

51. *Ibid.*, "Chickamauga," pp. 46–47.

52. *Letters*, p. 4.

53. *Ibid.*, p. 191.

54. *Ibid.*, Introduction, p. xxvi.

55. *Works*, II, *In the Midst of Life*, 27–45.

56. *Ibid.*, pp. 71–92.

57. *Works*, III, *Can Such Things Be?*, 13–43.

58. Ambrose Bierce, *In the Midst of Life* (New York: The Modern Library, 1927), Introduction by George Sterling, p. i. Just two weeks after completing this introduction, Sterling committed suicide.

59. Samuel Loveman, *Twenty-one Letters of Ambrose Bierce* (Cleveland: George Kirk, 1922), p. 4.

60. Fred L. Pattee, *A History of American Literature Since 1870* (New York: The Century Company, 1917), p. 379.

61. It is rather astonishing that he gave any space at all to Bierce, for as his letter to Walter Neale indicates, he was unsure as to Bierce's position as a writer and was somewhat doubtful about including him in his literary history. Pattee admits that he has not even seen, much less read, the *Collected Works* of Bierce which Neale published. The main purpose of this letter was to discover how the *Works* were selling so that Pattee could use this as a

criterion of Bierce's importance and worth as a writer—a writer worthy of being included in Pattee's book. Neale was so outraged by such a display of critical quackery that he did not even answer the letter; he merely waited until he brought out his own biography of Bierce and photographically reproduced the letter in his book.

62. Bierce, *In the Midst of Life*, Introduction by George Sterling, p. xiv.

63. *Letters*, pp. 74–75.

64. Adolphe de Castro, *Portrait of Ambrose Bierce* (New York: The Century Company, 1929). Danziger, a poseur with delusions of grandeur, changed his name to de Castro. His life of Bierce is a strange mélange of praise, contempt, and expression of jealousy, inspired to a certain extent by their quarrel as to which of them really wrote *The Monk and the Hangman's Daughter*.

65. *Works*, X, *The Opinionator*, "On Literary Criticism," 44.

66. *Ibid.*, p. 41.

67. *Ibid.*, pp. 42–43.

68. *Works*, V, *Black Beetles in Amber*, "To E. S. Salomon," 63.

69. Ambrose Bierce, *Write It Right* (New York and Washington: The Neale Publishing Company, 1909).

70. Pattee, *op. cit.*, p. 380.

71. *Letters*, p. 102.

72. *Ibid.*, p. 74.

73. Apparently, Pattee has Bierce confused with some other writer, for in his *A History of American Literature Since 1870*, p. 380, he says, "A few of his novels may be studied with profit as models of their kind. . . ."

74. Ambrose Bierce, *The Monk and the Hangman's Daughter* [and] *Fantastic Fables* (New York: Albert and Charles Boni, 1926), prefatory statement by Adolph de Castro [Gustav Adolf Danziger].

75. *Works*, X, *The Opinionator*, "Stage Illusion," 54.

76. *Ibid.*, p. 51.

77. *Ibid.*, p. 52.

Ambrose Bierce and the American Civil War

Daniel Aaron*

Abatiss, n. Embarrassing circumstances placed outside a fort in order to augment the coy reluctance of the enemy.

Army, n. A class of non-producers who defend the nation by devouring everything likely to tempt an enemy to invade.

Bayonet, n. An instrument for pricking the bubble of a nation's conceit.

Bomb, or Bomb-Shell, n. A besieger's argument in favor of capitulation, skillfully adapted to the understanding of women and children.

Foe, n. A person instigated by his wicked nature to deny one's merits or exhibit superior merits of his own.

Freedman, n. A person whose manacles have sunk so deeply into the flesh that they are no longer visible.

Ambrose Bierce,
The Enlarged Devil's Dictionary

Most northern writers who lived through the years of the American Civil War hated slavery, despised southern traitors, and welcomed the integrated nation destined to emerge after the federal victory, but their self-appointed roles as bards and prophets removed them too effectually from theaters of conflict. For reasons of age (many were in their thirties), temperament, health, family responsibilities, they disqualified themselves from military service and supported the Great Cause as soldiers of the pen.

The effusions of these warriors in mufti like Richard Henry Stoddard, Thomas Bailey Aldrich, George Henry Boker, and Edmund Clarence Stedman are forgotten with good reason. Although talented and in many ways sympathetic men, their elegies, eulogies, satires, and

*Reprinted by permission of the Department of English and American Literature and Language, Harvard University, from *Uses of Literature*, Monroe Engel, ed., Cambridge, Mass.: Harvard Univ. Press Copyright © 1973 by the President and Fellows of Harvard College (Harvard English Studies, 4). The essay has also appeared as a chapter in Daniel Aaron's *The Unwritten War. American Writers and the Civil War* (Knopf, 1973), reprinted by permission of the author.

ballads on the theme of war were largely rhymed propaganda ground out for the home front. A few of them made some effort to see the real war. Bayard Taylor, traveler, lecturer, and poet, visited some military camps before accepting a diplomatic post in Russia. Stedman wrote a vividly "literary" account of the Bull Run disaster for the *New York World* and reported the Union defeat at Ball's Bluff—his last glimpse of real battle.[1] Neither they nor the vehemently patriotic civilian writers broke through the smoke of ideology to behold the war's immensity and horror.

For literary men who took small interest in politics, the War was an annoying interruption,[2] and it was task enough to water the gardens of the muses during the four-year drought. "These war times are hard on authors," Bayard Taylor complained: "the sword of Mars chops in two the strings of Apollo's lyre."[3] It was also hard not to be caught up in the issues of the war or to ignore its presumed consequences. Whatever their political and aesthetic differences, the literary publicists belonged to the elect of "acute large-active minds" who saw in the war a chance to establish "a centralization of thoughts, feelings, and views on national subjects." They were the conscious and unconscious adjuncts of these scientists, scholars, clergymen, political theorists, journalists, and politicians bent upon converting "a loose aggregate of sovereign or semi-sovereign states" into "a single central object of love and devotion."[4]

The dream of a nation directed by an ideal aristocracy gave them an elevated view of the war and encouraged them not only to write poetic exhortations but also to campaign on the home front against Copperheads, to write and disseminate "correct" opinion to the nation's press, to address meetings and assemblies.[5] Toward the southern enemy they presented a stern collective face. None would have disagreed with Charles Eliot Norton's description of enemy leaders as "men in whom passions have usurped the place of reason, and whose understanding has been perverted, and well nigh, in moral matters, extinguished by long training in the seclusion of barbarism, and long use in the arts of self-deception."[6] All looked upon slavery as the ugly stigma of that barbarism, and while differing in their notions of the Negro and his capacities, they were ready to prolong the war if necessary to assure slavery's extinction. All, after first misgivings about the "ignorant, ungainly, silly, Western Hoosier,"[7] Abraham Lincoln, eventually backed him and in the end exalted him. He figured in their poems and orations as a benign distillation of the common man, but it is hard to imagine them any more at ease with Uncle Abe than with the common soldiers they sincerely but distantly applauded.

When Walt Whitman made his famous prediction that the real Civil War would never get into "the books," he was thinking, perhaps, of these genteel writers whose "perpetual, pistareen, pastepot work" omitted the terrors of the field and camp. A few writers, however (probably unknown to him) had a first-hand acquaintance with mass killing and organized atrocity and did put the "real War" into their books—the war that choked several millions with blood. One of them was Ambrose Bierce.

II

Ambrose Bierce not only choked on the blood of the Civil War. He practically drowned in it. For the remainder of his life it bubbled in his imagination and stained his prose.

Toward Grant, the "Butcher," in some of whose campaigns he had taken a microscopic part and whom he had seen shedding "the blood of the grape and grain abundantly" with his staff during the battle of Missionary Ridge,[8] Bierce maintained a reserved respect. He knew from experience, as Grant's toadies did not, that the General blundered on occasion. Nonetheless, in 1886 he memorialized the "admirable soldier" as a hard and cruel agent for a hard and cruel God.[9] Presumptuous civilians might try to invest the Civil War with divine intentions, to see "what the prophets say they saw." Too "simply wise" to dispute chance or fate, Grant submitted without any inward struggle to duty:

> The cannon syllabled his name;
> His shadow shifted o'er the land,
> Portentous, as at his demand
> Successive bastions sprang to flame!
>
> He flared the continent with fire,
> The rivers ran in lines of light!
> Thy will be done on earth—if right
> Or wrong he cared not to inquire.
>
> His was the heavy hand, and his
> The service of the despot blade;
> His the soft answer that allayed
> War's giant animosities.[10]

The eighteen-year-old Ambrose Bierce from northern Indiana, the second in his county to enlist after Lincoln's call to arms, was not the author Ambrose Bierce who wrote these lines. "When I ask myself what has become of Ambrose Bierce the youth, who fought at Chickamauga," he told a friend, "I am bound to answer that he is dead. Some little of him survives in my memory, but many of him are absolutely dead and gone."[11] The "deceased" Bierce was a country boy with a patchy education. Possibly some of the bookishness of his father, an ineffectual farmer, rubbed off on the son. A two-year apprenticeship as a printer's devil and several terms in a Kentucky military school may also have disciplined his mind. But when he was mustered into the Ninth Regiment of the Indiana Volunteers, nobody expected very much from him. His friends and neighbors knew him only as a solitary, undemonstrative boy who preferred books to games and who showed few signs of ambition or ability.

"At one time in my green and salad days," he later recalled, "I was sufficiently zealous for Freedom to be engaged in a four years' battle for its promotion. There were other issues, but they did not count much for me."[12] That was Bierce's way of saying he had once had illusions. The

Bierce clan was antislavery, and none more so than Lucius Verus Bierce, Ambrose's favorite uncle and the only member of the family of any public distinction. It was this same General Bierce of Akron who furnished his friend John Brown with supplies and weapons for Brown's Kansas business.[13] On the evening of Brown's execution, Lucius Bierce addressed a mass meeting in which he equated the martyr's alleged fanaticism, folly, madness, and wickedness with virtue, divine wisdom, obedience to God, and piety. John Brown, he predicted, would "rise up before the world with his calm, marble features, more terrible in death, and defeat, than in life and victory."[14] Whether or not his nephew read the oration, he applauded its sentiments. Eventually an older and disenchanted Bierce conjured up some retributive ghosts of his own.

III

Bierce's biographers agree the war was the central experience of his life to which he constantly returned, a time of bale and bliss, and an ordeal that brought some coherence to the hiterto random pattern of his youth. Of all the literary combatants of the Civil War, none saw more action or steeped himself so completely in the essence of battle.[15] For no other writer did it remain such an obsessive presence. "To this day," he wrote in 1887, "I cannot look over a landscape without noting the advantages of a ground for attack or defense . . . I never hear a rifle-shot without a thrill in my veins. I never catch the peculiar odor of gunpowder without having visions of the dead and dying."[16] The sight of Richmond in 1912 dejected him as it had Henry James when the author of *The American Scene* visited the city several years before. "True, the history is some fifty years old, but it is always with me when I am there, making solemn eyes at me."[17] There is no reason to question his quiet assertion that prefaces a recollection of Chickamauga, the graveyard of his idealistic youth: "I had served at the front from the beginning of the trouble, and had seen enough war to give me a fair understanding of it."[18]

Outside a few letters and diary notes, very little remains of Bierce's on-the-spot recording of the war years. His account of them is largely restrospective, often glazed with nostalgia and set down after he had trained himself to write. Yet thanks to an almost uncanny visual sense cultivated by his wartime duties as topographical engineer, he managed to fix in his mind the terrain he had traversed and to map his stories and sketches so that the reader can visualize every copse or ravine or stream he mentions. He also absorbed the business of war, the details of the soldier's trade conspicuously missing from the war chronicles of those who picked up their information second-hand. This "solidity of specification," as Henry James might say, gave his war fiction the "illusion of reality."

The word *illusion* is used advisedly here, because Bierce's tales of war are not in the least realistic; they are, as he doubtless intended them to be, incredible events occurring in credible surroundings. Triggered like traps, they abound in coincidences and are as contemptuous of the probable as any of Poe's most bizarre experiments. Bierce's soldiers move in a trance through a prefigured universe. Father and son, brother and brother, husband and wife, child and servant, separated by chance or conviction, murderously collide in accidental encounters. The playthings of some power, they follow a course "decreed from the beginning of time."[19] Ill-matched against the outside forces assailing them, they are also victimized by atavistic ones. Bierce's uncomplicated men-at-arms, suddenly commandeered by compulsive fear or wounded by shame, destroy themselves.

Yet each of Bierce's preposterous tales is framed in fact and touched with what Poe called "the potent magic of verisimilitude." Transitions from reality to sur-reality seem believable not only because the Civil War was filled with romantic and implausible episodes, but also because of the writer's intense scrutiny of war itself. The issues of the war no longer concerned him by the time he came to write his soldier stories. They had practically disappeared in the wake of history. But the physical and psychological consequences of constant exposure to suffering and death, the way men behaved in the stress of battle—these matters powerfully worked his imagination, for the war was only meaningful to Bierce as a personal experience. If war in general became his parable of pitifully accoutered man attacked by heavily armored natural forces, the Civil War dramatized his private obsessions.

IV

Like John W. DeForest, Bierce smuggled personal experiences into his fiction (the tales are usually laid in localities he had fought over), but he left no personal records so complete as De Forest's A Volunteer's Adventures. Bits of Autobiography, composed some time after the events described, touches only a few of the high points in Bierce's career as a soldier. All the same, it complements the war fiction and hints of his fiery initiation.

From the moment he enlisted, Bierce conducted himself like the trusty and competent soldiers who figure in his stories. The sketches are not self-celebrations, however, and tell little of his personal exploits; they are the emotion-tinted memories of an untranquil man. He looks back to "the autumn of that 'most immemorial year,' the 1861st of our Lord, and of our Heroic Age" when his regiment from the Indiana lowlands encamped in the Great Mountain country of West Virginia. During the first months of his " 'prentice days of warfare," he and his friends in the "Delectable Mountains" assumed the responsibility of personally subduing the rebel fiends. They felt omnipotent and free, in charge of their respective destinies. The proximity of the enemy added just the necessary "spice of danger." Only a few incongruities marred the idyll: a soldier named Abbot killed by "a nearly spent cannon shot" on which his name was stamped (an incident scarcely less improbable than one of Bierce's horrendous fictional coincidences) and the discovery of "some things—lying by the way side" whose "yellow-clay faces" would soon be made anonymous by rooting swine.[20]

Subsequent campaigns in the West seasoned the green recruit, and unremitting encounters with death raised first doubts in his mind about the propriety of dying "for a cause which may be right and may be wrong."[21] Bierce was attached to the Army of the Ohio under General Buell and took part in the dash from Nashville to assist Grant's mauled divisions at Pittsburg Landing. Shiloh, his first major battle, began with a sequence of exhilarating bugle calls, reached a climax in a tempest of hissing lead and "spouting fires" and ended in "desolation" and "awful silence." War was no longer new to him, but his surcharged recollection of confusion, of troops demented by shell-shock, of the night march when he and his men, soaked to the skin, stumbled in darkness over the bodies of the dead and near dead, testify to the sustained intensity of the impact: .

> Knapsacks, canteens, haversacks distended with soaken [sic] and swollen biscuits, gaping to disgorge, blankets beaten into the soil by the rain, rifles with bent barrels or splintered stocks, waist-belts, hats and the omnipresent sardine-box—all the wretched debris of the battle still littered the spongy earth as far as one could see, in every direction. Dead horses were everywhere; a few disabled caissons, or limbers, reclining on one elbow, as it were; ammunition wagons standing disconsolate behind four or six sprawling mules. Men? There were men enough; all dead, apparently, except one, who lay near where I had halted my platoon to await the slower movement of the line—a Federal sergeant, variously hurt, who had been a fine giant in his time. He lay face upward, taking in his breath in convulsive, rattling snorts, and blowing it out in sputters of froth which crawled creamily down his cheeks, piling itself alongside his neck and ears. A bullet had clipped a groove in his skull, above the temple; from this the brain protruded in bosses, dropping off in flakes and streams. I had not previously known one could get on, even in this unsatisfactory fashion, with so little brain. One of my men, whom I knew for a womanish fellow, asked if he should put his bayonett through him. Inexpressibly shocked by the cold-blooded proposal, I told him I thought not; it was unusual, and too many were looking.[22]

When Bierce wrote "What I Saw at Shiloh," he was already practicing to disguise the violence of his revulsion from organized killing by irony, understatement, and bravado. He succeeded no better than Hemingway. Like Sergeant Byring in "A Tough Tussle," the repugnance he felt toward the mangled dead was at once physical and spiritual, and his bitter joking about spilled guts and brains, his facetiousness in the presence of corrupted flesh, was his response "to his unusually acute sensibilities—his keen sense of the beautiful, which these hideous things outraged." Neither Bierce nor his sergeant found any dignity in death. "[It] was a thing to be hated. It was not picturesque, it had no tender and solemn side—a dismal thing, hideous in all its manifestations and suggestions."[23] The half-buried corpses at Shiloh angered him: "Their clothing was half burnt away—their hair and beard entirely; the rain had come too late to save their nails. Some were swollen to double girth; others shriveled to manikins. According to degree of exposure, their faces were bloated and black or yellow and shrunken. The contraction of muscles which had given them claws for hands had cursed each countenance with a hideous grin." And at the conclusion of this disgusting tableau, he burst out: "Faugh! I cannot catalogue the charms of these gallant gentlemen who had got what they enlisted for."[24]

The sight of men tumbling over like tenpins as the lead thudded against flesh, the piling up of bodies in "a very pretty line of dead," the postures of soldiers flattened out beneath "showers of shrapnel darting divergent from the unassailable sky," parodied the fracas between men and nature. Their fate and his was to wait "meekly to be blown out of life by level gusts of grape—to clench our teeth and shrink helpless before big shot pushing noisily through the consenting air." Neither Blue nor Gray was made to stand up to this kind of chastisement. In Bierce's Civil War, lead always scores "its old-time victory over steel," and the heroic invariably breaks "its great heart against the commonplace."[25]

At Chickamauga, the setting of one of his most macabre and powerful tales, he observed a fragment of the fierce, seesaw battle as a staff officer in General W. B. Hazen's command.[26] And at Pickett's Mill, too minor a disaster to find a place in Sherman's memoirs but important enough to be "related by the enemy," he stored up additional facts about the art of war. Here ignorant armies clashed by day. The Indiana veterans, unaware of what was going on in front of or behind them, fought alongside regiments of strangers. Their commander—"aggressive, arrogant, tyrannical, honorable, truthful, courageous"—had not flinched at the criminal order that would sacrifice his feeble brigade. His valorous troops, though virtually cut to pieces, pushed to the "dead-line," the stretch of "clear space—neutral ground, devoid of dead" beyond which men vulnerable to bullets could not pass. Veterans of this caliber and experience had by now learned almost instinctively to divine the hopeless and to retire in good order.[27]

Bierce survived a number of other engagements, only some of which he wrote about. "There are many battles in a war," he remarked, "and many incidents in battle: one does not recollect everything." The war itself, however, had pressed so deeply into his consciousness that he did not need to recollect it. Again and again he came back to it, sometimes to the accompaniment of rhetorical music. "Is it not strange," he asked, "that the phantoms of a blood-stained period have so airy a grace and look with so tender eyes?—that I recall with difficulty the danger and death and horrors of the time, and without effort all that was gracious and picturesque?" One suspects that it was not all that difficult for him to recall the terrors so meticulously and relentlessly recorded in his prose. What he desperately yearned for were his adventurous youth and his lost illusions. ("Ah, Youth, there is no such wizard as thou! Give me but one touch of thine artist hand upon the dull canvas of the Present; gild for but one moment the drear and somber scenes of today, and I will willingly surrender an other life than the one that I should have thrown away at Shiloh.") But he could not reproduce the ecstasy as authentically as the pain.[28]

V

The war left Ambrose Bierce stranded in a civilian world. He ungraciously adjusted to it, but between his retirement from the army and his disappearance into Mexico in 1913, he remained a prickly alien. The unformed (and he would have said "misinformed") youth emerged after four years of fighting as one of those "hardened and impenitent man-killers to whom death in its awfulest forms is a fact familiar to their every-day observation; who sleep on hills trembling with the thunder of great guns, dine in the midst of streaming missiles, and play cards among the dead faces of their dearest friends."[29] In short, he was a veteran, and no civilian who had not undergone this terrific initiation could claim membership in Bierce's mystic company.

The civilian—untested, insulated from the quintessential experience of violence and death—inhabited a different country and spoke in a different tongue. He was likely to be a patriot, an idealist, an amateur; he believed in God and Providence, hated the enemy, and had not an inkling of the soldier's austere trade.

"An Affair of the Outposts" personifies the civilian in the governor who for strictly political reasons comes from the "peaceful lands beyond the sea of strife" to visit Grant's bedraggled army after the battle of Pittsburg Landing. The governor misreads the hieroglyphics of war. To his unpracticed eye, the apparent disorder of the camp suggests "carelessness, confusion, indifference" whereas "a soldier would have observed expectancy and readiness."[30] Trapped in a melee, he is just unterrified enough to appreciate "the composure and precision" of the troops, but he is more shocked than enlightened by the sordidness of battle: "Even in his distress and peril the helpless civilian could not forbear to contrast it with the gorgeous parades and reviews held in honor of himself—with the brilliant uniforms, the music, the banners, and marching. It was an ugly and sickening business: to all that was artistic in his nature, revolting, brutal, in bad taste." The great man is rescued from capture by the heroic sacrifices of the Tenth Company but passes off his near misadventure with a witticism whose irony he is too obtuse to recognize: "At present—if you will permit an allusion to the horrors of peace—I am 'in the hands of my friends.' "[31]

In a society where such men held high place, war seemed superior to the indecencies of peace. The veterans, bestialized by battle and forced into the imbecile business of killing, evoked in Bierce a tenderness notably absent in his dealings with the rest of the world. It made no difference to him whether they broke under the ordeal or survived it; they contended against the uncontendable. The strong in his stories are always broken in any case. The men he most admired were stern paternal figures, like General Hazen, who made a religion out of duty, lived what they preached, and shared the fate of all who lived "a life of strife and animosities."[32] Such men were out of place in postwar America where civilian precepts and values suffocated the soldierly ones.

Bierce's idealism, although not completely extinguished at the end of the war, was already guttering. His work as a government treasury agent in Alabama in 1865 and a glimpse of corruption in New Orleans snuffed it out. Once he had believed in "a set of infinitely precious 'principles'—infallible criteria—moral solvents, mordant to all base materials." The carpetbaggers who enriched themselves and the ex-soldiers who looted "the people their comrades had offered their lives to bring back into the Union," helped out to rout such fancies from his mind.[33] "O Father of Battles," he begged in later years, "pray give us release/From the horrors of peace, the horrors of peace!"[34]

Corrupt civilians aroused his contempt, bloody-minded civilians his rage. Bierce never sympathized with the southern cause, but like Whitman he honored Confederate veterans as unfeignedly as he did his northern comrades in arms, for they belonged to his bloodied fraternity. "What glorious fellows they were . . . These my late antagonists of the dark days when, God forgive us, we were trying to cut one another's throat." So Bierce wrote long after when battle seemed to him a "criminal insanity."[35] He regretted his role of death-dealer and looked upon his former enemies as superior to the breed who survived them:

> They were honest and courageous foemen, having little in common with the political madmen who persuaded them to their doom and the literary bearers of false witness in the aftertime. They did not live through the period of honorable strife into the period of vilification—did not pass from the iron age to the brazen—from the era of the sword to that of the tongue and pen. Among them is no member of the Southern Historical Society. Their valor was not the duty of the non-combatants; they have no voice in the thunder of civilians and the shouting. Not by them are impaired the dignity and infinite pathos of the Lost Cause. Give them, these blameless gentlemen, their rightful part in all the pomp that fills the circuit of the summer hills.[36]

Bierce's tribute concluded his plea to provide markers for the shallow and forgotten graves of the Confederate dead. "Is there a man, North or South," he asked, "who would begrudge the expense of giving to these fallen brothers the tribute of green graves?" Apparently there were, just as there were the "Vindictives" of the Bloody-Shirt unwilling to return captured Rebel flags. He gently chided GAR veterans for fearing that concessions to old foes smacked of treason. He and his fellow soldiers had not fought to capture banners but to teach the South better manners. Let kings keep trophies, he said. "The freeman's trophy is the foeman's love,/Despite war's ravage."

> Give back the foolish flags whose bearers fell,
>   Too valiant to forsake them.
> Is it presumptuous, this counsel? Well,
>   I helped to take them.[37]

He was less genial to the superpatriots and self-righteous moralists, inflexible judges of right and wrong. Rejected ideas, he warned them, constantly double back to "mock the new"; they run "recurrent in an endless track." And angered by one who opposed the decorating of Confederate graves, Bierce wrote:

> The wretch, whate'er his life and lot,
>   Who does not love the harmless dead
>   With all his heart, and all his head—
> May God forgive him, *I* shall not.[38]

VI

The war educated Bierce, enlightened or undeceived him in the same sense that Melville's shattered veterans were enlightened by exploding shells and undeceived by bullets. It also left him a casualty, permanently warped and seared like one of Hawthorne's damned seekers who is crushed rather than tempered by revelation. A universe where such atrocities could happen remained hostile to him as did the God who allegedly managed human affairs. Once he had swallowed the "fascinating fallacy that all men are born equal," had believed that words meant what the dictionary said they did.[39] He had heard the cry for help when he was "young and full of faith" and in keeping with others of that "sentimental generation" had willingly taken more than his fair share of hard knocks. But "The Hesitating Veteran" asked himself in the light of the aftermath whether it had been worth it:

> That all is over now—the reign
>   Of love and trade still all dissensions,
> And the clear heavens arch again
>   Above a land of peace and pensions.

The black chap—at the last we gave
  Him everything that he had cried for,
Though many white chaps in the grave
  'Twould puzzle to say what they died for.

I hope he's better off—I trust
  That his society and his master's
Are worth the price we paid, and must
  Continue paying, in disasters;
But sometimes doubts press thronging round
  ('Tis mostly when my hurts are aching)
If war for Union was a sound
  and profitable undertaking.

No mortal man can Truth restore
  Or say where she is to be sought for.
I know what uniform I wore—
  O, that I knew which side I fought for![40]

Bierce the veteran did know what side he fought for even though Bierce the devil's lexicographer might treat the pastime of war with Biercean irreverence. If he knew little about the controversies leading up to the war when he enlisted, according to his friend and confidant Walter Neale, he decided "after he had reached years of discretion . . . that he had fought on the right side."[41] But the war turned him into a "hired assassin" and a bleak determinist. In his last visits to the battlefields—once in 1903 and again in 1913—retracing "old routes and lines of march" and standing "in my old camps," he tried but only partially succeded in recapturing the elation of what he called "my Realm of Adventure."[42] The ache of despair overmatched the pleasures of nostalgia.

By this time, Bierce's misanthropy was not "a reasoned philosophy of despair but a conditioned reflex."[43] His response to the war had always been intensely personal, never philosophical, and he generalized his pessimism into universal law. The war remained for Bierce hardly more than a lurid stage set for a private drama. It left the grander spectacle untouched and unfelt, but few writers registered the shock of war's terrors with a comparable fidelity.

Notes

1. E. C. Stedman, *The Battle of Bull Run* (New York, 1861).

2. R. H. Stoddard remarked almost petulantly that an anthology "of amatory verse from the best English and American poets" which he and Bayard Taylor were preparing might have succeeded but for the "impending shadow of our great Civil War," *Recollections Personal and Literary*, ed. Ripley Hitchcock (New York, 1903), p. 274. Some years later Stedman recalled how Stoddard, Taylor, and others "found their music broken in upon by the tumult of national war." *Poets of America* (Boston and New York, 1885), p. 379.

3. M. Hansen-Taylor and Horace Scudder, eds., *Life and Letters of Bayard Taylor* (Boston, 1895), I, 381.

4. Wolcott Gibbs to F. L. Olmsted, November 6, 1861 (Olmsted Papers, Library of Congress). In the same spirit, Stedman wrote to his mother in 1861: "So soon as this fight is over, we propose to shoot ahead of Great Britain in arms, navies, art, literature, health, and all other elements and appendages of national greatness," *Life and Letters*, I, 245.

5. Charles G. Leland, *Sunshine in Thought* (1862), facs. ed. (Gainsville, Fla.: B. Y. Spencer, 1959).

6. Norton to Olmsted, September 16, 1866 (Olmsted Papers, Library of Congress).

7. Leland, *Memoirs* (London, 1893), II, 22.

8. Paul Fatout, *Ambrose Bierce: The Devil's Lexicographer* (Norman, Okla.: Oklahoma University Press, 1951), pp. 48–49.

9. Carey McWilliams, *Ambrose Bierce: A Biography* (New York: Archon Books, 1967), p. 55.

10. *The Collected Works of Ambrose Bierce*, 12 vols. (New York and Washington, D.C.: Neale Publishing Company, 1909–1912), IV, 132.

11. Walter Neale, *Life of Ambrose Bierce* (New York: W. Neale, 1929), p. 158.

12. Fatout, *Ambrose Bierce*, p. 36.

13. "These were the identical weapons used in the Pottawatomie affair." McWilliams, *Ambrose Bierce*, p. 28. See also G. W. Knepper, *Travels in the Southland: The Journal of Lucius Verus Bierce*, 1822–1823 (Columbus, Ohio: Ohio State University Press, 1966), pp. 24–26.

14. McWilliams, *Ambrose Bierce*, p. 29.

15. Namely, at Shiloh, Murfreesboro, Stone River, Chattanooga, Kenesaw Mountain (where he was seriously wounded), Missionary Ridge, Franklin and in lesser engagements. Enlisting as a private, he rose to first lieutenant and upon his mustering out in January 1865 was brevetted major for distinguished service. He was often cited for bravery in the dispatches; experienced the excitement of capture, brief incarceration, and escape; and as a Treasury agent in postwar Alabama he once again participated in a kind of sporadic war.

16. Fatout, *Ambrose Bierce*, p. 159.

17. McWilliams, *Ambrose Bierce*, p. 311.

18. *Collected Works*, I, 270.

19. *Ibid.*, II, 76.

20. *Ibid.*, I, 225–233.

21. Fatout, *Ambrose Bierce*, p. 52.

22. *Collected Works*, I, 236, 256, 267, 269, 254–255.

23. *Ibid.*, III, 108–109.

24. *Ibid.*, I, 262.

25. *Ibid.*, I, 258, 259, 265.

26. 'In such circumstances the life of a staff officer of a brigade is distinctly 'not a happy one,' mainly because of its precarious tenure and the unnerving alternations of emotion to which he is exposed. From a position of that comparative security from which a civilian would ascribe his escape to a 'miracle,' he may be dispatched with an order to some commander of a prone regiment in the front line—a person for the moment inconspicuous and not always easy to find without a deal of search among men somewhat preoccupied, and in a din in which question and answer alike must be imparted in the sign language. It is customary in such cases to duck the head and scuttle away on a keen run, an object of lively interest to some thousands of admiring marksmen. In returning—well, it is not customary to return." "Killed at Resaca," *Collected Works*, II, 96.

27. *Ibid.*, I, 290, 284, 291.

28. *Ibid.* I, 324, 269.

29. "A Son of the Gods," *Collected Works*, II, 63.

30. Elsewhere Bierce observes: "An army in line-of-battle awaiting attack, or prepared to deliver it, presents strange contrasts. At the front are precision, formality, fixity, and silence. Toward the rear these characteristics are less and less conspicuous, and finally, in point of space, are lost altogether in confusion, motion, and noise. The homogeneous becomes heterogeneous. Definition is lacking; repose is replaced by an apparently purposeless activity; harmony vanishes in hubbub, form in disorder. Commotion everywhere and ceaseless unrest. The men who do not fight are never ready." *Ibid.*, II, 198. Here, perhaps, is an allegory of war and peace. After Appomattox, veteran and nonveteran alike wanted to instill some of this military discipline and precision into civilian life. Edward Bellamy's "Industrial Army" in *Looking Backward* is an example of such thinking.

31. *Ibid.*, 158, 164.

32. Fatout, *Ambrose Bierce*, p. 149.

33. McWilliams, *Ambrose Bierce*, pp. 67–68.

34. *Collected Works*, IV, 118.

35. *Ibid.*, I, 341.

36. *Ibid.*, XI, 398.

37. *Ibid.*, IV, 331–337.

38. *Ibid.*, V, 64.

39. *Ibid.*, III, 361.

40. *Ibid.*, IV, 116–118.

41. *Life of Ambrose Bierce*, p. 102. According to Neale, Bierce enlisted to free the slaves: "There was besides, the moral urge, the chivalric impulse, and the excuse to justify bloodshed. Of course, the dominating urge was lust for war, the opportunity for adventure, the call to the blood of youth" (193–194). Had Bierce known the Negro as well in 1861 as he did in 1906, "he might have been tempted to fight for the South—this jocosely" (190). And again: "He grew to dislike negroes intensely as a race, despite his fascination, although he did not extend his antipathies to individuals. But how he 'loathed their black hides, their filthy persons, and their odiferous [sic] aroma!' " (189). Neale, a Virginian, was deeply prejudiced against Negroes himself. His allegations about Bierce's distaste for blacks, Hindus, American Indians, Chinese, and Japanese must be taken with this in mind.

42. McWilliams, *Ambrose Bierce*, pp. 319–320.

43. S. C. Woodruff, *The Short Stories of Ambrose Bierce: A Study in Polarity* (Pittsburgh: University of Pittsburgh Press, 1964) p. 115.

The Bitterness of Battle:
Ambrose Bierce's War Fiction

Eric Solomon*

In his brilliant study, *The Art of Satire* (1940), David Worcester defines cosmic irony as the satire of frustration which has a particular relevance for post-Copernican man, who is no longer the center of his universe. Ambrose Bierce's short stories of war, "Tales of Soldiers" (1891), are vignettes of cosmic irony wherein man is brought to realize his insignificance in the face of the all-encompassing universe of war as well as the futility of all "normal" acts and aspirations. Only Stephen Crane has written as powerfully as Bierce about the shock of recognition brought on by the Civil War.

The keynote of Bierce's war fiction is frustration. His soldiers are chagrined by their limits of knowledge and their lack of control. As Bierce states in his military memoirs, *Bits of Autobiography*, "It is seldom indeed that a subordinate officer knows anything about the disposition of the enemy's forces . . . or precisely whom he is fighting. As for the rank and file, they can know nothing more of the matter than the arms they carry." (281) Man in war, afflicted by the failure of reason and the impact of collective suffering, is also unable to live up to his preconceived ideals. Again in the memoirs, we find Bierce telling us of a gallant charge that had been beaten back by a heavy fire: "Lead had scored its old time victory over steel; the heroic had broken its great heart against the commonplace. There are those who say that it is sometimes otherwise." (265) These two concepts, unreason and failure, provide the basis for the bitter irony of Bierce's brief, rapid anecdotes, which silhouette the blackest side of war.

The fifteen extremely short "Tales of Soldiers" included in the collection, *In the Midst of Life*, strike a mean between violently contrived naturalism—replete with disgusting ugliness and shocking coincidence—and the accumulation of exact, realistic, and factual observations of combat life. There can be no doubt that the author loads the dice in each of his tales. The theme of every story is the death of the good, the honest, and the brave. A Northern soldier kills his rebel father; a young enlisted man on guard duty discovers his brother's corpse; a gunner destroys his own house, murdering his wife and children. All the gestures

*Reprinted by permission of the author and the editor, *Midwest Quarterly*, 5 (October 1963–July 1964), 147–65.

of heroism turn out to be empty. Certainly the coincidences are over-emphasized for added ironic effect in these war stories as in all of Bierce's work. The mordant cynicism of *The Devil's Dictionary* and *Fantastic Fables*, the misanthropic savagery of Bierce's treatment of insanity and the supernatural in *Can Such Things Be?* do not lead to an objective point of view. Life is terrible, and war is the epitome of its misery.

War fits Bierce's philosophy perfectly. The very nature of combat that involves a heightening, a tension, an absurdity of situation, an incongruity that calls for satire, suits his dark approach. In Bierce's "Tales of Civilians" which make up the second half of *In the Midst of Life*, his stories seem labored and contrived. The writer must spend much more time to build up the situation than in the war stories, where the background may be taken for granted simply because war is war. The later stories become discursive—an almost fatal flaw for an epigrammatic method—since Bierce must describe the mining camps or the San Francisco social hierarchy; within the war context everything is understood at once. The military situation, by its nature rapid and simple, supplies its own foreshortening. Wilson Follett, perhaps Bierce's most acute critic, points out that the chief artistic weakness in his fiction comes from the substitution of an external irony for the irony inherent in the nature of things. War, with its own frame of irony, is the finest subject for "Bitter Bierce's" corruscating, witty excursions into fiction.

Bierce had ample opportunity to learn about war firsthand. He enlisted in the Ohio Volunteers at the age of nineteen, young enough for the ironies of war to become an integral part of his education. Bierce later spoke of his six years of soldiering as spent under a magic spell, "something new under a new sun." He was a success as a soldier. He rose through the ranks to become a sergeant, then a lieutenant, and finally, as a topographical engineer, he became an member of the staff of General W. B. Hazen. Bierce sums up his war experiences with an old soldier's quiet modesty: ". . . although hardly more than a boy in years, I had served at the front from the beginning of the trouble, and had seen enough of war to give me a fair understanding of it."

He was at Shiloh, Stone's River (Murfreesboro), Chickamauga, Kenesaw Mountain, and Franklin, among other engagements. Like almost every veteran who lives long enough, Bierce is able in his memoirs to cast a gloss of sentiment over army life, but he is realistic enough to comprehend that this warm sentiment is not called for. "Is it not strange" he reminisced, "that the phantoms of a bloodstained period have so airy a grace and look with so tender eyes?—that I recall with difficulty the dangers and death and horrors of the time, and without effort all that was gracious and picturesque?" We must not be misled by his fine war record and vintage memories. Bierce's war recollections are also sprinkled with the materials that go into his stories—the irony of a man named Abbot being killed by a shell with the foundry mark "Abbot" on it, or the ghastly sight of his dead comrades after they had been trampled by a herd of swine. While Bierce enjoyed the test of combat, the companionship and the excitement of war, he was revolted, intellectually, by the harsh brutalities of a repellent, paradoxical world.

Moving from memoir to fiction, Bierce found the short, almost elliptical story to be his ideal form. As critics have been quick to point out, Bierce learned a great deal from Edgar Allan Poe's theories of fiction. Like Poe, Bierce is highly selective, fixing upon the decisive, revealing moment. For example, he catches the instant of an execution in his famous "An Occurrence at Owl Creek Bridge," the intense immediacy of the discovery of cowardice and courage in the two protagonists of "Parker Adderson, Philosopher," or the momentary stasis in "A Horseman in the Sky," where a boy quietly presses the trigger and his father's body slowly falls into space.

Unquestionably, Bierce's plots are forced. Consider the manipulation for effect in "An Affair of Outposts." Here a young man, Armisted, informs the governor of his state that he wants a commission in the army in order to die in battle because his wife has taken up with some unknown person. Much later, the governor visits the battlefield, wanders too far, is endangered by an enemy attack, and saved by Armisted, who dies in the attempt—but not until both men realize that they share the knowledge that the governor is the villain of the piece. The bare plot outline, as always, hardly does justice to the story, which gains its effect from the conjunction of the civilian and military frames of reference and the bitingly sarcastic tone of the narrative. Yet this example shows how Bierce uses a highly unusual military situation that focuses the whole history of his characters onto one remarkable event. Since war is full of startling chances, the author's controlling hand is less obtrusive than it might be.

Although Bierce's figures are flat (to use E. M. Forster's term), each story expresses a deep psychological trauma, one that ends in madness or loss. Again, war is the proper setting for the intensified emotion Bierce presents. In war character becomes automatized, part of the military machine. Relying on this firm military context, Bierce easily sketches as much or as little of his heroes' past lives as he desires. The immediate impression is important in the war construct. So the hero of "An Occurrence at Owl Creek Bridge" is a spy who is about to be hanged—that much is germane to the story. We take for granted the reason for his being in this situation and what his beliefs are.

Bierce provides the barest minimum of character description:

> Peyton Farquhar was a well-to-do planter of an old and highly respected Alabama family. Being a slave owner and like other slave owners a politician, he was naturally an original secessionist and ardently devoted to the Southern cause. Circumstances of an imperious nature, which it is unnecessary to relate here, had prevented him from taking service with the gallant army . . .

Who he is makes little difference. How he reacts to war is important. Bierce's attitude towards plot and character may be cursory, but his fictional treatment of war is, with the exception of the work of Crane (and possibly Rudyard Kipling), the most extensive in nineteenth century English and American fiction. Bierce's subject is man in war. He does not heighten his fiction with the details of war in the manner of John W. De Forest or John Esten Cooke; rather he steeps his stories in the aura, the meaning of battle. Bierce captures the principle that lies behind the facts. He catches war at its sources, and he makes it an intensification of personal experience.

A remarkable aspect of Bierce's very short war stories is that in each one he manages to evoke the feeling of reality, the sense of fact and place that makes war not an abstract moral condition but a concrete physical actuality. Even in an allegory such as "A Son of the Gods," Bierce shows the solid circumstances of war, "the occasional rattle of wheels as a battery of artillery goes into position to cover the advance; the hum and murmur of the soldiers talking; a sound of innumerable feet in the dry leaves that strew the interspaces among the trees; hoarse commands of officers." He reproduces the serious minutiae of battle, the sound and impact of shells, the ugliness of death (his corpses, festering, with entrails spread on the ground, are as brutally portrayed as anything in the pages of Erich Remarque or Henri Barbusse), the boredom and the sweat, the mass movements and the isolation of the individual who "was alone . . . His world was a few square yards of wet and trampled earth about the feet of his horse." The war stories include all types of soldier: the gay, devil-may-care spy who cracks under pressure at the last moment; the serious young officer who obeys orders even when he knows he is killing his own men; the sensitive, poetic private who deserts when he finds his brother's dead body; the blindly courageous officer who is constantly attempting to prove his courage and repress his fear.

It is dark world, but there is a feeling of movement and excitement. "Color-bearers unfurled the flags, buglers blew the 'assembly,' hospital attendants appeared with stretchers. Field officers mounted and sent their impedimenta to the rear in care of Negro servants."

Bierce assumes that once the unique war world is created, his readers will themselves set the characters in their proper military context, as captain or private, cavalryman or infantryman. Bierce analyzes the matter of the uniqueness of the war situation brilliantly in his story "An Affair of Outposts." We have already mentioned the rather melodramatic plot of this tale. The particular quality of the story derives from the superb contrasting of the two worlds—the easy, ordered life of the governor, that enables him to carry a traditionally romantic conception of war in his mind, and the harsh, incongruous position of the soldier, that enforces a sardonic, anti-heroic outlook.

The governor and his staff, well-mounted and impeccably tailored, visit the fairly quiet combat area. "Things of charm they were, rich in suggestions of peaceful lands beyond a sea of strife. The bedraggled soldier looked up from his trench as they passed, leaned upon his spade, and audibly damned them to signify his sense of their ornamental irrelevance to the austerities of his trade." This coda of the story sets up the basic conflict. The author takes the position of a veteran dweller in the war world into which these others came as strange interlopers (such contempt for civilians becomes a familiar pattern in the angry war novels of the twentieth century, from John Dos Passos to John Horne Burns). The governor wanders too near the front and has to rush away—but he cannot escape the sight of the actualities of combat, the wounded struggling back, feebly dragging themselves to the cover of their comrades' fire. Now writing from the governor's angle of vision, Bierce sets forth his artistic credo as far as war is concerned:

> In all this there was none of the pomp of war—no hint of glory. Even in his distress and peril the helpless civilian could not forbear to contrast it with the gorgeous parades and reviews held in honor of himself—with the brilliant uniforms, the music, the banners, and the marching. It was an ugly and sickening business . . . revolting, brutal, in bad taste. . . . "Where is the charm of it all? Where are the elevated sentiments, the devotion, the heroism, the—?"

The author takes over at this point in the narrative and supplies the answer to the governor's question. The heroism is in the clear, deliberate voice of the captain, the austere devotion to duty that brings about a bayonet charge, savage hand-to-hand fighting, cutting, bludgeoning—and the death of the captain. The story ends with an added Biercean ironic twist: the cynical civilian is careless of all this dutiful military courage that saves his life. Yet this plot device also underlines the disparity between the honor of the battlefield and the deceit of the marketplace.

Bierce's fiction is tempered by his anti-romanticism, an attitude drawn from experience. The essay, "On a Mountain," compares the natural beauties of the Virginia landscape with the shocking sight of decaying corpses. Romance must give way to realism in the war setting:

> How romantic it all was; the sunset valleys full of visible sleep; the glades suffused and interpenetrated with moonlight . . . Then there was the "spice of danger" . . . As we trudged on we passed something—some things—lying by the wayside . . . How repulsive they looked with their blood smears, their blank, staring eyes, their teeth uncovered by contraction of the lips!

This conscious rejection of the glorious view of war that characterized nearly all war fiction before the shock novels of World War I is carried over into Bierce's stories. Although Bierce the essayist occasionally lets a nostalgic note creep into his work, in the fashion of Kipling or De Forest, Bierce the creator of fiction refuses to conceive any sentimental picture of war's glories. His heroes are not heroic; his cowards are not castigated.

In "One Kind of Officer," a condemnation of the entire military structure, Bierce merges plot and setting to show the irrationality of war. The general orders a captain of artillery to hold his position at all costs and to ask no questions. Obeying his orders to the letter, the captain fires on his own men. But the general is killed in the action, and the captain must be shot for carrying out his orders since there is no one to defend him. This mordant story is at an incredible distance from previous war fiction. Not even Emile Zola rigs his war plots in quite so nihilistic a manner. And Bierce's setting is equally anti-heroic. Rain, mud, rubber ponchos, dripping corpses—how different from the glittering pomp of Charles Lever's battle scenes! Bierce refuses to accept even a hint of the heroic. "Very repulsive these wrecks looked—not at all heroic, and nobody was accessible to the infection of their patriotic example. Dead upon the field of honor, yes; but the field of honor was so very wet! It makes a difference." It does indeed make a difference. The cosmic irony of a world out of joint leads to the use of certain special fictional techniques.

Bierce might be called the first really modern war writer working in the English language. With the exceptions of Tolstoy and Stendhal, nobody writing fiction in the nineteenth century sustained an ironic approach to war so consistently as Bierce did. There are five fictional methods in which he anticipates the writers of the next century: the treatment of time, the process of animism, the approach to nature, the use of religious symbolism, and, finally, the employment of the theme that was to be raised to its finest schematization by Stephen Crane, the development from innocence, through war, to experience.

It is to be expected that such tightly condensed tales as those of Bierce should demand a certain element of foreshortening. Characters are mere shadows; one action is usually the basis for the tale, and dialogue is held to a bare minimum. Bierce recognizes a basic fact of combat: that in an intense situation the time scheme is often upset; an event that seems to take an eternity may in reality happen in a matter of minutes, and the converse is equally possible.

An outstanding example of this first type of time-manipulation appears in Bierce's most frequently anthologized war story, "An Occurrence at Owl Creek Bridge." Like much of his writing, it is in essence a tour-de-force. The hero, Peyton Farquhar, is about to be hanged from a railroad bridge. Bierce supplies a mournfully slow, cadenced description of the bridge, the soldiers guarding it, the officer in charge, and the preparations for the hanging. Farquhar becomes conscious of the labored, measured passage of time when he hears a steady stroke sounding for all the world like a death knell; the noise comes from his watch. The trap is sprung, and first the author provides a flashback to Farquhar's previous life, then an increasingly tense narration of his escape from the noose, his rapid flight down the turbulent river, through the bullets of the sentinels and the grape-shot of the artillery. He makes good his escape, returns to his wife—and the last, shocking line utterly destroys the carefully wrought illusion. "Peyton Farquhar was dead; his body, with a broken neck, swung gently from side to side beneath the timbers of the Owl Creek Bridge."

The ordering of time, extending the felt experience far beyond the actual number of minutes involved, has become a commonplace in modern fiction. It is important in the context of the war genre because the extension of time to include the past histories and the future hopes of the participants in a military action has been an extremely effective technique for writers who must keep their focus on the battle circumstances in order to sustain the suspense, and yet move away in time and space from the physical restrictions of the battlefield to vary the effects.

The same device is used with even greater success in "One of the Missing," where a scout is crushed by a timber in a recently shelled barn. The narrator works from the scout's point of view, slowly drawing out the reveries, the mental agony, and the final abortive suicide attempt, before the soldier dies from the strain of his long isolation. For the ironic twist in the O. Henry manner that Bierce greatly enjoys, the narrative shifts to the victim's brother who looks at his watch the instant the barn is hit by the shell and automatically checks the timepiece again when he comes across the unrecognizable body of his brother Bierce accomplishes a double irony; the scout appears to have been dead a week, so great was the degenerative process of his fear; the watch indicates that only twelve minutes have passed. Again, sense of time supplies the macabre point to the story. Quite obviously, the shock effect is the product of Bierce's rather special sensibility. Still, the facts of war, where time is of transcendent importance, yet normally confused, where action may occur incredibly swiftly, or life may consist of tedious waiting—where, in short, time cannot be controlled by the individual—fits Bierce's treatment.

If "One of the Missing" would seem overly contrived in most settings, it does not seem out of place in war. We have but to compare Poe's "The Pit and the Pendulum" which is based on a similar stratagem. For all its horror and steady increase of suspense, Poe's tale has no connection with a realistic world. The Gothic terror of Poe, La Fanu, and Blackwood is, by definition, abnormal, and it calls for a suspension of disbelief. War is normally abnormal, so that the terror of Bierce's story receives the reinforcement of a thoroughly possible contemporary setting. Bierce can play with time in his war fiction and not destroy the illusion of reality.

In calling the Civil War the first modern war, military historians mean to draw attention to both the scale of manpower involved and the increased mechanization of weapons—the use of ironclad ships or railroad guns, for example. Throughout the fiction of the nineteenth century, from Fenimore Cooper and Sir Walter Scott to DeForest and Kipling, there has been a movement away from the positive view of war as an affair of glory to a consideration of it as an unpleasant necessity. The imagery of Ambrose Bierce and, to a far greater extent, Stephen Crane, supports the naturalistic conception of war.

There is a dual process observable in the war fiction of these two authors. First, they both lean heavily on the pathetic fallacy, the personification of inanimate objects. This animation is not new. As far back as Achilles' shield or Arthur's sword, Excalibur—or Natty Bumppo's rifle, "Kill-Deer"—weapons were given names and almost personal qualities. Animism is not a new technique, but Bierce and Crane anticipate its widespread use by modern war writers.

Language is further disrupted. Man is dehumanized, referred to either in terms of animals or machines. The modern war chronicler is attracted to violent imagery for the same reasons that motivated the metaphysical poets to seek out shocking and incongruous images to express their emotional disturbance over the changing world of the Renaissance. Bierce is equally disturbed by the absurdity of war which, after all, reverses the natural processes. It is against natural law to die young, and Bierce registers his complaint by reversing his imagery, turning men into beasts (as war does) and endowing the instruments of death with human attributes.

Any sensitive observer of army life immediately notices the fundamental irony of man's loss of individuality as he becomes part of the military machine. The most disturbing event in a young soldier's life is the realization that he is only the agent of another's volition. The machine is not only the metaphor of mass warfare, it is also the basis for the severest trauma of the civilian-soldier. In brief, the face of war changes in the nineteenth century, and the writers substitute a sardonically naturalistic picture for the shining armor and glowing hopes portrayed in earlier battle fiction. The hero is no longer the splendid chevalier who guides his horse over the highest barriers. He becomes, if the expression is permissible, the dogface who burrows deep in his fox-hole.

Bierce provides the first really extensive examples of this type of imagery in war fiction. He sets forth the rationale for animism in his memoirs. "There is something that inspires confidence in the way a gun dashes up to the front, shoving fifty or a hundred men to one side as if it said, 'Permit *me!*' Then it squares its shoulders, calmly dislocates a joint in its back, sends away its twenty-four legs and settles down . . ." (252). The fiction extends these images, often giving the impression that the guns are more important than the men in the war world. In a sentimental story by Thomas Nelson Page, for example, the survivors of a Confederate force at the war's end sadly bid farewell to the cannon which, under the names of Matthew, Mark, Luke, John, The Eagle, and The Cat, have become real personalities in the men's eyes. A cannon to Bierce is "something horrible and unnatural: the gun was bleeding at the mouth," or "The army's weapons seemed to share its military delinquency. The rattle of rifles sounded flat and contemptible."

To a similar extent, men in war are turned into beasts. A man with his jaw shot away has "the appearance of a great bird of prey crimsoned in throat and breast by the blood of its quarry." Bierce's wounded are always inarticulate; they crawl away like "a swarm of great black beetles." Equipment is their spoor; a trapped soldier is "conscious of his own rathood." Bierce chooses these images to convey his disgust with the whole process of war. He is particularly disturbed by the mutilated victims of the malignant weapons. The author expresses genuine compassion for "a writhing fragment of humanity, this type an example of crude sensation." In order to sustain the distance from his characters necessary for the ironic detachment he seeks, Bierce employs an imagery that shows contempt for men and admiration for guns—the reverse of his actual feeling.

What of nature itself in these passages? Bierce does not have the poet's eye for detail displayed by Crane. Instead, Bierce, the former topographical engineer, sets each story in an exactly planned and restricted composition. Relying on what von Clausewitz calls *Ortisinn*—sense of locality—Bierce puts his vignettes of war in a frame that includes a hill on which the observer is usually stationed (it is called an "acclivity," apparently Bierce's favorite word), and from which a long view stretches out over a field. A farmhouse is located on one side of the field, and a body of woods is behind the hill. There are variations, naturally, but Bierce is ordinarily satisfied with some such clearly defined stage for his military operations. His idea of nature is inconsistent. At times the landscape is indifferent. He shows the sheer beauty of the sight of a horseman poised on a cliff, outlined against the blue sky, looking down on a stream that runs through the valley below. Immediately after this vision, the horse and rider are plunged to their deaths. Or the natural setting is deliberately contrasted to the ugliness of the events it shelters: "He could imagine nothing more peaceful than the appearance of that pleasant landscape with its long stretches of brown fields over which the atmosphere was beginning to quiver in the heat of the morning sun." And in a moment, the observer of all this beauty will kill himself in a paroxysm of fear in order to escape an enemy attack!

As the attitude towards war grows more serious in nineteenth century fiction, a religious note creeps into the writing. Again, this is hardly a new departure, but rather a return to a much older tradition. The gods took part in the Homeric struggles; the Old Testament is packed with battles. As far back as the Old English *Dream of the Rood*, Christ has been portrayed as an heroic warrior. If the earlier historical novelists did not consider the spiritual side of war, Zola and Tolstoy constantly remind the reader that combat has its religious overtones.

Ambrose Bierce brings forth the religious motif in one of his finest, and least known, stories. "A Son of the Gods" is perhaps his most perfectly constructed war tale. It is a thinly disguised allegory. The story is told from the point of view of an anonymous soldier and is subtitled "A Study in the Present Tense." The atmosphere is heavy with the sense of mystery and silence that exists when the position of the enemy is unknown. The army is almost paralyzed, in a fog of hesitation and doubt, in awe of the incomprehensible.

The observer, a veteran staff-officer, is talking about the realities of war, and he employs the plainest terms, speaking of "an old saddle, a splintered wheel, a forgotten canteen." Suddenly, in sharp contrast, the narrator raises his eyes to see an anomalous entrant upon the subdued scene:

> . . . a young officer on a snow-white horse. His saddle blanket
> is scarlet. What a fool! No one who has ever been in action but
> remembers how naturally every rifle turns toward the man on
> a white horse . . . He is all agleam with bullion—a blue-and-
> gold edition of the poetry of war.

The old soldier's immediate reaction is one of mockery, he finds himself emotionally attracted to the figure. "But how handsome he is!—with what careless grace he sits his horse!"

Bierce combines the mystical religious connotations of this knight with the basic realities of the military problem. There is a hedge-lined wall on the top of a hill behind which the enemy may be stationed in force. The normal procedure would be to send out a body of skirmishers to prove the enemy's presence by drawing fire, but in this position it would mean annihiliation for those troops. So the young horseman, ten thousand eyes focused on him and the sun shining its benediction on his shoulder-straps, offers to sacrifice himself in place of the skirmishers. His act draws forth a spirit of ecstasy from the troops. The religious emotion inherent in Bierce's prose here recalls the intensity of Gerard Manley Hopkins' lyrics. As the officer rides on, "He is not alone—he draws all souls after him. But we remember that we laughed . . . Not a look backward. O, if he would but turn—if he could but see the love, the adoration, the atonement!"

The narrator pictures the burly commander-in-chief and the hardened killers who are accustomed to death in its ugliest forms—they are men who can play cards among the corpses of their comrades—and they are all equally involved with the fate of the young hero. The author does not attempt to conceal the young officer's symbolic configuration. " 'Let me pay all,' says this gallant man—this military Christ!"

The tone of pure enchantment is sustained perfectly up to this point. Having established the beauty and heroism of the act, the narration changes from the enchanted mood to one of direct suspense as the hero rides before the enemy guns and momentarily manages to escape their withering fire. Finally, after his horse has been shot down, the officer, still miraculously alive, signals with his sword to the watching troops that he has given his life for them. "His face is toward us. Now he lowers his hand to a level with his face and moves it downward, the blade of his sabre describing a downward curve. It is a sign to us, to the world, to posterity. It is a hero's salute to death and history."

If Bierce had ended his story here, it would exist as a remarkably sensitive and lyrical evocation of the spirit of sacrifice in war, a tale of sympathetic, elegiac loveliness—that would make war appear a thing of beauty. Bierce's philosophical approach to the realities of a war that is cruel and illogical will not allow such treatment of the religious theme to stand. Like much of later war fiction, "A Son of the Gods" must pervert the religious elements in order to remain true to the author's dark vision of war. We have qualified Bierce's philosophy as one of cosmic irony. One of the concomitants of this discipline is the certainty that God is an enemy, not a friend, of man. He is a careless God. Following such an ideology, Bierce needs to end his war story on a savagely ironic note.

The onlooking troops are brought to a state of religious frenzy by the hero's last sign to them. They break the rules of their world of war—since the knight is the symbol of another, supposedly higher world—and disobey their orders, charging in the direction of the dead body. The enemy opens fire, and by the time the preternaturally calm commander has the bugler sound the retreat, a mass of dead and wounded are left on the field. Taking the commander as an image of the father-God, and the officer the son-Christ, we see that the traditional sacrifice has been twisted out of shape. The Christ figure, whose action was planned to save even the skirmishers, has excited the army to such an extent that not only the skirmishers but also many other soldiers are killed *because* of the intended sacrifice. The most biting aspect of the irony is that the information was gained, and the officer's mission might have been a success. In war, however, not even religion obeys any rules—everything is perverted. The despondent voice of Bierce breaks through the narrator's sad cry of agony and anger that ends the story:

> Ah, those many, many needless dead! That great soul whose beautiful body is lying over yonder, so conspicuous against the sere hillside—could it not have been spared the bitter consciousness of a vain devotion? Would one exception have marred too much the pitiless perfection of the divine, eternal plan?

Throughout his war fiction, Bierce remains within the ethical system he has constructed. "A Son of the Gods" indicates that unless a writer has some sort of optimistic attitude towards war, the religious theme must show the horrible unreasonableness of a world whose real god is not Christ but Mars. Another piece, "The Story of a Conscience," emphasizes this point. Bierce follows the same routine, preparing the reader, through the tale of a spy who had once gratuitously saved his captor's life, for a moment of positive humanity. But the war ethic prevails; the spy who had once shown "a divine compassion" is shot, and his captor commits suicide. There can be no compromise with the illogic of war.

The archetypal character of modern war fiction is the innocent youth who gains an understanding of life through his war service. Many of Bierce's stories—"One Officer, One Man," or "The Mocking Bird," for example—examine the psychological problem of the extraordinary pressures brought about by the first introduction to war.

To express the innocence-to-experience theme, Bierce turns to the same mixture of realism and allegory used in "A Son of the Gods." "Chickamauga" carries the figure of the innocent back to its proper source, a six-year-old child. The story follows the adventures of a little boy who wanders away from home one sunny afternoon in wartime. It becomes immediately clear that the child, clutching a wooden sword and endowed with an inherited love of military books and pictures, represents the idea of romantic war, since, ". . . this child's spirit, in bodies of its ancestors had for thousands of years been trained to memorable feats of discovery and conquest." One aspect of the story is sheer parody. The little boy is a dreamer who savagely destroys his enemies, slashing to the right and to the left with his sword, until he is suddenly terrified—by a rabbit. Thus reality—and a reversed reality at that for the rabbit is the least frightening of beasts—ruins his game for a time, and he goes to sleep amid a strange, muffled sound of thunder.

He awakes to see a procession of revoltingly wounded men staggering bloodily through the woods. This, too, is reality, but the innocent who only comprehends the romance of war finds these victims of combat less terrible than one rabbit. He laughs with glee at the clownish antics of these agonized creatures, and even mounts one, a man whose jaw has been shot away. The little boy goes to the head of the column of dying and mutilated men and leads them forward to the gestures of his wooden sword. "Surely such a leader never before had such a following."

Bierce continues the dreadful parody of reality almost to the breaking point. The child's lack of experience is emphasized; he does not recognize drowned men for what they are, nor notice the signs of a great retreat. The innocent must learn the truth, however, and Bierce destroys the maddening illusion in two swift strokes. The boy, a knight on a quest, leads his troops towards the red glow of a fire. Eager to add fuel to the flames, he searches for wood, but everything he finds is too heavy. "In despair he flung in his sword—a surrender to the superior forces of nature. His military career was at an end." His first understanding of reality comes from the comprehension of his own inferiority in the face of nature's indifference, and he gives up his romantic dreams of military conquest.

Bierce has an additional irony in reserve, moreover. The child discovers that the burning dwelling is his own home. He comes upon the Goya-like scene of his mother's disgusting and dismembered corpse. The romantic vision of war died when the sword went into the fire. Now the sickening reality of everything he has been experiencing is brought home to the boy. Bierce compounds the irony with a third note of horror by making the child a deaf-mute. The shock of the story is overwhelming, but the author's meaning is clear. War is not what it seems to be in books and pictures. Only experience, personal experience, can wipe out the false impression and teach the essentials of war. Like all those caught up in war, the child learns the tremendous disparity between the vision and the actuality.

Ambrose Bierce never loses sight of the incongruous and the shocking aspect of war. The illusion-reality theme runs throughout his war stories. His grim portrait of combat anticipates the modern attitude towards war, but the compressed force of his war stories has never been equalled.

The Wry Seriousness of "Owl Creek Bridge"

F. J. Logan*

Ambrose Bierce's "An Occurrence at Owl Creek Bridge" has a history of both popularity and critical inattention.** The result is misreading. The story has languished in anthologies, chiefly those used in secondary schools, perhaps because it has been so frequently offered as an action tale of extreme power written by an otherwise unfamiliar Civil War writer.

It is fitting that, if Bierce's slender popular reputation must rest on any one story, it should rest on this one since it is among his best; it is unfortunate that the story should be generally valued for its accidents and not its essence—that the fine Biercean imagination, grisly wit, and poignant irony should be slighted or overlooked entirely—and that it should be most often read, as Cleanth Brooks and Robert Penn Warren read it, as a war yarn with a gimmicky ending, a reverse O. Henry twist.[1]

Because "Owl Creek Bridge" is still misunderstood, a correction is in order. Recent evidence of this general misunderstanding is a puzzling article by Fred H. Marcus titled "Film and Fiction: 'An Occurrence at Owl Creek Bridge.' " Professor Marcus sees the story as a "narrowly homogenized Gothic tale of horror," "spiced by authorial intrusions of sardonic observation."[2] He has noticed two of Bierce's more important sentences ("What he heard was the ticking of his watch." "He was a Federal scout."), and contends that here "the horror reaches its apogee in the terse closing phrase which flares like luminous evil over the preceding lines" (p. 15); and that "the eerie light illuminates section I and maintains the chill mood of Bierce's horror tale" (p. 16). The persona's observation

*Reprinted by permission of the author and the editor, *American Literary Realism*, 10, No. 2 (Spring 1977), 101–13.
**I have contended elsewhere ("The Development of Ambrose Bierce's Prose Style," diss. University of Alberta, Edmonton, 1974) that Ambrose Bierce was, during the last century, the West Coast's premier stylist and wit. Implicit in this contention are two others: that his work merits a careful rereading, and that such a rereading will make obvious the injustice of Bierce's low and little reputation. That he was more than a post-Civil War anomaly, more than a California curiosity, more than a man who, as Twain so snidely put it, wrote "acceptably for the magazines"—this I have not room to demonstrate. But if I cannot here demonstrate Bierce's genius I can at least strongly suggest it by reading one of his works with the care which, it should soon become apparent, that work so richly deserves.

that Farquhar was evidently "no vulgar assassin" reflects Bierce's "social consciousness of caste" (p. 16), according to Marcus (this is one of the story's three themes, as Marcus reads it); and Farquhar's post-imaginary-plunge hypersensitivity reveals "man's usual insensitivity to the vibrant, throbbing life pulsating about him" (p. 17). Marcus reviews a cinematic adaptation of the story following this observation, and closes his article with the reflection that, since the filmmaker used a number of details which "trivialize death," and since this "trivializing of death suggests contemporary events only too clearly," *therefore*, "the late nineteenth-century story becomes highly relevant to our time and place" (p. 23).

This most shopworn and factitious of all conclusions puts a period to ten pages of what Bierce and every good Biercean reader would surely brand as "bosh." In those places where Marcus is neither obvious, nor silly, nor trite, he is dead wrong. He is wrong about the protagonist, the story, and the intended effect of the story on the reader; and he is therefore wrong about Bierce. In those places where his meaning is accessible he seems to be arguing that "Owl Creek Bridge" is a sensational thriller a la Poe (probably the most widely held interpretation of the story). I will show that it is not.

The story is, incidentally, an action tale; *essentially*, its concern is with what may be loosely called philosophical questions: it is a speculation on the nature of time and on the nature of abnormal psychology, particularly on processes of abnormal perception and cognition. The story also explores or exploits epistemological issues and the logic upon which this epistemology rests. So the story is philosophy, but it is satire as well—two kinds: first, it is a burlesque of the orthodox war yarn in which the hero's death or survival is noble and significant; and second, it is thus in effect a lampoon-in-progress against those who, expecting the usual war yarn, mistake "Owl Creek Bridge" for their standard fare and overlook its central concerns. And its ending is thus a sharp rap across the sensibilities for "that cave-bat, 'the general reader,' " dealt in punishment for woolgathering.[3]

For the reader, to the extent that he likes and is like Farquhar, to the extent that he ignores reason and irony, to the extent, that is, that he does not really *read*, the end of the story is a sad shock. Would Bierce purposely lampoon the inattentive? Yes. He detested "bad readers—readers who, lacking the habit of analysis, lack also the faculty of discrimination, and take whatever is put before them, with the broad, blind catholicity of a slop-fed conscience or a parlor pig."[4]

Bierce, by the way, was himself a *close* reader. For example, in an essay written in 1903 titled "The Moon in Letters" (*Works*, IX, 58–67), he takes a number of authors to task for their "private systems of astronomy," for "their ignorance of what is before their eyes all their blessed lives." After listing several celestial impossibilities in a novel by H. Rider Haggard, he says,

A writer who believes that the new moon can rise in the east soon after sunset and the full moon at ten o'clock; who thinks the second of these remarkable phenomena can occur twenty-four hours after the first, and itself be followed some fourteen hours later by an eclipse of the sun—such a man may be a gifted writer, but I am not a gifted reader.

The novelist William Black has been even less attentive than Haggard:

> In dismissing Black I cannot forbear to add that even if the moon could rise in the south; even if rising into the dome when it should be setting . . . [etc.] . . . I have found similar blunders in the poems of Wordsworth, Coleridge, Schiller, Moore, Shelley, Tennyson and Bayard Taylor. Of course a poet is entitled to any kind of universe that may best suit his purpose, and if he could give us better poetry by making the moon rise "full-orbed" in the northwest and set like a "tin sickle" in the zenith I should go in for letting him have his fling. But I do not discern any gain in "sweetness and light" from these despotic readjustments of the relations among sun, earth and moon, and must set it all down to the account of ignorance, which, in any degree and however excusable, is not a thing to be admired.

Similarly, here is Bierce once more on the primacy of precision: "We think in words; we cannot think without them. Shallowness or obscurity of speech means shallowness or obscurity of thought."[5] And this is an application of that dictum:

> The other day, in fulfillment of a promise, I took a random page of [Howells'] work and in twenty minutes had marked forty solecisms—instances of the use of words without a sense of their importance or a knowledge of their meaning—the substitution of a word that he did not want for a word that he did not think of. Confusion of thought leads to obscurity of expression. . . . Words are the mechanism of thought. The master knows his machine, and precision is nine parts of style. This fellow Howells thinks into the hopper and the mangled thought comes out all over his cranky apparatus in gobs and splashes of expression."[6]

The point to this digression is to establish at the outset the certainty that Bierce as reader demanded accuracy, and therefore the high probability that Bierce as writer provided it. Lawrence Berkove and Mary Grenander have urged us to read this man's fiction with *care*; and I am contending that "Owl Creek Bridge" is not, *pace* Marcus and nearly all other critics good and bad and indifferent, some sort of hysterical gothic horripilator; it is, on the contrary, as tightly controlled and meticulously organized as any story is likely to be. Bierce knew what he was doing—among other things, here, dispensing fine satiric comment, and seeing to it that the story's protagonist gets his fair share.

I

Poor Peyton Farquhar—"such an attractive figure: brave, sensitive, highly intelligent. . . . It is," Stuart Woodruff mourns, "the tragic waste of such a man which engages our sympathies."[7] Woodruff is mistaken: Farquhar is not brave, he is foolhardy; he is not sensitive, he is callous ("a civilian who was at heart a soldier, and who in good faith and without too much qualification assented to at least a part of the frankly villainous dictum that all is fair in love and war"); and he is not highly intelligent. He is, as we shall see, rather stupid.

Farquhar, poised on the bridge, "looked a moment at his 'unsteadfast footing.' "[8] If recognized as an allusion, this must have seemed a mere gratuitous one to readers for the last eighty years, because no one, so far as I know, has bothered to follow up this little tag. It is worth following up. Here is the allusion in the context (Worcester trying to placate Harry) of *Henry IV, Part I:*

> Peace cousin, say no more.
>   And now I will unclasp a secret book,
> And to your quick-conceiving discontents
> I'll read you matter deep and dangerous,
> As full of peril and adventurous spirit
> As to o'er-walk a current roaring loud
> On the unsteadfast footing of a spear.

Harry is interested:

> If he fall in, good night. Or sink, or swim!
> Send danger from the east unto the west,
> So honor cross it from the north to south,
> And let them grapple! O the blood more stirs
> To rouse a lion than to start a hare.
>   *Northumberland.* Imagination of some great exploit
> Drives him beyond the bounds of patience.
>   *Hotspur.* By heaven methinks it were an easy leap
> To pluck bright honor from the pale-fac'd moon,
> Or dive into the bottom of the deep,
> Where fadom-line could never touch the ground,
> And pluck up drowned honor by the locks . . . (I.iii.197–205)

So by means of his short allusion Bierce has strongly suggested Farquhar's pedigree: he is a sort of latter-day Warmspur, not as splendid and formidable as Harry, but just as restive and foolhardy. What other evidence have we that this is so, that Farquhar is a satiric object?

We have the burlesques. Here, for example, is the beginning of the story's second section:

> Peyton Farquhar was a well-to-do planter, of an old and
> highly respected Alabama family. Being a slave owner and like

other slave owners a politician he was naturally an original
secessionist and ardently devoted to the Southern cause. Circumstances of an imperious nature . . . had prevented him
from taking service with the gallant army that had fought the
disastrous campaigns ending with the fall of Corinth, and he
chafed under the inglorious restraint, longing for the release of
his energies, the larger life of the soldier, the opportunity for
distinction. That opportunity, he felt, would come, as it comes
to all in war time. Meanwhile he did what he could. No service
was too humble for him to perform in aid of the South, no
adventure too perilous for him to undertake.

Now I read this as a thumbnail burlesque of martial rhetoric: words
like "gallant," "inglorious," "opportunity," "distinction," and "adventure" begin cropping up immediately.[9] They are symptoms of
Farquhar's terminal "Walter Scott disease," as Mark Twain called it.
Bierce's inclusion in this *mimesis* of alliteration ("longing . . . release . . .
larger . . . life") helps the burlesque along by inflating these words and
phrases, rendering them emptier than they inherently are, giving
them—to borrow Bierce's own metaphor from a different context—"the
martial strut of a boned turkey." This calls attention to them and thus to
the irony lurking within them (Hemingway fans will note resemblances
here). Bierce emphasizes his burlesque with the figure *isocolon*, here, the
hoariest of encomia for the stay-at-home ("No service . . . too humble, no
adventure too perilous"), and follows this with a sentence epitomizing
chivalric fatuity: the Federal scout asks for a drink of water, and "Mrs.
Farquhar was only too happy to serve him with her own white hands."

John Kenney Crane has mistaken satire for mawkishness. He assures
us that "it is, of course, the blatant sentimentality that mars the story,"
and it is presumably such passages as these which lie at the root of his objection.[10] Crane assumes that the vocabulary is Bierce's, but there is no
reason why he should. To assume that stupid words necessarily signify
authorial obtuseness is to ignore the author's option of addressing his
readers indirectly; such words may well be a sign of authorial astuteness,
as they are here in section two of "Owl Creek Bridge."

Let me emphasize this point. No one, for example, has objected to
James Joyce's occasionally sounding like his characters: "But wasn't Maria
glad when the women had finished their tea and the cook and the dummy
had begun to clear away the tea-things!"[11] When reading sentences like
this, noboby accuses Joyce of being himself a dummy; everybody assumes
that this is masterly first person narrative couched in the third person;
nobody doubts his genius, much less his competence.

If Joyce, why not Bierce? Why assume that what strikes us as Victorian gingerbread would not have struck Bierce as contemporary treacle?
Why not give him the benefit of the doubt? As it turns out, however, there
is no need to do so; nearly everything about the sickly Victorian novel, in-

cluding the hackneyed "white hands" convention, did strike Bierce as being tiresome frippery. In "The Captain of 'The Camel,' " for example,
starving mariners are reduced to eating volumes of current genteel fiction, with the result that

> Our diction consisted, in about equal parts, of classical allu-
> sion, quotation from the stable, simper from the scullery, cant
> from the clubs, and the technical slang of heraldry. We
> boasted much of ancestry, and admired the whiteness of our
> hands whenever the skin was visible through a fault in the
> grease and tar.[12]

The irony, then, is Bierce's; the timidity, triteness, and inanity are Farquhar's. The words are not the author's but the character's, and they
establish him as part villain manqué, part fool. The flaws Crane finds in
the story are flaws in Farquhar's character, and Gordon W. Cunliffe, in
writing that "the sympathy evoked by the description of the main figure is
here [in section two] confirmed," would have been correct had he written
not "confirmed," but "cancelled."[13]

"I will ease my heart/Albeit I make a hazard of my head"
(1H4.I.iii.127–128). These are Hotspur's words, but they could serve,
with the simple substitution of "neck" for "head," as Farquhar's motto.
Obsessed with honor, he neglected the "dusty horseman," neglected to ask
him about his regiment, and so forth—to see if this man were what he
seemed. "Gray-clad" is good enough for Farquhar. And when the
horseman tells him that the piled driftwood "is now dry and would burn
like tow," Farquhar's reaction (inferred from his subsequent predica-
ment) is like Harry's: "Why, it cannot choose but be a noble plot!" (I.
iii.277). As an unreflecting and ingenuous glory hunter, who reveals his
tragicomic flaw in his lexicon, who wears his soldierly heart on his sleeve,
and who seems never to have heard (though "all is fair," though he is
himself an agent) that there exists such folk as spies, Farquhar gets what is
coming to him:

> His neck was in pain and lifting his hand to it he found it hor-
> ribly swollen. He knew that it had a circle of black where the
> rope had bruised it. His eyes felt congested; he could not close
> them. His tongue was swollen with thirst; he relieved its fever
> by thrusting it forward from between his teeth into the cold
> air. How softly the turf had carpeted the untraveled
> avenue—he could no longer feel the roadway beneath his feet!

Here Bierce's own tongue is thrust firmly in his cheek, and we can catch a
clear echo, particularly in the last sentence here, of his charnel wit. This
almost jovial description of the hanged man, plus the burlesque, plus the
allusion to Farquhar's literary lineage, make it obvious that for Bierce he
is negligible and expendable, and fair satiric game.

But Farquhar is, like Henry Fleming, Gulliver, Hotspur, Huck, a satiric vehicle as well as a satiric object. If Farquhar is all too human, as the euphemism has it, then his executioners, the Union company, are all too inhuman. This is how Bierce presents them. This is how, in so doing, he maintains the necessary semblance of neutrality toward his characters, but also, having discouraged sympathy for Farquhar, retains the reader's interest in him. Farquhar, however much a figure of fun he may be, is definitely a human character. We know something about him, as a man; but of the Union soldiers, as men, we know nothing.

Biercean *metonymy* is at work here. It is distinct and distinctive enough in his war writing, that Lars Ahnebrink has called it a "process of animism."[14] Bierce invented this technique (just as he invented the drastic fictional distortion of time). This value of this "process of animism"—which might better be called a "process of deanimism"—is this: by confounding men with things, Bierce, and later Stephen Crane, were able to convey in a subtle but telling manner man's insignificance and subhumanity in his own horrendous conflicts. The latter-day Union soldiers are introduced in terms of the arms they bear, as extensions of their weapons. Just as Farquhar's vice and folly make him liable to lampooning, so the soldiers' apparent lack of any feeling or thought makes them liable to the same. And that is what they get. The sentinels at either end of the bridge and facing outward stand in the "support" position with their rifles. They are not spectators but merely blockades; they "might have been statues to adorn the bridge." The main body of the company stands "staring stonily, motionless," with their rifles at "parade rest," lined up like the tree trunks of the stockade. A lieutenant stands with his hands folded over the hilt of his sword. The captain stands silently.

This tableau is the machine of death in repose. In action it is hardly less regular, suggesting as it does the automata that emerge from the works of Swiss town hall clocks to elaborately chime the hours (an apposite suggestion, since Bierce's main theme is the concept of time, and since his protagonist becomes a "pendulum.") A robot-like series of movements transposes the sergeant and the captain; a nod from the captain removes the sergeant from the plank and precipitates Farquhar. This is the rhetorical trope *hypotyposis*, mimicry of acts, another Biercean favorite.

And these robot-like actions are conveyed by and reflected in a pattern of robot-like sentences and phrases ("The preparations . . . the two . . . The sergeant . . . These movements . . . the end . . . This plant . . . the arrangement"). Such a flatfooted series—article/subject, article/subject—reads like an army training manual on the field-stripping of rifles.[15] Here is more jargon. Bierce has allowed his military persona (for that is the speaker as the story opens) to drift into a burlesque of military diction. The denatured and clumsy language both describes the graceless maneuvers and blurs their significance. This is *mimesis*, again, and it functions with the *metonymy* and the *hypotyposis* to make

Bierce's point, unobtrusively but effectively, about the soldiers. Further-more, this burlesque complements Farquhar's jingoism, already noted, which comes a page later. The jargons interact, military litotes with military hyperbole, revealing the weaknesses of each. The language is ob-jective but the anti-war message is subjective indeed, and the passages together constitute another example of dry and rarefied Biercean wit. "Humor is a sweet wine," he tells us elsewhere, "wit a dry; we know which is preferred by the connoisseur."[16] "Owl Creek Bridge" contains vintage wit, is vintage satire. But it is more than satire; it is philosophy.

II

"A man stood upon a railroad bridge in northern Alabama, looking down into the swift water twenty feet below." This is the first sentence. A few lines later, the "man," Farquhar, is again gazing at the water which we already know is "swift," and he watches it "swirling" and "racing madly" below. Then:

> A piece of dancing driftwood caught his attention and his eyes followed it down the current. How slowly it appeared to move! What a sluggish stream!

The "swift" stream has suddenly turned "sluggish." Bierce is tampering with time in these latter three sentences, for each reflects a different point of view.

The water is swift. What thoughts this current calls up for the doomed man are at first open to conjecture since we are still observing Farquhar and his surroundings, not yet observing through him. The point of view is limited, the narrator acutely perceptive but disinterested. We are met with a series of uncertainties which communicate the narrator's limitations. Things beyond the moment and the field of vision are not definitely known, and the narrator is careful to separate, precisely, sur-mise from certainty: the captain is definitely a captain because he is in the uniform "of his rank," but the sergeant "*may*" (my emphasis) in civil life have been a deputy sheriff—and then again he may not have been; there is no way to be sure. Also, because the railroad was "lost to view" in the forest after a hundred yards, the narrator can only infer from military usage that "doubtless there was an outpost farther along." Similarly, Far-quhar was "apparently" thirty-five years old, "evidently" no vulgar assassin, and a civilian and planter "if one might judge from his habit."

Bierce's handling of this persona—a man who knows what he knows and what he does not—is as deft as it is unobtrusive. But despite this per-sona's seeming objectivity and anonymity, we can still know a bit about him because his language gives him away. For example, he is (the irony indicates) slightly amused: "The liberal military code makes provision for hanging many kinds of persons, and gentlemen are not excluded." And this raises another point: this persona seems to know a great deal about the military. In the first part of section one we are treated to explanations of martial code, etiquette, usage, terms, and postures. In brief, the story's title and its first section smack of the general officer's memoirs—perhaps those of an old soldier who is at heart a *litterateur*.

This military observer (to refer again to the three sentences quoted above) notices the object catching Farquhar's attention and Farquhar's eyes following that object; this limited observer becomes an omniscient one in the next sentence, and is thus able to relate how this object appears to Farquhar; and in the third sentence the observer again becomes limited, but it is now a different observer, Farquhar himself. The reversal is complete. (And this is only the first of what becomes a pattern of such reversals, ranging from minute [the three sentence about-face], through extensive [the intrusion of the omniscient narrator—and reality—into fancy, at the close of each section], to all-inclusive [the last such intrusion, the whiplash ending].) This momentary but significant glance through Farquhar's eyes sets a precedent; the character has become, briefly, a second persona, and may do so again.

These three sentences merit a bit more attention. Bierce signals this reversal, accompanies and helps accomplish it, by supplanting prose with near-verse for as long as the reversal takes. Sentence one begins with four iambs ("A piece of dancing driftwood caught"); sentence two consists of the same ("How slowly it appeared to move!"); and sentence three begins with two trochees ("What a sluggish stream!"). That is the meter. The first sentence's *d*-alliteration gives way to the *s*-alliteration of sentences two and three. Bierce varies this alliteration in the last two words, slowing them, by juxtaposing *s*- and *sh*- sibilants, thus joining sound to sense; it is impossible to articulate, quickly, "sluggish stream."

We are now and momentarily inside the protagonist's brain, and that brain is definitely malfunctioning. In the next paragraph, the first full one on page thirty, the ticking of Farquhar's watch becomes to his ears thunderous, and more and more infrequent. ("No reader," Professor Marcus assures us, "could possibly fail to be reminded of Poe's story of 'The Tell-Tale Heart' " [p. 15]; Marcus does not, however, say why an essentially unlike and woefully inferior story should so inevitably come to mind, and one must therefore assume that he is simply resorting to the easy and stereotypic but wrong preconceptions that preclude an adequate reading of Bierce—in this instance, the persistent misconception that Bierce aped Poe.) Again we are perceiving through Farquhar. The sound "seemed" both distant and close, but then the interposed consciousness of the omniscient narrator again disappears; the intervals of silence did not "seem to grow," they "*grew*" and the sound "*increased*" (my emphases). It is, must be, his own brain, with thoughts being "flashed" upon it, that misinterprets this subdued and regular sound, and thus flaws the narrative. (Professor Marcus, however, does not think this is a disguised first person intrusion because he has discovered that the whole story is told by—and this would have pleased Bierce—an "omniscient author" [p. 14]. One might point out to him, though—without quibbling over the distinction between "author" and "narrator"—that his "omniscient author" is at times strangely ignorant: "What he heard was the ticking of his watch." "What a sluggish stream!"). As Farquhar's mind works at ever higher speed everything else correspondingly slows, and we should be prepared for, not an escape, but a hallucination.

And this is what fascinated Bierce: the grim possibility that there is no death which is mercifully instantaneous since ordinary time may not apply. Mary Grenander, in her Twayne book on Bierce (Ch. 11, n. 5), first found this intriguing and revealing passage in his essay on the then new electric chair:

> The physicians know nothing about it; for anything they know to the contrary, death by electricity may be the most frightful torment that it is possible for any of nature's forces or processes to produce. The agony may be not only inconceivably great, but to the sufferer it may seem to endure for a period inconceivably long. That many of the familiar physical indications of suffering are absent (though "long, shuddering sighs" and "straining at the straps" are not certainly symptoms of joy) is very little to the purpose when we know that electricity paralyzes the muscles by whose action pain is familiarly manifested. We know that it paralyzes all the seats of sensation, for that matter, and puts an end to possibilities of pain. That is only to say that it kills. But by what secret and infernal pang may not all this be accompanied or accomplished? Through what unnatural exaltation of the senses may not the moment of its accomplishing be commuted into unthinkable cycles of time?[17]

Hence Farquhar, his senses "exalted and refined," in his "unthinkable arcs of oscillation."

Later in this essay Bierce comes to the point: "Theories of the painlessness of sudden death appear to be based mostly upon the fact that those who undergo it make no entries of their sensations in their diaries" (p. 266). The third section of "Owl Creek Bridge Bridge" is a fictional attempt at just such a diary.

And logic is our guide through its mad pages. How do we know what we know? Bierce raises the epistemological question subtly but persistently. Indeed the whole story is "a lesson in perspective," as Stuart Woodruff so aptly titled his consideration of it. Or, what comes to the same thing, it is an exercise in "the faculty of discrimination," a faculty dormant or absent in both Farquhar and "bad readers."

There is an initial, strange uncertainty: could a man—however "exalted and refined" his "organic system"—see a million distinct blades of grass, and the dewdrops on each blade, and the prism in each drop, and the colors in each prism? Not likely. Thomas Erskine is probably right in saying that most readers accept this "outrageous hyperbole."[18] But there is no excuse for such readers—Marcus among them—to do so, because Farquhar's perceptions are, in the strict sense of the word, preposterous.

And Bierce even points this out, as directly as he is able; Farquhar's senses are making "record of things never before perceived." This is the rhetorical trope *adianoeta*, deliberate ambiguousness, a Biercean favorite. Here it enables Bierce to ask his reader, indirectly but pointedly, perceived by whom? If by Farquhar only, then to make this explicit, "they had" should appear between "things" and "never." But the wording as it is leaves the question barely open: it may be only Farquhar who has never sensed such things; it may well be that no human being has ever sensed them; probably no percipient creature has ever done so. The conclusion following the latter two interpretations is obvious, and these two are supported by the record of Farquhar's astonishing sensations.

Could he (to take another example) hear a water spider's legs moving on the same flood in which he is now ostensibly immersed? Could he hear this above the rush of the torrent and the rasp of his own half-strangled breathing? Perhaps; very probably not—despite Professor Marcus's conviction that, were it not for our "usual insensitivity," we could, just as Farquhar did, thrill to this "vibrant, throbbing, pulsating," albeit infinitesimal, "life." "A fish slid along beneath his *eyes* and he *heard* the rush of its body parting the water" (my emphases). Bierce's phrasing suggests that Farquhar comes close to a synaesthetic experience here, that not only does he hear the inaudible but he does so with his eyes, and this at a time when he is supposedly bending every effort to stay alive. Again, however, this may not be absolutely impossible.

But when we are told that as he surfaced he could see the bridge and the fort (that is, he was far enough downstream for such a comprehensive view), but that the figures on the bridge were at this distance gigantic; and when we are told that at this distance he could see the eye and the color of the eye of the soldier who is shooting at him (which feat is in itself extremely improbable), although this man is to Farquhar a *silhouette*—by definition a dark featureless form in outline—then we must conclude that the gray eye is Farquhar's own, that it is turned inward, and that the "visible world" of which he is the "pivotal point" is also all his own. We *know* that Farquhar could not have seen these last two sights for the same reason we know that God can make neither a colossal midget nor a square circle.

No critic, so far as I know, has caught these two clear logical contradictions. And Woodruff, moving from a consideration of things he thinks *could* not have happened—seeing the dewdrops, etc.—to a consideration of things that did not happen, even quotes part of the passage in question: "Excited soldiers, silhouetted 'against the blue sky,' shout and gesticulate, Farquhar is spun and buffeted by the current, shots spatter all around him and he dives 'as deeply as he could.' " Woodruff comments: "It is this kind of specific detail [presumably including the eye in the silhouette and the gigantic soldiers in the distance] that keeps persuading the reader that perhaps the impossible has happened, that the rope did break and that soon Farquhar will be safe in the forest."[19]

Not so. Farquhar is hallucinating and we know it. But, one may object, he is doing so too quickly: he is compressing an imaginary twenty-four hours into a fraction of a second.

Yet this is of course just Bierce's point. He makes it in his electric chair essay; he makes it implicitly throughout the story, beginning with the preposition *at* in the title; he makes it explicitly in the story's last sentence, ruling out any possibility of the comparatively slow death by strangulation: Farquhar had a "broken neck" and his dreaming was therefore done in an instant. Bierce, with his passion for precision and concision, would hardly have included such a detail inadvertently. No. Farquhar's death sentence was (and note the typically Biercean irony in this word's connotation) *"commuted"* only in the sense that death by electrocution may be "commuted"—that is, subjectively. "Swift" Owl Creek and the perceived behavior of the watch tell us that Farquhar's mind was accelerating (geometrically, in the manner of the falling body that he is) in proportion to the world's apparent deceleration; as real time left to him dwindles to nothing, subjective time expands this remnant, maintaining the balance. This is the hypothesis for the "careful and analytic record of" Farquhar's "sensations at every stage of his mischance"; this is the logical foundation for Bierce's "*A Diary of Sudden Death; By a Public-Spirited Observer on the Inside.*"[20] Farquhar is the guinea pig; Bierce is the real "student of hanging."

The theoretical arrow of Zeno is a good analogy here since the story's premise can be understood as a corollary of this ancient conundrum. Zeno's arrow never reached its target because, before it could do so, it had first to traverse half the distance, then half the remaining distance, etc., with eighths, sixteenths, thirty-seconds, sixty-fourths, and so on, endlessly interposing themselves. The arrow can get very close, but since a mathematical line has only location and direction, and not area, one can always be squeezed in half way between approaching point and static plane. For the archer this would be sufficiently discouraging. But when he reflects that his arrow can never get more than half-way anywhere, then he will realize that the shaft can never even leave the bow and that motion is impossible; and he will trudge sadly home. Zeno's assumption is that space is infinitely divisible; Bierce's, that time is infinitely divisible. It follows that if the human brain could perform that function and thus generate its own reprieve-in-progress, then death would be impossible, and Farquhar, thinking "with the rapidity of lightning," would be forever *in extremis*—immortal in some private fifth dimension.

Woodruff writes, toward the close of his discussion of the story, that "somehow the reader is made to participate in the split between imagination and reason, to *feel* the escape is real while he *knows* it is not."[21] Woodruff is right, but his "somehow" could be improved upon. My suggestion is that the story gets much of its power from the opposition of two logics, that this is the submerged origin of Woodruff's "split." Bierce pairs unanswerable philosophical logic with the implacable logic of natural law. To Farquhar, death cannot be real so the escape must be; to the Biercean reader, the reader who keeps his eyes open and his sympathies in check, who therefore sees the series of gross improbabilities, contradictions, and shifts in point of view, to such a reader it is just the other way around—because the human brain, even a first-rate one, cannot perform the function of dividing time infinitely. The shaft hits home and the man's neck breaks.

To sum up: Bierce knew what he was doing, and we can know what he did. He did not write a Radcliffean cliff-hanger, nor a soap operetta, nor a slam-bang action yarn. All the evidence, both inside and outside the story, points the other way. The logic lets us know that we are participating in a hallucination, and that whatever else the reality behind the hallucination may be, it is not tragedy. This is simply the record of an "occurrence"—a rehearsal of the way things are. But it is also a broad hint at the warless way life should be, as well as an imaginative guess at the way death may be.

And it is superb art. Brooks and Warren ask, expecting the answer *no*, "is the surprise ending justified; is it validated by the body of the story; is it, in other words, a mere trick, or is it expressive and functional?"[22] We do not drink fine wine to quench thirst; we do not read Bierce to kill time. Brooks and Warren expected mediocrity, read the story accordingly, and misunderstood this masterpiece of fiction—complaining, as they do, about the sad lack of "meaningful irony" and so forth.[23] One might as reasonably dismiss a lofty vintage, gulped from the bottle, for the bitterness of its lees. The correct answer to Brooks and Warren's question is a resounding *yes*. Yes, the ending is justified, validated, expressive, and functional because the story's satiric content requires it, because the story's premise demands it, and because, realizing these necessities, Bierce took care that the ending should be in the beginning and throughout. Stephen Crane, as good a reader and critic as he was a writer, did *not* misunderstand "Owl Creek Bridge": "That story has everything," he wrote.[24] "Nothing better exists."

Notes

1. *Understanding Fiction*, 2nd ed. (NY: Appleton, 1959), short excerpt rpt. in *From Fiction to Film/Ambrose Bierce's* "An Occurrence at Owl Creek Bridge," ed. Gerald R. Barrett and Thomas L. Erskine, Dickenson Literature and Film Series, No. 2 (Encino, Calif.: Dickenson, 1973), pp. 52, 53.

2. *California English Journal*, 7 (February 1971), 14–23; first quotations pp. 15, 14 resp.

3. "Emma Frances Dawson," s.v. "The Reviewer," *The Collected Works of Ambrose Bierce*, 12 vols. (NY: Neale, 1909), X, 167.

4. "Prattle," The San Francisco *Argonaut*, 22 June 1878.

5. "The Matter of Manner," *Works*, X, 59.

6. "Prattle," The San Francisco *Wasp*, 17 February 1883.

7. *The Short Stories of Ambrose Bierce/A Study in Polarity* (Pittsburgh: Pittsburgh U Press, 1964), p. 156.

8. "An Occurrence at Owl Creek Bridge," s.v. "In the Midst of Life," *Works*, II, 30. All subsequent references to this edition.

9. Thomas L. Erskine has noted that "Farquhar has unrealistic ideas about war," in his essay "Language and Theme in 'An Occurrence at Owl Creek Bridge,' " Barrett and Erskine, p. 71; and Cathy N. Davidson, having perceived this earlier, rightly points out that this passage of the story contains mostly meaningless words. Her analysis "Literary Semantics in the Fiction of Ambrose Bierce" will appear in a forthcoming issue of *ETC., A Review of General Semantics* (San Francisco).

10. "Crossing the Bar Twice: Post-Mortem Consciousness in Bierce, Hemingway, and Golding," *Studies in Short Fiction*, 6 (Summer 1969), 363.

11. "Clay," *Dubliners* (1916; rpt. NY: Viking, 1962), p. 101.

12. "The Ocean Wave," *Works*, VIII, 234–235.

13. "An Occurrence at Owl Creek Bridge." *Insight*, 1 (1962), rpt. in Barrett and Erskine, p. 56.

14. *The Beginnings of Naturalism in American Fiction* (Cambridge: Harvard U Press, 1950). Ahnebrink thinks it likely that Crane read *Soldiers and Civilians* before writing *Red Badge of Courage*: he bolsters this contention by quoting from a Crane letter: "I deeply admire some short stories by Mr. Bierce" (p. 103).

15. Erskine has noticed this too: the passage reads, he says, "like 'How To' instruction with short, choppy sentences, step-by-step chronological order—only the numbers are missing" (p. 71).

16. "The Opinionator," *Works*, X, 101.

17. "The Chair of Little Ease," *Works*, XI, 365–366. It is worth noting that this essay's title is the colloquial term for the instrument of the slow and most horrible of deaths, impalement.

18. "Language and Theme in 'An Occurrence at Owl Creek Bridge,' " in Barrett and Erskine, p. 71.

19. Woodruff, p. 158.

20. "The Chair of Little Ease," pp. 366–367.

21. Woodruff, p. 157.

22. Brooks and Warren, p. 52.

23. p. 153.

24. R. W. Stallman and Lillian Gilkes, *Stephen Crane/Letters* (NY: New York U Press, 1960), pp. 139–140, n. 94.

Bierce's Turn of the Screw:
Tales of Ironical Terror

M. E. Grenander*

Sponge-like, the glamorous life and elusive personality of Ambrose Bierce have absorbed the attention of scholars, who have studied the author instead of his literary output. Accordingly, such off-hand critical judgments as the numerous writers on Bierce have offered are usually either wrong, or right for the wrong reasons. For example, in the Autumn, 1954, issue of the *Hudson Review*, Marcus Klein pauses in the midst of an article discussing the hatefulness of Ambrose Bierce to break a parenthetical lance on the collective heads of those who dismiss Bierce's stories as mere imitations of Poe's. For the Bierce stories are, according to Mr. Klein, "unlike the satin horrors of Poe" because "they did a job. They drew an indictment. They served."

Mr. Klein's conclusion immediately sets him up in opposition to a long line of critics and literary historians, of varying degrees of scholarship, who have either tried to establish, or subscribed blindly to, the thesis that Bierce was a follower of Poe. The attempt began in Bierce's own lifetime, and never failed to arouse his articulate wrath and his stout disclaimers that his tales had really been sired by Poe. On September 6, 1909, he wrote Silas Orrin Howes with wry irony: "If I had left the tragic and the supernatural out of my stories I would still have been an 'imitator of Poe,' for they would still have been stories; so what's the use?"[1]

Bierce's repeated denials of Poe's influence on his tales did not, however, prevent a succession of reviewers and critics from continuing to trace this same illegitimate genealogy. The effort reached its solemn apotheosis in Arthur Miller's scholarly attempt to establish the bar sinister in the ancestry of Bierce's stories. In an article in *American Literature* (May, 1932) entitled "The Influence of Edgar Allan Poe on Ambrose Bierce," Mr. Miller marshalled an imposing array of similarities between the work of the two men, but offered no proof that Bierce "borrowed" from Poe. And the recent *Times Literary Supplement* issue on American literature (September 17, 1954) was only following conventional pro-

*Reprinted by permission of the editor, *Western Humanities Review*, and by M. E. Grenander, who has authorized two minor corrections in the text. From *Western Humanities Review*, 11 (Summer 1957), 257–64.

cedure in treating the two authors together as part of our national tradition of dark horror.

Hence Mr. Klein's heresy is a welcome corrective to an uncritical bromide which has been accepted more or less on faith by generations of readers. But the grounds on which Mr. Klein bases his conclusion are disturbing in their implications. For few writers have been more insistent than Bierce that it was *not* the function of literature to do a job, draw an indictment, or serve. These chores he relegated to journalism, for which, despite the very good living it paid him ($100 a week from William Randolph Hearst), he had only contempt. But literature was something else again. "The Muse will not meet you if you have any work for her to do"[2] is a characteristic statement of Bierce's views on the subject.

Nevertheless, despite what I consider his false premises, I believe Mr. Klein to have arrived at a sound conclusion, for I think it is demonstrable that Bierce's stories are completely "unlike the satin horrors of Poe," though for aesthetic rather than didactic reasons. In the first place, besides his tales of horror Bierce wrote other types: comic stories, tales of pathos, stories of tragic pity, etc. In the second place, when we do concentrate on his horror tales we find that they differ specifically from Poe's in a way that has not yet been analyzed and that constitutes them as a distinct form, an examination of which yields illuminating differentiae. I therefore propose, in this essay, to scrutinize some of Bierce's tales of terror and to show in what way their form differs from that of Poe's.

Briefly, I believe that Bierce's unique contribution to the development of the short story is the particular way in which he combined irony with terror. In any terror tale, the emotional effect is basically an intense degree of fear. Poe uses all the devices at his command to enhance and increase it to a climactic crescendo, relying heavily, for example, on bizarre settings: a lonely decayed old house on the brink of a miasmal tarn, a torture chamber of the Spanish Inquisition, a subterranean tomb in the vaults of an ancient family castle.

Bierce's method, however, was quite different. He added an ironic twist,[3] which rests primarily on a certain kind of relationship between plot and character, so that we feel an intense fear coupled with a bitter realization that the emotion is cruelly inappropriate. What emerges is really a new form. Poe's tales of terror are nearly all simple in plot and cumulative in their emotional impact; Bierce's best ones are complex in plot and involve an element of irony in their emotional effect.

Bierce's handling of irony was, moreover, highly individual. Most authors who have cultivated it—O. Henry comes instantly to mind—have done so by manipulating the manner of representation. In other words, the narrator self-consciously conceals or holds back vital bits of information until he can spring them on the unsuspecting reader—often with little regard for the demands of probability in either plot or character—at a point in the representation where he thinks they will achieve their maximum effect of surprise. (The revelation is frequently so unexpected, and rests on so slight a foundation of probability, that not uncommonly the effect can, indeed, be more accurately described as stupefaction.) When this technique is applied to the terror story, we get what might be termed "the ironical tale of terror."

Bierce was not above using this artificial device. But in his best stories, the irony lies not in a self-conscious coyness on the part of the narrator, but in a certain relationship between a given character and the incidents of the plot. Hence I have chosen to call these stories, not ironical tales of terror, but tales of ironical terror, since the irony is not a factitious thing tacked on by the narrator, but an integral part of the action itself.

How is this effect of ironical terror achieved? Fundamentally, it depends on a firm psychological grasp of the connection between intellectual, emotional, and sensory factors in the human personality. In Bierce's tales of ironical terror, a character's reaction to given circumstances involves all three of these factors. First, he has an intellectual awareness of a dangerous situation—typically one which he believes threatens his life or his honor. Second, this knowledge arouses in him an emotion of fear, deepening to terror, and frequently thence to madness. Third, this emotional involvement results in a particular kind of physical reaction—usually a tremendous heightening and acceleration of sensory perceptions, the latter often indicated by a slowing-up of subjective time.

Obviously the base of this psychology is the intellectual awareness of danger. Just as obviously this psychology could be used in a good nonironical horror story showing the steadily increasing effects of terror on the protagonist. (As matter of fact, this is the kind of story Poe writes.) Bierce, however, makes the intellectual awareness on which the whole psychology of his protagonist's terror rests a wrong one; hence all the emotional and sensory reactions which follow are erroneous, and the reader's perception of this gruesome inappropriateness to the facts of the real situation is what gives their peculiar distillation of horror to the Bierce tales.

Let us say that a character sees a deadly snake in his bedroom. He "knows" that the snake's bite will be fatal. This intellectual perception results in an emotional reaction of fear. Or suppose that a man, after a long absence, returns home and sees his cherished wife running to meet him. He "knows" that they will soon be reunited; consequently he "feels" joy. In either of these cases, the intellectual perception is accurate and the emotional reaction proper and appropriate. But suppose that in the second example, the man sees a woman running to meet him who he thinks is his wife; she is in fact, however, a neighbor who is hurrying to tell him of his wife's death. His emotional reaction in this case will be the same as in the former—i.e., joy; but the effect of the story will be ironical, since his intellectual perception is inaccurate and his emotional reaction therefore painfully inappropriate.

That this relationship between thought and emotion was an integral part of Bierce's interpretation of human pyschology and not a factitious schema superimposed on his stories by the present writer is indicated by comments he made in two letters. Writing to his protégé, George Sterling, on January 29, 1910, he said: "You know it has always been my belief that one cannot be trusted to feel until one has learned to think." And to Percival Pollard he wrote, on July 29, 1911: "To feel rightly one must think and know rightly."[4]

The story "One Kind of Officer" probably isolates more clearly than any other the importance of the intellectual perception of danger to Bierce's psychology. Although I conceive this tale to be one of retributive tragedy rather than one of terror, I introduce it at this point because it shows the tremendous importance Bierce puts on a character's "knowledge" of a situation. In this story even the army, for example, has a subconscious kind of knowledge: "Beneath the individual thoughts and emotions of its component parts it thinks and feels as a unit. And in this large, inclusive sense of things lies a wiser wisdom than the mere sum of all that it knows." Hence the men "had a dumb consciousness that all was not well" and "felt insecure," while the officers "spoke more learnedly of what they apprehended with no greater clearness."[5]

But Captain Ransome, who is in "conditions favorable to thought," understands the situation with greater precision. General Cameron, however, has told him: "It is not permitted to you to know *anything*"—an order which Ransome takes quite literally and repeats to Lieutenant Price. Cameron, we discover, has been tragically mistaken in thinking Ransome "too fond of his opinion," for the captain commits the fatal error of acting contrary to knowledge he himself possesses. With the "mechanical fidelity" which all the army is showing that day, Ransome does no more than his duty, callously following orders and consciously slaughtering his own men. And he must pay the price for his lethal actions: when General Masterson asks him if he does not know what he had been doing, he admits his knowledge. Masterson, shocked, says: "You know it—you know that, and you sit here smoking?"

Ransome tries to excuse himself on the grounds of following orders, even though they ran counter to his knowledge, but when he turns to Lieutenant Price (General Cameron has been killed) with the query, "Do you know anything of the orders under which I was acting?" Price, who has also been told it was not permitted him to know *anything*, says: "I know nothing." And Ransome is doomed by the same kind of officer he himself is: one who obeys orders mechanically, knowing they are wrong, and sends men to their death in the process.

"One Kind of Officer" is unique among Bierce's stories, not for its irony—that is typical—but because the protagonist does not act on his knowledge. For typically in a Bierce story the character acts, or reacts, all too thoroughly on the basis of the best knowledge that he has, irony arising because his knowledge is fatally wrong.

The situation in terror stories must be one that will arouse fear; hence it must either be dangerous or be thought dangerous. Bierce's best tales of ironical terror can be divided into two groups: those in which the actual situation is harmful, with the protagonist conceiving it to be harmless and reacting accordingly; and those in which the actual situation is harmless, with the protagonist conceiving it to be harmful and reacting accordingly. In either of these groups, the reader may share the protagonist's misconception of the situation, not realizing the truth until the end of the story; or he may realize all along that the protagonist is wrong. What the reader's grasp of events will be is controlled by the method of narration.

In the first category come such stories as "An Occurrence at Owl Creek Bridge"[6] and "Chickamauga." In both, the protagonist thinks himself safe in what is really a harmful situation. Peyton Farquhar's sensations in "Owl Creek Bridge"[7] are at first "unaccompanied by thought. The intellectual part of his nature was already effaced; he had power only to feel." Suddenly, however, "the power of thought was restored; he knew that the rope had broken and he had fallen into the stream. . . . His brain was as energetic as his arms and legs; he thought with the rapidity of lightning." He thinks (wrongly) that he has made a miraculous last-minute escape from being hanged.

The child in "Chickamauga"[8] believes that the group of maimed and bleeding soldiers he comes upon is "a merry spectacle," which reminds him "of the painted clown whom he had seen last summer in the circus." He fails to recognize his home when he sees its blazing ruins, and thinks them a pleasing sight.

Accompanying these intellectual misunderstandings are emotional reactions which are gruesomely inappropriate. Farquhar eagerly makes his way homeward (he thinks), joyfully anticipating a reunion with his wife. The boy in "Chickamauga" has a gay time playing with the pitiful specimens he comes upon, "heedless . . . of the dramatic contrast between his laughter and their own ghastly gravity." He even tries to ride pig-a-back on one of the crawling and broken soldiers, and he dances with glee about the flaming embers of his home.

In both stories the protagonist also has unusual physical reactions. Farquhar's senses are preternaturally acute: "Something in the awful disturbance of his organic system had so exalted and refined them that they made record of things never before perceived." He feels each ripple of water on his face; he sees the veining of individual leaves in the forest on the bank of the river, the insects on them, and the prismatic colors of the dew in the grass. He even sees through the rifle sights the eye of the man on the bridge who is firing at him. And he hears "the humming of the gnats . . .; the beating of the dragon-flies' wings, the strokes of the water-spiders' legs," the rush of a fish's body. Accompanying all this is the slowing up of time; the interval between his falling and suffocating is "ages," and the ticking of his watch is so strong and sharp it "hurt[s] his ear like the thrust of a knife."

The "Chickamauga" boy, on the other hand, has senses which are subnormally dull. He is a deaf-mute, a fact which accounts for his sleeping through the battle: "all unheard by him were the roar of the musketry, the shock of the cannon." When he recognizes the torn and mangled body of his dead mother, and a belated understanding bursts upon him, he can express himself only by "a series of inarticulate and indescribable cries—something between the chattering of an ape and the gobbling of a turkey—a startling, soulless, unholy sound, the language of a devil."

In "An Occurrence at Owl Creek Bridge," the reader does not realize the true state of affairs until the end of the story. In "Chickamauga," he is constantly aware of the true situation and the irony of the boy's reaction to it; the narrator tells us immediately: "Not all of this did the child note; it is what would have been noted by an elder observer." For this reason, in "Chickamauga" the horrific effect is stronger, and the ironic element in it is maintained more consistently from beginning to end. We are not conscious, as we are in "Owl Creek Bridge," of the narrator's manipulation of point of view. We lose the element of surprise at the end; we gain a more powerful and more constant emotional effect.

In the second group of stories—represented by "One of the Missing," "One Officer, One Man," and "The Man and the Snake"[9]—the technique of ironic terror is reversed. A basically harmless (or at least, not very harmful) situation is misinterpreted as an extremely perilous one; the protagonist has all the emotional reactions which would be appropriate to a situation of terrible danger, and the story concludes with his death.

Jerome Searing in "One of the Missing" is convinced that a loaded rifle, set on a hair-trigger and pointed directly at his forehead, will go off if he makes the slightest move. In "One Officer, One Man" Captain Graffenreid not only misinterprets his situation, he misinterprets his own character. Thinking himself a courageous man, "his spirit was buoyant, his faculties were riotous. He was in a state of mental exaltation." But after the shooting starts, "his conception of war" undergoes "a profound change. . . . The fire of battle was not now burning very brightly in this warrior's soul. From inaction had come introspection. He sought rather to analyze his feelings than distinguish himself by courage and devotion. The result was profoundly disappointing." In his change from ignorance to knowledge of his own character, he realizes his cowardice, but he still thinks he is engaged in a dangerous battle.

In "The Man and the Snake" Harker Brayton thinks the reptile under his bed a real one which is trying to hypnotize him with its malevolent glare. At first he is "more keenly conscious of the incongruous nature of the situation than affected by its perils; it was revolting, but absurd." He thinks of calling the servant, but it occurs to him "that the act might subject him to the suspicion of fear, which he certainly did not feel." Then he considers the offensive qualities of the snake: "These thoughts shaped themselves with greater or less definition in Brayton's mind and begot action. The process is what we call consideration and decision. It is thus that we are wise and unwise." But he overestimates his own powers of emotional resistance, and makes a fatal mistake: " 'I am not so great a coward as to fear to seem to myself afraid.' "

In all these cases, the protagonist reacts emotionally to what he thinks is a situation of extreme jeopardy. Jerome Searing is a brave man, and as he creeps forward on his scouting expedition, his pulse is "as regular, his nerves . . . as steady as if he were trying to trap a sparrow." When he sees the rifle pointed at his head and remembers he has left it cocked, he is "affected with a feeling of uneasiness. But that was as far as possible from fear." Gradually, however, he becomes conscious of a dull ache in his forehead; when he opens his eyes it goes away; when he closes them it comes back. He grows more and more terrified. As he stares at the gun barrel, the pain in his forehead deepens; he lapses into unconsciousness and delirium.

> Jerome Searing, the man of courage, the formidable enemy, the strong, resolute warrior, was as pale as a ghost. His jaw was fallen; his eyes protruded; he trembled in every fibre; a cold sweat bathed his entire body; he screamed with fear. He was not insane—he was terrified.

Captain Graffenreid, as he hears his men laughing at his cowardice, burns with "a fever of shame," and "the whole range of his sensibilities" is affected. "The strain upon his nervous organization was insupportable." Agitation also grips Brayton, though he is a reasonable man. The snake's horrible power over his imagination increases his fear, and finally he, too, screams with terror.

In these stories, as in those of the first group, the protagonists react with unusual physical sensations. Searing "had not before observed how light and feathery" the tops of the distant trees were, "nor how darkly blue the sky was, even among their branches, where they somewhat paled it with their green. . . . He heard the singing of birds, the strange metallic note of the meadow lark." Time slows up, space contracts, and he becomes nothing but a bundle of sensations:

> No thoughts of home, of wife and children, of country, of glory. The whole record of memory was effaced. The world had passed away—not a vestige remained. Here in this confusion of timbers and boards is the sole universe. Here is immortality in time—each pain an everlasting life. The throbs tick off eternities.

Captain Graffenreid, in his state of terror, grows "hot and cold by turns," pants like a dog, and forgets to breathe "until reminded by vertigo." Harker Brayton is also affected physically. When he means to retreat, he finds that he is unaccountably walking slowly forward. "The secret of human action is an open one: something contracts our muscles. Does it matter if we give to the preparatory molecular changes the name of will?" His face takes on "an ashy pallor," he drops his chair and groans.

> He heard, somewhere, the continuous throbbing of a great drum, with desultory bursts of far music, inconceivably sweet, like the tones of an aeolian harp. . . . The music ceased; rather, it became by insensible degrees the distant roll of a retreating thunder-storm. A landscape, glittering with sun and rain, stretched before him, arched with a vivid rainbow framing in its giant curve a hundred visible cities.

The landscape seems to rise up and vanish; he has fallen on the floor. His face white and bloody, his eyes strained wide, his mouth dripping with flakes of froth, he wriggles toward the snake in convulsive movements.

All three men die of their fright: Brayton and Searing from sheer panic; Graffenreid a suicide because he can no longer tolerate the disorganization of his nervous system. But all their terror and pain was needless—Searing's rifle had already been discharged; Graffenreid's battle was a minor skirmish; Brayton's snake was only a stuffed one with shoe-button eyes. In these stories, as in "Chickamauga" and "An Occurrence at Owl Creek Bridge," Bierce has given the terror an ironic turn of the screw.

Notes

1. Unpublished letter, HM 10255, quoted by permission of the Henry E. Huntington Library, San Marino, California.

2. Letter to Blanche Partington, August 28, 1892, *The Letters of Ambrose Bierce*, ed. Bertha Clark Pope (San Francisco: The Book Club of California, 1922), p. 10.

3. Carey McWilliams has recognized this fact: "His stories are, with a few exceptions, not concerned with terror so much as they are with a sort of mocking and ironic fright, a fear inspired in the reader by the clever manipulation of phrase and scene. . . ." See the Introduction to Carroll D. Hall's *Bierce and the Poe Hoax* (San Francisco: The Book Club of California, 1934), p. v.

4. Manuscripts of both letters are in the Henry W. and Albert A. Berg Collection of The New York Public Library. Permission to quote from them was given by the Library.

5. All story quotations are from Vol. II, *In the Midst of Life*, of *The Collected Works of Ambrose Bierce* (New York and Washington: The Neale Publishing Co., 1909–12). "One Kind of Officer" is on pp. 178–96.

6. For an interesting, though less artistic, parallel to "Owl Creek Bridge" see Daphne du Maurier's "The Split Second," in *Kiss Me Again, Stranger* (Garden City, New York: Doubleday & Company, Inc., 1953), pp. 233–80.

7. *Works*, II, 27–45.

8. *Ibid.*, pp. 46–57.

9. *Ibid.*, pp. 71–92, 197–208, 311–23.

Bierce's "The Death of Halpin Frayser": The Poetics of Gothic Consciousness

William Bysshe Stein*

> Mind, n. A mysterious form of matter secreted by the brain. Its chief activity consists in the endeavor to ascertain its own nature, the futility of the attempt being due to the fact that it has nothing but itself to know itself with.
>
> *The Devil's Dictionary*

Whatever its European origins and whatever its reflections of the unresolved dualism of the Protestant sensibility, the Gothicism of American fiction remains an artistic phenomenon. Almost as if by dynastic succession, Brown, Poe, Hawthorne, James, and Bierce labor to bring larger stretches of the chartless domain of human consciousness under control of the word. The exorcizing of the demons and ghosts of dream, reverie, fantasy, nightmare, and compulsion is for each of them an irresistible challenge to invent a narrative method that will magically effect a conjunction of the subjective and objective worlds. But unlike literary critics, not one of these writers presumes to call the one illusory and the other real. With the exception of Brown who learned the same lesson from, I think, Sterne, they learn from one another that the practice of fiction is an art of illusion far more reliable than the artifact of history in revealing the essentially ahistorical activity of the mind. Accordingly, they undertake to create discrete worlds of rhetoric that incarnate the meaning of experience in their reconstruction of the process of consciousness. Beginning with Brown and continuing through Bierce (or even Faulkner), they manipulate the language of prose as if composing poetry, intent upon allowing the mind to speak in the multiple idioms in which it thinks or thinks it thinks. For them the perception of anything has little to do, ultimately, with the faculty of reason which, as scientists are beginning to realize, is simply a pragmatic instrument—a convenient and useful mental habit for condensing a combination of noted, half-noted, and un-

*Reprinted by permission of the author and the editor, *Emerson Society Quarterly*, 18 (Second Quarter, 1972), 115–22.

noted observations into an expedient crutch for carrying on the clumsy business of life. Or, put in another perspective, these practitioners of Gothicism, each in his own way, attempt to capture all the associations and dissociations of thought that merge into a single perception of what is called reality. In spite of his swaggering penchant for sensationalism, Bierce is a virtuoso in the handling of this "poetics" of consciousness—and no more so than in "The Death of Halpin Frayser" with its baffling rhetorical orchestration.

I

In the first three chapters the use of the "poetics" of consciousness is conspicuous yet baffling, and in the fourth and last chapter, except for a teasing flourish of poetic fancy in the first paragraph, inconspicuous yet revealing. This masking reflects a carefully planned strategy for the resolution of the action. The story is finally filtered through the minds of conventional stereotypes of rationality—the sheriff Holker (a pun on "holk," to dig or turn things up), who manipulates clues with the empty zeal of a checker player, and the detective Jaralson (perhaps a pun on "son of jarl," suggesting an "eagle-eye"), who is a kind of caricature of Sherlock Holmes in his dogmatic omniscience on irrelevant matters. They reduce the process of reason to a pattern of absurd cause and effect far more terrifying in its implications than Halpin Frayser's dream that he is murdered by the vengeful ghost of his jealous mother.

To achieve this astonishing reversal, Bierce, a connoisseur of red herrings with the odor of mockery, dangles an epigraph, attributed to Hali, under the nose of the typical reader of ghost and horror tales. It sets up the motif of the soulless creature that will appear to strangle the hero, albeit in a dream. Then with a backward glance at Shakespeare and the enduring wisdom of his remark that "The lunatic, the lover, and the poet/Are of imagination all compact," Bierce establishes the seasonal setting of the action on a "dark night in midsummer."[1] Here it must be remembered that in his dream Halpin Frayser becomes a poet—what kind probably has to be determined by the derivation of Halpin from "elfin." Nor is this sleight-of-hand nonsense on his part (or mine). It simply follows the logic of a definition in *The Devil's Dictionary*, a parody of Descartes; *cogito ergo sum* that converts the faculty of thought into a wayward mischief-maker: "I think that I think, therefore I think that I am."[2] Or put another way, consciousness is an "elfin phraser"; whatever its mode of expression, it makes fools of us all. The etymological pun, however, is no doubt a verbal ploy that Bierce employs to alert the curiosity of anyone who, after a few readings of the story, begins to realize that Bierce's rhetorical hocus-pocus disguises an obsession with the uncharted avenues of perception.

Indeed, even for the reader who comes to this horror tale willing to suspend disbelief in the marvels of the supernatural, the substance of the next paragraph of narration may well serve to deflect the inclination:

He [Halpin Frayser] lived in St. Helena, but where he lives now is uncertain, for he is dead. One who practices living in the woods with nothing under him but the dry leaves and the damp earth, and nothing over him but the branches from which the leaves have fallen and the sky from which the earth has fallen, cannot hope for great longevity, and Frayser had already attained the age of thirty-two. There are persons in this world . . . and far away the best persons, who regard that as a very advanced age. They are the children. (p. 1)

As the lore of spiritualism and theosophy ("but where he lives . . .") collides with mythic cosmogony ("the sky from which . . .") and then dissolves into the enchanted world of the *puer aeternus* ("They are the children"), Bierce deliberately short-circuits any attempt on the part of the reader to set up a consistent train of associations. Seen in the perspective of the entire story, this tactic undermines the plausibility of the three solutions to Halpin Frayser's murder that the narrator presents: the hero as a victim of the soulless ghost, of the second husband of his mother, or of his own misguided mind. The cryptic references invalidate the authority of the motif of incest jealousy, the psychological extension of the content of the epigraph. They also controvert the sheriff's logical reconstruction of the crime and the parody of Descartes' radical separation of mind and body. However, the disconcerting, if not confusing, exposition at issue rings with a solemnity that precludes an outright dismissal of its importance, particularly when contrasted with the narrator's later whimsical and sardonic intrusions. As subsequent analysis will show, it functions to reveal Bierce's vision of the individual as a fragment of cosmic consciousness. To the extent the act of creation is an embodiment of divine thought as capricious as the rhetoric suggests, then the dead Halpin Frayser lives on as an orphaned mind. Nor is it difficult to understand why the children of the world take for granted this inescapable fate. They play out the fiction that existence is real while knowing full well that consciousness in its human expression is no more than a dream in the endless cycle of reciprocal becoming and passing away because for them death and life are ultimately the same. Of course, this explanation directly reflects the epigraph to this essay; that is, how can the isolated thought ever apprehend the process that produced the thought in the infinite regression of cause and effect underlying the endless manifestations of cosmic consciousness.

The hugger-mugger of Bierce's preceding commentary leads directly into the apparently prosaic circumstances of Halpin Frayser's nightmare. Lost in the hills and barred from any descent by impenetrable "thickets of manzanita" (apple trees, p. 2), he at last falls asleep "near the root of a large madrono" (mother tree, p. 2). Here surrogates of the tree of knowledge and tree of life are polarized in order to externalize the way ego consciousness sinks into the womb of unconsciousness and seeks an escape from the vexations of insecurity. For next the narrator proceeds to describe the expulsion from the paradise of infantile bliss—the awakening to the uncertainties of existence:

> It was hours later, in the very middle of the night, that one of God's mysterious messengers, gliding ahead of the incalculable host of his companions sweeping westward with the dawn line, pronounced the awakening word in the ear of the sleeper, who sat upright and spoke, he knew not why, a name, he knew not whose.   (p. 2)

The trite, gushing rhetoric reduces the diurnal paradigm of creation to a parody of the providential "let there be light" of Genesis, for the inscrutable name, "Catherine Larue" (p. 1) hints at the virtual impossibility of ever arriving at a comprehension of the divine mind. The subversion of the sacred also echoes in the casual reference to the witching hour ("in the very middle of the night," p. 2) especially in connection with the semantics of rue (the herb of grace used to exorcise demons and also used by witches for the opposite reason, in the latter instance as implied in Halpin Frayser's poem). As a mock epiphany, the passage debases the validity of mystical perception, relating all such insights to cultivated modes of consciousness. This explication finds corroboration in Halpin Frayser's reaction to the strange event: "Halpin Frayser was not much of a philosopher, nor a scientist. The circumstance that, waking from a deep sleep at night in the midst of a forest, he had spoken a name aloud did not arouse an enlightened curiosity to investigate the phenomenon. He thought it odd . . ." (p. 2). The careful differentiation between Halpin Frayser's discrimination and the hypothetical discernment of a philosopher or a scientist clearly indicates that Bierce categorizes the mental responses of individuals in accordance with conditioned outlooks on so-called reality. In effect, he argues that what we take for the mind is for the most part a culturally inherited mind—an externally imposed method of thinking.

The description of the outset of Halpin Frayser's dream confirms this assumption, as again an incongruous rhetorical intrusion alerts the reader to heed the character of thought: "in the land Beyond the Bed surprises cease from troubling and the judgment is at rest" (p. 2). What this implies is that during sleep the silenced voices of other levels of consciousness assert their right to speak. And it is this psychoscape that the hero now trods: "a road less traveled, having the appearance, indeed, of having been long abandoned, because, he thought, it led to something evil, yet he turned into it without hesitation, impelled by some imperious necessity" (p. 2). What he thinks at this point expresses less the actuality of circumstances than the fear of an encounter with an unknown aspect of his being. Thus the threat to the security of an accepted order of self-knowledge evolves into a premonition of evil. As Bierce later indicates, Halpin Frayser has been trained to be a lawyer, and as a consequence in this particular situation of the dream he resorts to the simplistic cause-and-effect logic that explains everything but resolves nothing. Even granting that the sudden manifestation of the destroying mother seems to support the assumption of impending malevolence, the vision also belongs to an established outlook on things that is not necessarily connected with any Oedipal complex.

The unreliability of Halpin Frayser's responses emerges in his interpretation of the voices heard along the unused road:

> As he pressed forward he became conscious that his way was haunted by invisible existences whom he could not definitely figure to his mind. From among the trees on either side he caught broken and incoherent whispers in a strange tongue which yet he partly understood. They seemed to him fragmentary utterances of a monstrous conspiracy against his body and soul.   (p. 2)

The qualifications about the identity of the unseen creatures and about their intentions hardly lend credence to his impressions. He sees in his imagination the auditory apparitions of the received cultural formula of good and evil, of God withstanding the devil. Yet there is an incongruity in this association, the linking of "body and soul," that bespeaks the presence of a voice long repressed by tyrannical routines. As this subsequent envisagement of the struggle with the ghost suggests, it is the voice of body whose language takes the form of physical activity. When the dominance of pragmatic consciousness relaxes in a crisis of existence, it achieves freedom of expression:

> [H]is mind was still spellbound, but his powerful body and agile limbs, endowed with a blind, insensate life of their own resisted stoutly and well. For an instant he seemed to see this unnatural contest between a dead intelligence and a breathing mechanism only as a spectator . . . then he regained his identity almost as if by a leap forward into his body, and the straining automaton had a directing will. . . . (p. 8)

The casual "seemed" (Bierce's controlling word in modulating the hero's impressions of the dream) clearly casts doubt on Halpin Frayser's interpretation of the experience. On the other hand, his envisagement of the restoration of his identity isolates the uncensored reaction to the struggle, dramatizing the inseparable union of the mind and the body. As the description of the momentary alienation indicates, the ego consciousness derives its identity from its physical vessel, the sanctuary so desperately reclaimed. Despite adding an abstract purpose to the energetic motions of the body, the ego still serves the primary instinctual impulse of the body to survive. Thus the so-called automaton automates thought, not vice versa. The machine which thinks in "Moxon's Master" is the correlative of this line of action; and probably to a greater degree than any other Gothic specialist in mental terror, Bierce intuitively perceives the cybernetic mechanisms of human biology.

The redefinition of the monitoring power of intelligence is clearly foreshadowed in Bierce's ironical account of Halpin Frayser's attempts to translate the language of the flesh and blood (the chemistry of dread) into a usable illusion of logic. Falling back upon the retributive fiction of conventional Christian morality, he proceeds to create another fiction upon its foundation: "All this . . . *seemed* not incompatible with the fulfillment of a natural expectation. It *seemed* to him that it was all in expiation of some crime which, though conscious of his guilt, he could not rightly remember. To the menaces and horrors of his surroundings the consciousness was an added horror" (p. 3; italics mine). Of course, here Bierce teasingly invites an association with Halpin Frayser's alleged Oedipal complex and its burden of inward anxiety and guilt. But as the gist of the quotation suggests, it is the bent of his individualized consciousness that induces the estrangement within his dream. He restricts his vision of life to what he has been taught to think it is, not to what it is—a reciprocal interplay of a mind lodged in the body and of a body intertwined in the convolutions of the brain. His refusal to come to terms with the incarnate thought of body (and the machine of the cyberneticists) explains why he becomes a poet; he seeks to remake himself in the making of a poem: " 'I will not submit unheard. There may be powers that are not malignant traveling this accursed road. I shall leave them a record and an appeal. I shall relate my wrongs, the persecutions that I endure—I, a helpless mortal, a penitent, an unoffending poet!' Halpin Frayser was a poet only as he was a penitent: in his dream" (p. 3). But Halpin Frayser is not even a poet in his dream: he is a lawyer. The fragment of consciousness that he takes for his mind is the product of the roboting memory of his education. It is he who curses the road of his traveling mind. It is he who is his own murderer. The gruesomely Gothic Gongorism of his poem adds the final touch of grotesque comedy to his ordained fate:

> Conspiring spirits whispered in the gloom
> Half-heard, the stilly secrets of the tomb.
>   With blood the trees were adrip; the leaves
> Shone in the witchlight with a ruddy bloom.
>
> I cried aloud!—the spell, unbroken still,
> Rested upon my spirit and my will.
>   Unsouled, unhearted, hopeless and forlorn,
> I strove with monstrous presages of ill!   (p. 13)

He is what he makes himself—an echo of borrowed consciousness.

II

Commonly Bierce launches the action of his Gothic exercises *in medias res*, and then at the point of climax (in this case the manifestation of the supposed ghost of the mother) disrupts the continuity of the horror sequence with a restrospect. Devisedly (and often flippantly) clumsy and mechanical, this formula of suspense calls attention to itself but for an ulterior purpose. It usually is the vehicle of a revelation crucial to the understanding of the previously delineated states of consciousness, and is thus a test of a reader's perception. As in the case of this story, what is treated dismissively or ironically is far more important than what invites careful scrutiny, to wit, "the sexual element" in the relations between Halpin Frayser and his mother (p. 6). The exposition so depressed involves a summary of the hero's social background and heredity, both a target of implicit ridicule:

> The Fraysers were well-to-do. . . . Their children had the social and educational opportunities of their *time and place*, and had responded to good associations and instruction with agreeable manners and cultivated minds. Halpin . . . was perhaps a trifle spoiled. He had the double disadvantage of a mother's assiduity and a father's neglect. Frayser *père* was what no Southern man of means is not—a politician. His country . . . made demands upon his time . . . so exacting that to those of his family he was compelled to turn an ear, partly deafened by the thunder of the political captains and the shouting, his own included.   (pp. 4–5; first italics mine)

Obviously, Halpin Frayser's sensibility is a product of his conditioning, even like his father's. He inherits a pattern of stock responses, intellectual and emotional, that reflect the ethos of the time and the place. "Dreamy, indolent, and rather romantic" (p. 5), he is further taught to believe "that in him the character of the late Myron Bayne, a maternal great-grandfather, had revisited the glimpses of the moon—by which orb Bayne had in his lifetime been sufficiently affected to be a poet of no small Colonial distinction" (p. 5). In effect, Bierce dictates the scenario of the dream in the context of these quotations. Along with his training in law, environment and heredity (or their spurious influences) shape the protagonist's male ego and, by extension, the romantic attachment to his mother who "was herself a devout disciple of the late and great Myron Bayne" (p. 5). Surely, the pun on the name of the grandfather presages a curse on Halpin Frayser—a "myronic" fatality, bitter as myrrh, despite the fact that "myron" is a chrism. Just as in the play on the hero's name, the cynical frivolity of the planted association with Byron traces poetic inspiration to a quirk of consciousness, to a search for a disinherited sense of being.

Significantly, Myron Bayne figures importantly in the situation that Bierce contrives to titillate the sensibilities of Freudian critics—the Oedipus complex. This involves a Gothic subterfuge on the part of the mother to keep her son from going to California on legal business. What it suggests is that Halpin Frayser is the surrogate of the grandfather, a displacement for his mother's romantic attachment to a figure warmer in emotions than her husband:

> Grandfather Bayne had come to me in a dream, and standing by his portrait . . . pointed to yours on the wall [.] And when I looked it seemed I could not see the features; you had been painted with a face cloth, such as we put upon the dead. Your father has laughed at me, but you and I, dear, know that such things are not for nothing. And I saw below the edge of the cloth the marks of hands on your throat. Perhaps you have another interpretation. Perhaps it does not mean you will go to California. Or maybe you will take me with you.   (p. 6)

But for all the blatant foreshadowing of the implacable succubus of the dream, this dialogue is a red herring. It betrays the mother's feeling for the son, not his for her. Indeed, Halpin Frayser without being a politician is not unlike his father in adapting to the "odd notions of duty" decreed by his professional persona (p. 7). Furthermore, as Bierce points out in Halpin Frayser's reaction to the sinister portent of his departure, the latter is totally unaware of his mother's perverted love: "[T]his ingenious interpretation of the dream *in the light of newly discovered evidence* [of his legal case] did not wholly commend itself to the son's more logical mind . . . it foreshadowed a more simple and immediate, if less tragic, disaster than a visit to the Pacific coast. It was Halpin Frayser's impression that he was to be *garroted on his native heath*" (p. 6; italics mine). Apparently some oversight in his handling of a case has left him open to the threat of revenge. Which is to say that the figure of his dream is his client in the dissociated form of the mother. So much then for the incest guilt so easily misread into the equivocal account of his nightmare.

But if that crux is resolvable in a distortion of memory, such is not the case with the action of the fourth chapter, which centers on the putative unraveling of the murders of Halpin Frayser and his mother. Indeed, at the outset Bierce's omniscient narrator plays around with a description that comments equally on weather and whether:

> A warm, clear night had been followed by a morning of drenching fog. At about the middle of the afternoon of the preceding day a little whiff of light vapor—a mere thickening of the atmosphere, *the ghost of a cloud*—had been observed clinging to the western side of Mount St. Helena, away up along the barren altitudes near the summit. It was so thin, so diaphanous, so *like a fancy made visible*, that one would have said: "Look quickly! in a moment it will be gone."   (p. 8; italics mine)

The deliberate reversal of the continuity of time, the inversion of the usual connotations of night and day, the implicit pun on vapor, the dream ghost lurking in the ghost of a cloud, and the notion of a materialized fancy (an optical illusion in tether to a fiction of the imagination): these observations all mock the self-reliance of rational thought and sensory perception. Moreover, the lyrical ecstasy of the breathless moment so readily shared with the reader collapses into a nonsensical joke. A dense fog immediately forms as the wisp of a cloud joins "small patches of mist that appeared to come out of the mountain side on exactly the same level, with an intelligent design to be absorbed" (p. 9).

Properly, Bierce brings a pair of manhunters into the narrative on the morning after this weather develops, as they set out on a journey to lift the fog of mystery surrounding the murder of a woman (Mrs. Frayser) by her second husband (Branscom). And once more the narrator enjoins the reader to share a moment of pointless mutual superiority in awareness: "They [Holker the sheriff and Jaralson the detective] carried guns on their shoulders, yet no one having knowledge of such matters could have mistaken them for hunters of bird or beast" (p. 9). As the plot thickens in the unthickening fog, white turns black in the movement of the two men towards their destination, though in a kind of educative jest:

> "The White Church? Only a half mile farther," the other [Jaralson] answered. "By the way," he added, "It is neither white nor a church; it is an abandoned schoolhouse, gray with age and neglect. Religious services were once held in it—when it was white, and there is a graveyard that would delight a poet."   (p. 9)

Counterpointing the narrator's subversion of the tone of the story (though not Bierce's cynical disdain for the power of thought), Jaralson's reversals of anticipation signal a total *reductio ad absurdum* of a commonsensical resolution of the mystery of Halpin Frayser's murder. Like the principals of the main plot, the detective also suffers from a perceptual quirk. The manipulated conjunction of methodical literality and romantic sentiment projects the peculiar balance of reason and emotion that enters into his judgments of factual reality. As the one faculty colors the functions of the other, he exercises as little control over his associations as Halpin Frayser.

In effect, both find themselves dominated by equivalent patternings of consciousness. One a lawyer and the other a detective, they build their outlook on the dislocations of life from similar points of view, and in a grimly hilarious coincidence Myron Bayne's Gothic poetry feeds the yearnings of their imagination. This strategy of identity is contrived to cast as much doubt upon Jaralson's objectivity in criminal investigation as Halpin Frayser's subjectivity in the nightmare characterization. Ordinary thought, at least from Bierce's standpoint, differs not a whit from the dream fantasy. Although Jaralson's purpose in coming to White Church is to find the grave of Mrs. Frayser who has been murdered by her second husband, it is hardly a wonder that he discovers the dead body of the son sprawled by the headboard. Nor, by the same token, is it unpredictable that Holker stumbles upon the manuscript of Halpin Frayser's poem. This convergence of plot and subplot rehearses the usual scenario of the horror tale on the verge of resolution, but that convention does not actually apply in this story.

For when the narrator describes the strangled body of the protagonist, the unsaid and the unanswered beg for scrutiny, especially since the two manhunters immediately jump to the conclusion that he has been murdered by Branscom: "The body lay upon its back, the legs wide apart. One arm was thrust upward, the other outward; but the latter was bent acutely, and the hand was near the throat. Both hands were tightly clenched. The whole attitude was that of a desperate but ineffectual resistance to—what?" (p. 12). Yet these and other gruesome details are taken in "almost at a glance" by the two men (p. 13). They fail to heed the message of the clenched, confessional hands—the answer to the unanswered questions of the story and a cross-reference to the dream in which the body, responding to the promptings of its own irrepressible language, usurps the authority of the mind. This parallel finds support in the terror, similar to Halpin Frayser's, that begins to overwhelm Jaralson. Like Frayser, he also feels haunted by a phantom murderer, the figure of the Branscom conjured up in his imagination. Bierce insistently draws attention to this condition in the description of his physical movements: "making a vigilant circumspection of the forest, his shotgun held in both hands and at full cock"; " 'The work of a maniac,' he said, without withdrawing his eyes from the enclosing wood"; "[He] continued scanning the dim gray confines of their narrow world and hearing matter of apprehension in the drip of water from every burdened branch" (p. 13). Thus Bierce urges the reader to note the correspondence in the state of consciousness of the awake Jaralson and the dreaming Halpin Frayser.

The purpose behind this rhetorical strategy emerges when Holker reads aloud from the latter's poem: for Jaralson's dogmatic identity of its author establishes the voice of the verse as a flow of consciousness that transcends person, time, and place: " 'Myron Bayne, a chap who flourished in the early years of the nation—more than a century ago. Wrote mighty dismal stuff; I have his collected works. The poem is not among them, but it must have been omitted by mistake' " (p. 14). Here Bierce's use of the casual "dismal" (etymologically, to cause dread or consternation) associates the voice with an impulse of life hostile to the norms of ordinary awareness. As such, it speaks for the body, for all the desires of liberation from cultural automatism that receive expression in the rebellious language of poetry, fantasy, murder, and dream. Thus the gathering at White Church, the dead and the living, marks the convergence in and out of time of all the characters in the story who have been lured into traveling the forbidden road of consciousness so dramatically evoked in the recorded dream and poem.

Accordingly, Bierce next deftly concretizes the specious factuality of historical identity in the dialogue that follows the discovery of Mrs. Frayser's grave marker, " 'Larue, Larue!' exclaimed Holker, with sudden animation. 'Why, that is the real name of Branscom—not Pardee. And—bless my soul! how it all comes to me—the murdered woman's name had been Frayser' " (p. 14). Constantly delineated as incurious and unimaginative, Holker personifies the limitations of empirical reason. For all his piecing together of evidence, nothing has been solved. The still un-captured Branscom or Larue (surrogate of the Oedipal son) is no more or less a murderer than Mrs. Frayser in her son's dream or Myron Bayne in the ecstasies of morbid inspiration or Jaralson in arresting an assassin. If there is a criminal at large, he is for Bierce the creator of the mind of man: the trickster God (Descartes' *Dieu trompeur*) who delights in betraying every aspiration for truth or certitude that the creatures of His creation harbor in their thoughtless thought. For it is the sound of that thought, echoing out of the spaceless and timeless distances of consciousness, that Holker and Jaralson hear or think they hear emanating out of the forest. The sound actually originates at the source of all consciousness and records the pitiless indifference of the creator of all things for the fragments of His consciousness. This horrifying cry, always keyed to the bitter frustrations of human thought, is the signature of American Gothicism—the subjective condition of the ingrained Puritan sensibility of the American even when he is in the grip of the consoling illusion of self-reliance. And this is the nightmarish voice that haunts the fiction of Brown, Poe, Hawthorne, James, and Bierce. Listen attentively: it sounds loudest in the silences of the sun under the supreme manifestation of the illusion-making Word.

Notes

1. *Ghost and Horror Stories of Ambrose Bierce* (New York, 1964), p. 1 Hereafter all parenthetical page references are to this edition.

2. *The Devil's Dictionary* (New York: Dolphin Book, n. d.), entry under Cartesian.

Selected Bibliography of Works
By and About Ambrose Bierce*

PRIMARY SOURCES

I. Books by Ambrose Bierce, including some contemporary editions of Bierce's work (arranged chronologically)

Grile, Dod (pseud.). *The Fiend's Delight*. London: John Camden Hotten, [1873].

———. *Nuggets and Dust*. London: Chatto and Windus, [1873].

———. *Cobwebs from an Empty Skull*. George Routledge and Sons, 1874.

Herman, William (pseud. [in collaboration with T. A. Harcourt and W. Rulofson]). *The Dance of Death*. 3rd ed. San Francisco: Keller, 1877.

Bowers, Mrs. J. Milton (pseud.). *The Dance of Life: An Answer to The Dance of Death*. San Francisco: San Francisco News Co., 1877.

Bierce, Ambrose G. *In the Midst of Life*. London: Chatto and Windus, 1892.

———. [in collaboration with Gustav Adolph Danziger]. *The Monk and the Hangman's Daughter*. Chicago: F. A. Schulte, 1892.

———. *Black Beetles in Amber*. San Francisco: Western Author's Publishing Co., 1892.

———. *Can Such Things Be?* New York: Cassell, 1893.

———. *In the Midst of Life—Tales of Soldiers and Civilians*. New York: Putnam, 1898.

———. *Fantastic Fables*. New York: Putnam, 1899.

———. *Shapes of Clay*. San Francisco: W. E. Wood, 1903.

———. *The Cynic's Word Book*. New York: Doubleday, 1906.

———. *A Son of the Gods and A Horseman in the Sky*. San Francisco: Paul Elder, 1907.

———. *The Shadow on the Dial and Other Essays*. Ed. S. O. Howes. San Francisco: A. M. Robertson, 1909.

———. *The Collected Works of Ambrose Bierce*. 12 Vols. New York: Neale, 1909.

*© Cathy N. Davidson, 1980.

———. *Write It Right: A Little Blacklist of Literary Faults.* 1909; rpt. New York: Union Library Assoc., 1940.

———. *Ambrose Bierce's Civil War.* Ed. William McCann. New York: Sagamore Press, 1957.

———. *The Collected Writings of Ambrose Bierce.* Ed. Clifton Fadiman. New York: Citadel Press, 1960.

———. *Ghost and Horror Stories of Ambrose Bierce.* Ed. E. F. Bleiler. New York: Dover, 1964.

———. *The Enlarged Devil's Dictionary.* Comp., ed. Ernest Jerome Hopkins. Garden City, N.Y.: Doubleday, 1967.

———. *The Ambrose Bierce Satanic Reader: Selections from the Invective Journalism of the Great Satirist.* Ed. Ernest Jerome Hopkins. Garden City, N.Y.: Doubleday, 1968.

———. *The Complete Short Stories of Ambrose Bierce.* Ed. Ernest Jerome Hopkins. Garden City, N.Y.: Doubleday, 1970.

———. *The Stories and Fables of Ambrose Bierce.* Ed. Edward Wagenknecht. Owing Mills, Md.: Stemmer House, 1977.

———. *Skepticism and Dissent. Selected Journalism from 1898–1901.* Ed. Lawrence I. Berkove. Ann Arbor: Delmas, 1980.

II. Published Letters

Chittick, V. L. O. "Holograph Treasures in the Reed College Library Adams Collection, III." *Reed College Notes,* 9 (April 1947).

Containing Four Ambrose Bierce Letters. [New York: Charles Romm, 1923].

Grenander, M. E. "Ambrose Bierce and Charles Warren Stoddard: Some Unpublished Correspondence." *Huntington Library Quarterly,* 23 (May 1960), 261–92.

———. "H. L. Mencken to Ambrose Bierce." The Book Club of California *Quarterly News Letter,* 22 (Winter 1956), 5–10.

———. "A London Letter of Joaquin Miller to Ambrose Bierce." *Yale University Library Gazette,* 46 (October 1971), 109–16.

———. "Seven Ambrose Bierce Letters." *Yale University Library Gazette,* 32 (July 1957), 12–18.

Jackson, Hartley E. and James D. Hart. *Battlefields and Ghosts.* [Palo Alto, California]: The Harvest Press, 1931.

Loveman, Samuel, ed. *Twenty-one Letters of Ambrose Bierce.* Cleveland: George Kirk, 1922.

[McWilliams, Carey.] "A Collection of Bierce Letters." *University of California Chronicle,* 34 (January 1932), 30–48.

McWilliams, Carey, "Ambrose Bierce and His First Love." *Bookman,* 75 (June 1932), 254–59.

———. "New Letters of Ambrose Bierce." *Opinion,* 2 (May 1930), 3–4.

Pope, Bertha Clark, ed. *The Letters of Ambrose Bierce.* San Francisco: The Book Club of California, 1922.

Ridgely, J. V. "Ambrose Bierce to H. L. Mencken." The Book Club of California *Quarterly News Letter*, 26 (Fall 1961), 27–33.

Scholnick. Robert J. " 'My Humble Muse': Some New Bierce Letters." *Markham Review*, 5 (1976), 71–75.

Slade, Joseph W. " 'Putting You in the Papers': Ambrose Bierce's Letters to Edwin Markham." *Prospects*, 1 (1975), 335–68.

Williams, Stanley T. "Ambrose Bierce and Bret Harte." *American Literature*, 27 (May 1945), 179–80.

III. Bibliographies

"Bierce, Ambrose." *Articles on American Literature, 1900–1950*. Ed. Lewis Leary. Durham, N.C.: Duke Univ. Press, 1954, pp. 21–22.

Blanck, Joseph. "Ambrose Gwinnett Bierce, 1842–1914(?)." *Bibliography of American Literature*. New Haven: Yale University Press, 1955. I, 216–27.

Fatout, Paul. "Ambrose Bierce (1842–1914)." *American Literary Realism*, 1 (Fall 1967), 13–19.

Gaer, Joseph, ed. *Ambrose Gwinett [sic] Bierce, Bibliography and Biographical Data*. California Literary Research, Monograph No. 4, California Relief Administration: 1935. Mimeographed. Rpt. New York: Burt Franklin, 1968.

Grenander, M. E. "Ambrose Bierce, John Camden Hotten, *The Fiend's Delight*, and *Nuggets and Dust*." *Huntington Library Quarterly*, 28 (August 1965), 353–71.

Monteiro, George. "Addenda to Gaer: Bierce in the *Anti-Philistine*." *PBSA*, 66 (1972), 71–72.

———. "Addenda to Gaer: Reprintings of Bierce's Stories." *PBSA*, 68 (1974), 330–31.

SECONDARY SOURCES

I. Books

Atherton, Gertrude. *Adventures of a Novelist*. New York: Liveright, 1932.

Boynton, Percy H. *Literature and American Life*. Boston: Ginn, 1936.

———. "Ambrose Bierce." *More Contemporary Americans*. Chicago: Univ. of Chicago Press, 1927.

Brooks, Van Wyck. *The Confident Years: 1885–1915*. New York: E. P. Dutton, 1952.

———. *Emerson and Others*. New York: E. P. Dutton, 1927.

Canby, Henry Seidel. *The Age of Confidence: Life in the Nineties*. New York: Farrar, Straus, 1934.

Cooper, Frederic Taber. "Ambrose Bierce." *Some American Story Tellers*. New York: Holt, Rinehart & Winston, 1911.

Cummins, Ella Sterling. *The Story of the Files: A Review of California Writers and Literature*. Issued under the auspices of the World's Fair Commission of California. San Francisco, 1893.

de Castro, Adolphe. *Portrait of Ambrose Bierce*. New York: Century, 1929.

de Ford, Miriam Allen. *They Were San Franciscans*. Caldwell, Idaho: Caxton Printers, 1951.

Fatout, Paul. *Ambrose Bierce: The Devil's Lexicographer*. Norman: Univ. of Oklahoma Press, 1951.

———. *Ambrose Bierce and the Black Hills*. Norman: Univ. of Oklahoma Press, 1956.

Grattan, C. Hartley. *Bitter Bierce: A Mystery of American Letters*. Garden City: Doubleday, 1929.

Grenander, M. E. *Ambrose Bierce*. New York: Twayne, 1971.

Hall, Carroll D. *Bierce and the Poe Hoax*. San Francisco: Book Club of California, 1943.

Hicks, Granville. *The Great Tradition: An Interpretation of American Literature since the Civil War*. 2nd ed. revised. New York: The Macmillan Co., 1935.

Josephson, Matthew. *Portrait of the Artist as American*. New York: Harcourt, Brace & World, 1930.

Littell, Robert. "Bitter Bierce." *Read America First*. New York: Harcourt, Brace & World, 1926.

Markham, Edwin. *California the Wonderful*. New York: Hearst's International Library, 1910.

McWilliams, Carey. *Ambrose Bierce: A Biography*. New York: A. and C. Boni, 1929.

Mencken, H. L. "Ambrose Bierce." *Prejudices: Sixth Series*. New York: Alfred A. Knopf, 1927.

Neale, Walter. *Life of Ambrose Bierce*. New York: Walter Neale, 1929.

Noel, Joseph. *Footloose in Arcadia: A Personal Record of Jack London, George Sterling, Ambrose Bierce*. New York: Carrick and Evans, 1940.

Pollard, Percival. *Their Day in Court*. New York and Washington: Neale Publishing Co., 1909.

Smith, Edward H. "The Ambrose Bierce Irony." *Mysteries of the Missing*. New York: The Dial Press, 1927.

Smith, Paul Jordan. "Ambrose Bierce." *On Strange Altars: A Book of Enthusiasms*. New York: A. and C. Boni, 1924.

Snell, George. *The Shapers of American Fiction: 1798–1947*. New York: E. P. Dutton, 1947.

Starrett, Vincent. *Ambrose Bierce*. Chicago: Walter M. Hill, 1920.

———. "Ambrose Bierce." *Buried Caesars: Essays in Literary Appreciation*. Chicago: Corvici-McGee, 1923.

Sterling, George. *The Testimony of the Suns*. San Francisco: The Book Club of California, 1927.

Walker, Franklin. *Ambrose Bierce: The Wickedest Man in San Francisco*. San Francisco: Colt Press, 1941.

———. *San Francisco's Literary Frontier*. New York: Alfred A. Knopf, 1939.

Ward, Alfred C. "Ambrose Bierce: 'In the Midst of Life.' " *Aspects of the Modern Short Story, English and American*. London: Univ. of London Press, 1924.

Weeks, George F. *California Copy*. Washington: Washington College Press, 1928.

Wiggins, Robert A. *Ambrose Bierce*. Univ. of Minnesota Pamphlets on American Writers, No. 37. Minneapolis: Univ. of Minn. Press, 1964.

Wilson, Edmund. *Patriotic Gore: Studies in the Literature of the American Civil War*. New York: Oxford Univ. Press, 1962.

Woodruff, Stuart C. *The Short Stories of Ambrose Bierce: A Study in Polarity*. Pittsburgh: Univ. of Pittsburgh Press, 1964.

II. Articles

Aaron, Daniel. "Ambrose Bierce and the American Civil War." In *Uses of Literature*, ed. Monroe Engel. Harvard English Studies, 4. Cambridge: Harvard Univ. Press, 1973, pp. 115–31.

Anderson, David D. "Can Ohio and the Midwest Claim Ambrose Bierce?" *Ohioana Quarterly*, 16 (1973), 84–88.

Andrews, William L. "Some New Ambrose Bierce Fables." *American Literary Realism*, 8 (August 1975), 349–52.

Bahr, Howard W. "Ambrose Bierce and Realism." *The Southern Quarterly*, 1 (July 1963), 309–30.

Barry, R. "The Mystery of Ambrose Bierce." *Mentor*, 9 (June 1921), 34.

Bierce, Helen. "Ambrose Bierce at Home." *American Mercury*, 30 (December 1933), 453–58.

Bishop, Morris. "The Mystery of Ambrose Bierce." *New Yorker*, 26 February 1949.

Bower-Shore, Clifford. "Ambrose Bierce." *Bookman*, 78 (1930), 283–84.

Boyd, E. Rev. of *Bitter Bierce: A Mystery of American Letters* by C. Hartley Grattan. *Outlook*, 151 (1929), 470.

Braddy, Haldeen. "Ambrose Bierce and Guy de Maupassant." *American Notes and Queries*, 1 (1941), 67–68.

———. "Trailing Ambrose Bierce." *American Notes and Queries*, 1 (1941), 5–6, 20.

Cann, Louis Gebhard. "Ambrose Bierce: A Rejected Guest." *Stratford Journal*, 2 (1918), 38–48.

Clemens, William M. "The Art of Ambrose Bierce." *The Biblio*, 4 (July 1924), 676–77.

Cooper, Frederic Taber. "Ambrose Bierce, An Appraisal." *Bookman*, 33 (July 1911), 471–78.

Crane, John Kenny. "Crossing the Bar Twice: Post-Mortem Consciousness in Bierce, Hemingway, and Golding." *Studies in Short Fiction*, 6 (1968), 361–65.

Davidson, Cathy N. "Literary Semantics and the Fiction of Ambrose Bierce." *ETC., A Review of General Semantics*, 31 (September 1974), 263–71.

de Castro, Adolphe. "Ambrose Bierce as He Really Was." *American Parade*, 1 (October 1926), 28–44.

de Vree, Freddy. "Ambrose Bierce." *Kunst and Culture*, 1 (May 1975), 24.

Dibble, R. F. "Ambrose Bierce." *Overland Monthly*, 85 (1927), 327.

Dickson, S. B. "Ambrose Bierce, Cynical Poet and Philosopher of Old San Francisco." *Sunset Magazine*, 63 (1929), 15–16.

East, H. M., Jr. "Bierce—The Warrior Writer." *Overland Monthly*, 65 (June 1915), 507–509.

"English Tribute to the Genius of Ambrose Bierce." *Current Opinion*, 63 (June 1915), 427.

Fatout, Paul. "Ambrose Bierce, Civil War Topographer." *American Literature*, 26 (November 1954), 391–400.

———. "Ambrose Bierce Writes About War." The Book Club of California *Quarterly News Letter*, 16 (Fall 1951), 75–79.

Field, B. S., Jr. "Ambrose Bierce as a Comic." *Western Humanities Review*, 31 (Spring 1977), 173–80.

Follett, Wilson. "Ambrose Bierce: An Analysis of the Perverse Wit that Shaped His Work." *Bookman*, 68 (1928–29), 284–89.

———. "Ambrose, Son of Marcus Aurelius." *Atlantic Monthly*, 160 (July 1937), 32–42.

———. "Bierce in His Brilliant Obscurity." *New York Times Book Review*, 11 October 1936, pp. 2, 32.

Fraser, Howard M. "Points South: Ambrose Bierce, Jorge Luis Borges, and the Fantastic." *Studies in Twentieth-Century Literature*, 1 (1977), 173–81.

French, Joseph Lewis. "Ambrose Bierce." *Pearson's Magazine*, 39 (1918), 245–47.

Friedrich, Otto. "The Passion of Death in Ambrose Bierce." *Zero*, 2 (1956), 72–94.

Frink, Maurice M. "A Sidelight on Ambrose Bierce." *Book Notes*, 1 (1923), 154.

Garnett, Porter. "Poetics, Bierce and Sterling." *Pacific Monthly*, 18 (1907), 553–58.

Goldstein, J. S. "Edwin Markham, Ambrose Bierce, and *The Man With the Hoe*." *Modern Language Notes*, 58 (1943), 165–75.

Grattan, C. Hartley. "Biography of a Journalist." *Saturday Review*, 18 August 1951, p. 11.

Grenander, M. E. "Ambrose Bierce and *Cobwebs from an Empty Skull: A Note on BAL 1100 and 1107.*" *PBSA*, 69 (1975), 403–06.

———. "Ambrose Bierce Describes Swinburne." *Courier*, 14 (1977), 22–26.

———. "Bierce's Turn of the Screw: Tales of Ironical Terror." *Western Humanities Review*, 11 (Summer 1957), 257–63.

Gribble, Francis. "The Ambrose Bierce Mystery." *Biblio*, 4 (1924), 673–75.

Harding, Ruth. "Mr. Boythorn-Bierce." *Bookman*, 61 (1925), 636–43.

Harris, Leon. "Satan's Lexicographer." *American Heritage*, 28 (1972), 56–63.

Harte, Walter Blackburn. "A Tribute to Ambrose Bierce." *Biblio*, 4 (1924), 680–81.

Highsmith, James M. "The Forms of Burlesque in *The Devil's Dictionary.*" *Satire Newsletter*, 7 (1970), 115–27.

Kazin, Alfred. "On Ambrose Bierce and 'Parker Adderson, Philosopher.' " In *The American Short Story*. Ed. Calvin Skaggs. New York: Dell, 1977, pp. 26–35.

Kenton, Edna. "Ambrose Bierce and 'Moxon's Master.' " *Bookman*, 62 (1925), 71–79.

Klein, Marcus. "San Francisco and Her Hateful Ambrose Bierce." *Hudson Review*, 7 (Autumn 1954), 392–407.

Lambert, Mary. "A Trio of California Poets." *Pacific Town Talk*, 18 December 1897, pp. 26–27.

Leary, Lewis. "Bierce in Business." *Saturday Review*, 9 June 1956, p. 20.

Littell, Robert. "Bitter Bierce." *New Republic*, 40 (1924), 177.

Logan, F. J. "The Wry Seriousness of 'Owl Creek Bridge.' " *American Literary Realism*, 10 (Spring 1977), 101–113.

Lovett, R. M. "Five Books on Ambrose Bierce." *American Literature*, 1 (January 1930), 434–39.

Martin, Jay. "Ambrose Bierce," In *The Comic Imagination in American Literature*. Ed. Louis D. Rubin, Jr. New Brunswick: Rutgers Univ. Press, 1972, pp. 195–205.

McCann, William. "Introduction." *Ambrose Bierce's Civil War*. New York: Henry Regnery, 1956.

McLean, Robert C. "The Deaths in Ambrose Bierce's 'Halpin Frayser.' " *PLL*, 10 (1974), 394–402.

McWilliams, Carey. "Ambrose Bierce." *American Mercury*, 16 (February 1929), 215–22.

———. "Ambrose Bierce and His First Love." *Bookman*, 75 (June 1932), 254–59.

———. "Introduction." *The Devil's Dictionary*. New York: Sagamore Press, 1957.

———. "The Mystery of Ambrose Bierce." *American Mercury*, 22 (March 1931), 330–37.

———. "Roosevelt Johnson Becomes Reminiscent." *Overland Monthly*, 85 (December 1927), 367.

Millard, Bailey. "The Launching of a Famous Poem." *Bookman*, 27 (May 1908), 267–72.

———. "Personal Memories of Bierce." *Bookman*, 40 (July 1915), 653–58.

Miller, Arthur M. "The Influence of Edgar Allan Poe on Ambrose Bierce." *American Literature*, 4 (May 1932), 130–50.

Monaghan, Frank. "Ambrose Bierce and the Authorship of *The Monk and the Hangman's Daughter.*" *American Literature*, 2 (1931), 337–49.

"Mr. Bierce's War Club." *Bookman*, 30 (October 1909), 124–25.

Nathan, George Jean. "Ambrose Light." *American Mercury*, 2 (1934), 2.

Nations, Leroy J. "Ambrose Bierce: The Gray Wolf of American Letters." *South Atlantic Quarterly*, 25 (1926), 253–68.

O'Brien, Matthew C. "Ambrose Bierce and the Civil War: 1865." *American Literature*, 48 (1976), 377–81.

Oehser, P. H. "Ambrose Bierce's Centenary." *Saturday Review*, 21 November 1942, p. 11.

Partridge, Eric. "Ambrose Bierce." *London Mercury*, 16 (1927), 625–38.

Poore, E. G. "Ambrose Bierce's Last Tilt with Mars." *New York Times Magazine*, 1 January 1928.

"Prophetic Powers of Ambrose Bierce." *Bookman*, 30 (October 1909), 120–22.

Prussia, George. "Ambrose Bierce." *The Wave*, 22 September 1894, p. 13.

Rideing, William H. "A Corner of Bohemia." *Bookman*, 32 (February 1911), 620–29.

Roth, Russell, "Ambrose Bierce's 'Detestable Creature.' " *Western American Literature*, 9 (1974), 169–76.

Scheffauer, Herman. "The Death of Satire." *The Living Age*, 278 (July 1913), 82–90.

Snell, George. "Poe Redivivus." *Arizona Quarterly*, 1 (1945), 49–57.

Solomon, Eric. "The Bitterness of Battle: Ambrose Bierce's War Fiction." *Midwest Quarterly*, 5 (1963–64), 147–65.

Stein, William Bysshe. "Bierce's 'The Death of Halpin Frayser': The Poetics of Gothic Consciousness." *Emerson Society Quarterly*, 18 (1972), 115–22.

Sterling, George. "The Shadow Maker." *American Mercury*, 6 (1925), 10–19.

———. "The Wine of Wizardry." *Cosmopolitan*, 43 (1909), 551–56.

Thomas, Jeffrey F. "Ambrose Bierce." *American Literary Realism*, 8 (Summer 1975), 198–201.

"*Two Essayists.*" *The Nation*, 89 (September 1909), 306–07.

"The Underground Reputation of Ambrose Bierce." *Current Literature*, 47 (September 1909), 279–81.

Weimer, David R. "Ambrose Bierce and the Art of War." In *Essays in Literary History*. Ed. Rudolph Kirk and C. F. Main. New York: Russell and Russell, 1964, pp. 229–38.

Wilson, Edmund. "Ambrose Bierce on The Owl Creek Bridge." *New Yorker*, 27 (8 December 1951), 159–70.

Wilt, Napier. "Ambrose Bierce and the Civil War." *American Literature*, 1 (November 1929), 260–85.

III. Reviews

"Another Attempt to Boost Bierce Into Immortality." *Current Opinion*, 65 (September 1918), 184–85.

Rev. of *The Collected Works, Vol. I. The Atheneum*, 3 July 1909, p. 8.

Rev. of *The Collected Works, Vol. II. The Atheneum*, 26 March 1910, p. 367.

Rev. of *The Collected Works, Vol. III. The Atheneum*, 11 June 1910, p. 702.

Rev. of *The Collected Works, Vol. VII–X. The Atheneum*, 16 September, 1911, pp. 322–23.

Hubbard, Elbert. Rev. of *The Collected Works*, Vol. I. *The FRA*, 3 (May 1909), 29–31.

Rev. of *In the Midst of Life. The Atheneum*, 20 February 1892, p. 241.

Rev. of *In the Midst of Life. The Nation*, 66 (March 1898), 225.

Rev. of *In the Midst of Life. The Nation*, 107 (August 1918), 232.

Monahan, Michael. "Our Greatest Poet." *The Papyrus*, 1 (October 1907), 1–8.

Smith, H. Greenbough. "Bierce's Devil Dictionary." *The Biblio*, 4 (July 1924), 678–80.

IV. Dissertations

Berkove, Lawrence Ivan. "Ambrose Bierce's Concern with Mind and Man." Diss. Pennsylvania 1962.

Brazil, John Russell. "Literature, Self, and Society: The Growth of a Political Aesthetic in Early San Francisco." Diss. Yale 1975.

Davidson, Cathy N. "The Poetics of Perception: A Semantic Analysis of the Short Fiction of Ambrose Bierce." Diss. S.U.N.Y. (Binghamton) 1974.

Emmons, Winfred S. "The Materials and Methods of American Horror Fiction in the Nineteenth Century." Diss. Louisiana State 1952.

Finn, Eugene C. "Ambrose Bierce and the Journalization of the American Short Story." Diss. St. John's 1954.

Francendese, Janet Malverti. "Ambrose Bierce as Journalist." Diss. N.Y.U. 1977.

Grenander, M. E. "The Critical Theories of Ambrose Bierce." Diss. Chicago 1948.

Hill, Larry Lew. "Style in the Tales of Ambrose Bierce." Diss. Wisconsin 1973.

Hodgson, Helen E. "Four Short Stories of Ambrose Bierce: A Critical Edition." Diss. Denver 1973.

Kocher, Richard Luke. "Fear and Dilemma in the War Stories of Ambrose Bierce." Diss. Southern California 1978.

Kummer, George N. "Percival Pollard: Precursor of the 'Twenties.' " Diss. N.Y.U. 1947.

Logan, F. J. "The Development of Ambrose Bierce's Prose Style." Diss. Alberta 1974.

Rubens, Philip Maurice. "The Literary Gothic and the Fiction of Ambrose Gwinett Bierce." Diss. Northern Illinois 1976.

Sheller, Harry Lynn. "The Satire of Ambrose Bierce: Its Objects, Forms, Devices, and Possible Origins." Diss. Southern California 1945.

Smith, Rebecca. "The Civil War and Its Aftermath in American Fiction, 1861–1899." Diss. Chicago 1932.

Suhre, Lawrence R. "A Consideration of Ambrose Bierce as Black Humorist." Diss. Pennsylvania State 1972.

Woodruff, Stuart Cowan. "The Short Stories of Ambrose Bierce: A Critical Study." Diss. Connecticut 1962

INDEX